THE TERRACOTTA FIGURINES AND RELATED VESSELS

*Enthroned Cybele (**59**)*

UNIVERSITY MUSEUM MONOGRAPH 86

GORDION SPECIAL STUDIES II
G. Kenneth Sams, Series Editor

THE TERRACOTTA FIGURINES AND RELATED VESSELS

Irene Bald Romano

Published by
THE UNIVERSITY MUSEUM
Philadelphia
1995

Design, editing, production
  Publications Department
  The University Museum

Printing
  Science Press
  Ephrata, Pennsylvania

Library of Congress Cataloging-in-Publication Data

  (University Museum monograph; 63-)
  Companion set to The Gordion excavations.
  Summary in Turkish, (v. 1)
  Map on lining papers.
  Errata slip inserted.
  Includes bibliographical refereces and indexes.
  Contents: v. 1. Nonverbal graffiti, dipinti, and stamps / Lynn E. Roller—v. 2.
The terracotta figurines and related vessels / Irene Bald Romano.
  1. Gordion (Extinct city)   2. Turkey—Antiquities.   3. Graffiti—Catalogs.   4. Pottery—Marks—Catalogs.   5. Trademarks—Catalogs.   6. Pottery, Ancient—Turkey—Catalogs.   I. Roller, Lynn E.   II. Romano, Irene Bald.   III. Series: Gordion special studies; 63, etc.
ISBN 0-93471-870-9 (v. 1)
ISBN 0-92417-129-4 (v. 2)

Copyright © 1995
THE UNIVERSITY OF PENNSYLVANIA MUSEUM
of Archaeology and Anthropology
Philadelphia
All rights reserved
Printed in the United States of America

Printed on acid free paper

to

David Gilman Romano
Katherine MacLeod Romano
Elizabeth Scott Romano
and
Sarah Gilman Romano

Contents

LIST OF ILLUSTRATIONS AND FIGURES ix
LIST OF TABLES ix
LIST OF PLATES xi
ACKNOWLEDGMENTS xiii
EDITOR'S PREFACE xiv
ABBREVIATIONS xv
BIBLIOGRAPHY xvii
INTRODUCTION 1
I. CATALOGUE 4
    Introduction to Catalogue 4
    Animal Vessels: Central Anatolian (**1-18**) 5
    Plastic Vessels: Greek or Greek-Inspired (**19-34**) 9
    Bust-Flower Thymiateria: Locally Manufactured (**35-51**) 17
    Kybele and Related Types (**52-64**) 22
    Females (**65-96**) 29
        Standing (**65-76**) 31
        Seated (**77** and **78**) 36
        Protomes (**79**) 36
        Heads (**80-94**) 37
        Other Fragments (**95** and **96**) 41
    Males (**97-107**) 41
        Deities (**97-105**) 41
        Other (**106** and **107**) 45
    Unidentifiable Humans (**108** and **109**) 46
    Masks (**110-114**) 46
    Animals: Central Anatolian and Non-Central Anatolian (**115-155**) 49
        Central Anatolian-Manufactured (**115-121**) 51
        Large Quadrupeds (**122-130**) 53
        Large Quadrupeds Attached to Plinths (**131** and **132**) 54
        Yoked or Harnessed Quadrupeds (**133-135**) 55
        Wheeled Quadruped (**136**) 55
        Other Quadrupeds (**137-148**) 56
        Birds (**149-152**) 58
        Imports (**153-155**) 58

Miscellaneous (**156-171**) 59
    Vehicles and Wheels (**156-161**) 59
    Boots or Shoes (**162-168**) 61
    Other (**169-171**) 63
II. TERRACOTTA DEPOSITS 65
III. CONCLUSIONS 71
CONCORDANCE 82
TURKISH SUMMARY 85
INDEX 87
FIGURES
PLATES

List of Illustrations and Figures

Illustration 1.	Reconstruction of a Bust-Flower Thymiaterion	17
Figure 1.	General Site Plan of Gordion	
Figure 2.	Early Phrygian City Mound	
Figure 3.	Middle Phrygian City Mound	
Figure 4.	Late Phrygian City Mound	
Figure 5.	Reconstructed Floor Plan of Chamber of Tumulus P	
Figure 6.	"Level 2 House"	
Figure 7.	Pottery Establishment and Adjoining Structures	

List of Tables

Table 1.	Chronological Chart	50
Table 2.	Types of Gordion Figurines and Their Chronology	73

List of Plates

Frontispiece	Enthroned Cybele (**59**)
Color Plate I.	Painted Figurines (**33, 52, 66, 68, 76, 111**)
Color Plate II.	Drawings of Boots/Shoes (**163, 164, 165, 167, 168**)
Plate 1.	Animal Vessels (**1-2**)
Plate 2.	Animal Vessels (**3-5**)
Plate 3.	Animal Vessels (**6-9**)
Plate 4.	Animal Vessels (**10-13**)
Plate 5.	Animal Vessels (**14-18**)
Plate 6.	Plastic Vessels (**19-23**)
Plate 7.	Plastic Vessels (**24-26**)
Plate 8.	Plastic Vessels (**27**)
Plate 9.	Plastic Vessels (**28-30**)
Plate 10.	Plastic Vessels (**31-34**)
Plate 11.	Bust-Flower Thymiateria (**35-37**)
Plate 12.	Bust-Flower Thymiateria (**38-42**)
Plate 13.	Bust-Flower Thymiateria (**43-49**)
Plate 14.	Bust-Flower Thymiateria (**50-51**)
Plate 15.	Kybele and Related Types (**52**)
Plate 16.	Kybele and Related Types (**52**)
Plate 17.	Kybele and Related Types (**53-56**)
Plate 18.	Kybele and Related Types (**57-59**)
Plate 19.	Kybele and Related Types (**60-64**)
Plate 20.	Standing Females (**65-66**)
Plate 21.	Standing Females (**67-68**)
Plate 22.	Standing Females (**69-73**)
Plate 23.	Standing Females (**74-76**)
Plate 24.	Females (**77-81**)
Plate 25.	Females (**82-83**)
Plate 26.	Females (**84-89**)
Plate 27.	Females (**90-96**)

Plate 28.   Males (**97-99**)
Plate 29.   Males (**100-103**)
Plate 30.   Males (**104-106**)
Plate 31.   Unidentifiable Humans (**107-109**)
Plate 32.   Masks (**110-114**)
Plate 33.   Animals (**115-130**)
Plate 34.   Animals (**131-144**)
Plate 35.   Animals (**145-155**)
Plate 36.   Miscellaneous: Vehicles and Wheels (**156-161**)
Plate 37.   Miscellaneous: Boots and Shoes (**162-165**)
Plate 38.   Miscellaneous (**166-171**)
Plate 39.   Comparable Figurines from Other Sites
Plate 40.   Comparable Figurines from Other Sites
Plate 41.   Comparable Figurines from Other Sites

Acknowledgments

I am grateful to many who have provided assistance in all stages of the preparation of this volume, most especially to the following members of the Gordion project: Keith DeVries, Jean Carpenter Efe, Ann Gunter, Ellen Kohler, Lynn Roller, G. Kenneth Sams, Karen Vellucci, Robert and Frances Vincent, and Frederick A. Winter.

For their generous time in reading drafts of this manuscript, examining photographs and making useful comments, I owe much gratitude to Richard Nicholls, G. Kenneth Sams, Dorothy Burr Thompson, Jaimee P. Uhlenbrock and Frederick A. Winter. In addition, Richard Green was most helpful in providing information on theatrical masks from the photo archives in Sydney, Australia, and Elsbeth B. Dusenbery kindly provided a photograph and information about the Samothracian Erotes (cf. **104**). I am very appreciative of the careful and patient assistance of Jean Donohoe, who entered the manuscript into a computer, edited, checked references and prepared indices; and of Chrisso Boulis, who assisted with the final copy of the manuscript. To Laurie Tiede I am grateful for her editorial guidance.

I am also deeply indebted to my colleagues in Turkey who extended to me their hospitality or facilitated my study of terracotta figurines from many sites in the summer of 1981: Ekrem Akurgal in Ankara; Nuşin Askari at the Istanbul Archaeological Museum; Kudret Ata, Ayfer Aker and Meral Gözübüyük at the General Directorate of Antiquities and Museums in Ankara; Selahattin Erdemgil in Selcuk; the late Kenan Erim at Aphrodisias; Crawford Greenewalt at Sardis; Pontus Hellström at Labraunda; Kubilay Nayir and Rafet Dinç at the Manisa Museum; Azize and Edip Özgür at the Antalya Museum; Wolfgang Radt at Pergamon; Raci Temizer at the Museum of Anatolian Civilizations in Ankara.

The expert photographic work under difficult conditions was done by Robert and Frances Vincent, and the careful restored drawing of the bust-flower thymiaterion on Ill.1 and the pencil drawings of the boots on Color Plate II were the work of Jean Carpenter Efe.

Financial support for various phases of this study and the preparation of this volume was provided by the Gordion excavation project and The University Museum (1978, 1979, 1987); the American Research Institute in Turkey (1981 traveling fellowship); and the University of Pennsylvania Research Foundation (1985 award).

POSTSCRIPT

The writing and editing by the author of this manuscript were completed in December 1988 and no bibliographic references (except where forthcoming volumes meanwhile have become published) or additional data have been incorporated after that date. Since that date this manuscript has been held by the Publications Department of The University Museum in order that other volumes in the Gordion series could be published.

In 1990, the author published a brief article summarizing the Hellenistic terracotta figurines from Gordion in J. P. Uhlenbrock, *The Coroplast's Art: Greek Terracottas of the Hellenistic World*. New Paltz/New Rochelle: College Art Gallery/A. D. Coratzas (pp. 102-106).

Editor's Preface

The publication of the excavations made under the direction of Rodney S. Young takes another important step forward with the present study by Dr. Irene Bald Romano of the terracotta figurines and related plastic vessels found between 1950 and 1973. Ranging in date from the Bronze Age down into Roman times, the collection overall shows an impressive richness and diversity, as are characteristic of other significant categories of small finds awaiting publication (e.g., glass, seals and sealings, and lamps).

The current importance and centrality of Gordion for the archaeology of west-central Anatolia, especially in the first millennium B.C., is as apparent with the terracottas as it is with other categories of finds. Without the evidence of Gordion, archaeology would have no real sense of the range of imported and local terracottas present in the region, particularly from the sixth century B.C. on. By the same token, Gordion suffers in being a type site, in that comparative material within the region is sorely limited. It is thus impossible, given the present state of knowledge, to know whether Gordion was at all unusual in the level of imported Greek terracottas that reached the site. Similarly, the Anatolian products often leave the question of whether they were made in or around Gordion or in other coroplastic centers that have so far gone undetected. As is true of the Gordion publication series in general, Dr. Romano's study looks to future discovery in Central Anatolia.

The centerpiece of the study is the corpus of Hellenistic terracottas. As one important result of his very first season of excavation, Rodney Young identified a level of abandoned, sometimes burned Hellenistic buildings with the deserted settlement that Manlius Vulso encountered when he came to Gordion in 189 B.C. Livy, in his account of Manlius' campaign, described the town as being "filled with an abundance of all things." That remark would appear to be supported in part by the coroplastic wealth of the once thriving town, both the imported Greek goods and those that were made on the spot following Greek models, as the kilns and molds demonstrate. Beyond their intrinsic worth, the terracottas from this historically dated level will make a major contribution to Hellenistic art and its chronology, a field that is notoriously reliant on stylistic criteria for dating. The corpus also gives insight into the human currents and influences that existed in one town of Hellenistic Anatolia. The terracottas reflect the cultural presence of Phrygians, Greeks, Celts, and perhaps other elements as well, and in so doing they yield a microcosmic view of the Hellenized East.

For the research in Turkey that led to this publication, we express deep gratitude to the Turkish Ministry of Culture, and especially to the General Directorate for Antiquities and the Directorate of the Museum of Anatolian Civilizations in Ankara. We are also most grateful to the National Endowment for the Humanities for support of the preparation of this volume and, as always, to the University of Pennsylvania Museum and its Department of Publications.

G. Kenneth Sams
September 1994

Abbreviations

AA	*Archäologischer Anzeiger*
AAA	*Athens Annals of Archaeology*
ADOG	*Abhandlungen der Deutscher Orient-Gesellschaft*
AJA	*American Journal of Archaeology*
AnatSt	*Anatolian Studies*
AntCl	*L'antiquité classique*
AntP	*Antike Plastik*
ArchEph	*'Archaiologikè 'Ephemerís*
ArchNews	*Archaeological News*
ARV	*Attic Red-Figure Vase-Painters* (Beazley 1963)
ASAtene	*Annuario della R. Scuola archeologica di Atene*
AvP	Altertümer von Pergamon
AZ	*Archäologische Zeitung*
BCH	*Bulletin de correspondance hellénique*
BdA	*Bollettino d'arte*
Belleten	*Belleten Türk Tarih Kurumu*
BICS	*Bulletin of the Institute of Classical Studies, University of London*
BMMA	*Bulletin of the Metropolitan Museum of Art, New York*
BMQ	*British Museum Quarterly*
BSA	*British School at Athens, Annual*
CA	*Classical Antiquity* (University of California Press)
CVA	*Corpus Vasorum Antiquorum*
GEFR	Gordion Excations Final Reports
GSS	Gordion Special Studies
IstMitt	*Mitteilungen des deutschen archäologischen Instituts, Abteilung Istanbul*

JdI	*Jahrbuch des (k). deutschen archäologischen Instituts*
JGS	*Journal of Glass Studies*
JHS	*Journal of Hellenic Studies*
JHS-AR	*Journal of Hellenic Studies, Archaeological Reports*
METU	Middle East Technical University
MonAnt	*Monumenti Antichi*
NB	Gordion Excavation Notebook
OIP	Oriental Institute Publications
RA	*Revue archéologique*
TürkArkDerg	*Türk Arkeoloji Dergisi*
TürkTarDerg	*Türk Tarih Arkeologya ve Etnografya Dergisi*
UPMB	*University of Pennsylvania Museum Bulletin*
WVDOG	*Wissenschaftliche Veröffentlichung en der Deutschen Orient-Gesellschaft*

Bibliography

Albizzati, C.	1928	"Agalmation Kythereias." *AntP* (Festschrift für Walther Amelung). Berlin and Leipzig: Walter de Gruyter.
Alexander, C.	1930	"A Recently Acquired Terra Cotta Statuette." *BMMA* 25: 242-244.
Allègre, F.	1889	*Étude sur la déesse grecque Tyché*. Paris: Ernest Leroux.
Allen, R. E.	1983	*The Attalid Kingdom: A Constitutional History*. Oxford: Clarendon Press.
Allen, T. W., ed.	1952	*Homeri Opera V*. Oxford: Clarendon Press.
Anderson, G.	1980	*The Common Cemetery at Gordion*. Ph.D. dissertation, Bryn Mawr College.
Arik, R. O.	1934	"Karalar Hafriyati." *TürkTarDerg* 2: 102-167, 308 ff.
Arik, R. O. and J. Coupry	1935	"Les tumuli de Karalar et la sépulture du roi Deiotarus II." *RA* 6, ser. 5: 133-151.
Bayburtluoğlu, C.	1977	*Erythrai* II: *Pişmis Toprak Eserler: Terracottas in Erythrai*. Ankara: Türk Tarih Kurumu Basimevi.
Beazley, J. D.	1929	"Charinos: Attic Vases in the Form of Human Heads." *JHS* 49: 38-78.
	1963	*Attic Red-Figure Vase Painters*. 2d ed. Vol. 2. Oxford: Clarendon Press.
Belin de Ballu, E.	1972	*Olbia: cité antique du littoral nord de la Mer noire*. Leiden: E. J. Brill.
Bell, M.	1981	*Morgantina Studies* I: *The Terracottas*. Princeton: Princeton University Press.
Berger, E., ed.	1982	*Antike Kunstwerke aus der Sammlung Ludwig* II: *Terrakotten und Bronzen*. Basel: Archäologischer Verlag.
Besques, S., *et al.* (see also S. Mollard-Besques)	1985	"Cinquante ans de découvertes et de travaux sur les figurines de terre cuite grecques et romaines." *RA* 1: 77-114.
Bielefeld, E.	1950-51	"Eros in der Blüte." *AA* 65-66: 47-73.
Bittel, K.	1963	"Phrygisches Kultbild aus Boğazköy." *AntP* 2: 7-22.
Bittel, K.; H. Naumann; and H. Otto	1967	*Yazilikaya: Architektur, Felsbilder, Inschriften und Kleinfunde*. WVDOG, Bd. 61. Osnabrück: Otto Zeller.
Blinkenberg, C.	1931	*Lindos, fouilles de l'acropole 1902-1914* I: *Les petits objets*. Berlin: Walter de Gruyter.
Boardman, J.	1962-63	"Greek Archaeology on the Shores of the Black Sea." *JHS-AR* 1962-63: 34-51.

	1967	*Excavations in Chios, 1952-1955: Greek Emborio.* British School at Athens, Supp. Vol. 6. London: Thames and Hudson.
Boardman, J., and J. Hayes	1966	*Excavations at Tocra, 1963-1965: The Archaic Deposits* I. British School of Archaeology at Athens, Supp. Vol. 4. London: Thames and Hudson.
Boehlau, J.	1898	*Aus ionischen und italischen Nekropolen.* Leipzig: B. G. Teubner.
Boehmer, R. M.	1972	*Boğazköy-Hattuşa 7: Die Kleinfunde von Boğazköy.* WVDOG, Bd 87. Berlin: Gebr. Mann.
	1979	*Boğazköy-Hattuşa 10: Die Kleinfunde aus der Unterstadt von Boğazköy*: Grabungskampagnen, 1970-1978. Berlin: Gebr. Mann.
Breitenstein, N.	1941	*Catalogue of the Terracottas, Danish National Museum.* Copenhagen: E. Munksgaard.
Brixhe, C., and M. Lejeune	1984	*Corpus des inscriptions paléo-phrygiennes.* Paris: Institut Français d'Études Anatoliennes, Mémoire No. 45.
Buluç, S.	1979	*Ankara Frig Nekropolünden üç Tümülüs Buluntulari.* Eylül: Doçentlik Tezi.
Burkert, W.	1979	*Structure and History in Greek Mythology and Ritual.* Berkeley and London: University of California Press.
	1985	*Greek Religion.* tr. J. Raffan. Cambridge, Mass.: Harvard University Press.
Burr, D. (see also D. B. Thompson)	1934	*Terracottas from Myrina in the Boston Museum of Fine Arts.* Vienna: A. Holzhausens nachfolger.
Canarache, V.	1969	*Masks and Tanagra Figurines Made in the Workshops of Callatis (Mangalia).* Constanta: Muzeul de Arhelogie Constanta.
Caner, E.	1983	*Prähistorische Bronzefunde XIV,8: Fibeln in Anatolien* I. Munich: C. H. Beck'sche.
Catling, H. W.	1981-82	"Archaeology in Greece, 1981-82." *JHS-AR* 1981-82: 3-62.
Coja, M.	1961	"Alcuni aspetti della coroplastica ellenistica di Histria." *Dacia* 5: 213-232.
Conze, A., and P. Schazmann	1911	*Mamurt-Kaleh: ein Tempel der Göttermutter unweit Pergamon. JdI* Ergänzungsheft 9. Berlin: Georg Reimer.
Cook, J. M.	1983	*The Persian Empire.* New York: Schocken Books.
Crome, J. F.	1934	"Ausgrabungen in Larisa am Hermos in Frühjahr 1934: die Kleinfunde." *AA* 49: 392-410.
Crome, J. F.; E. Gren; L. Kjellberg; and B. Meyer-Plath	1942	*Larisa am Hermos* III: *Die Kleinfunde.* Berlin: Walter de Gruyter.
Daux, G.	1958	"Nouvelles de Myrmèkion." *BCH* 82: 351-352.
Devreker, J., and M. Waelkens	1984	*Les fouilles de la Rijksuniversiteit te Gent à Pessinonte, 1967-1973.* IA-B, Dissertationes Archaeologicae Gandenses XXII. Brugge: De Tempel.
DeVries, K.	1988	"Gordion and Phrygia in the Sixth Century B.C." *Source* 7(3/4): 51-59.
	1990	"The Gordion Excavation Seasons of 1969-1973 and Subsequent Research." *AJA* 94: 371-406.

	forthcoming	*The Pre-Hellenistic Greek Pottery*. GEFR. Philadelphia: The University Museum, University of Pennsylvania.
Diehl, E.	1964	"Fragmente aus Samos." *AA* 79: 494-611.
Dragendorf, H.	1903	*Theraeische Graeber* (= Hiller von Gaertringen, *Thera* 2.). Berlin: Georg Reimer.
Ducat, J.	1963	"Les vases plastiques corinthiens." *BCH* 87: 431-458.
	1966	*Les vases plastiques rhodiens archaiques en terre cuite*. Paris: E. de Boccard.
von Duhn, F.	1877	"Griechische Reliefs." *AZ* 35: 139-175.
Edwards, G. R.	1959a	"The Gordion Campaign of 1958: Preliminary Report." *AJA* 63: 263-268.
	1959b	"Gordion Report, 1958." *TürkArkDerg* 9(1).
	1975	*Corinth* VII,3: *Corinthian Hellenistic Pottery*. Princeton: American School of Classical Studies.
Fischer, F.	1963	*Boğazköy-Hattuşa* IV: *Die hethitische Keramik von Boğazköy* WVDOG, Bd. 75. Berlin: Gebr. Mann.
Frel, J.	1971	"The Rhodian Workmanship of the Alexander Sarcophagus." *IstMitt* 21: 121-124.
Gabrici, E.	1913	"Cuma." *MonAnt* 22: entire volume.
Goldman, H.	1950	*Excavations at Gözlü Küle, Tarsus I: The Hellenistic and Roman Periods*. Princeton: Princeton University Press.
Greenewalt, C. H. Jr.	1966	*Lydian Pottery of the Sixth Century* B.C.: *The Lydion and Marbled Ware*. Ph.D. dissertation, University of Pennsylvania.
	1971	"An Exhibitionist from Sardis." pp. 29-46 in D.G. Mitten *et al.*, eds., *Studies Presented to G. M. A. Hanfmann*. Mainz: Philipp von Zabern.
Gualandi, G.	1979	"Sculture di Rodi." *ASAtene* 54 (n.s. 38, 1976): 7-257.
Gunter, A. C.	1991	*The Bronze Age*. GEFR III. Philadelphia: The University Museum, The Unversity of Pennsylvania.
Hansen, E.	1971	*The Attalids of Pergamon*. Ithaca: Cornell University Press.
Haspels, C. H. E.	1951	*Phrygie: exploration archéologique* 3: *La cité de Midas, céramique et trouvailles diverses*. Paris: E. de Boccard.
	1971	*The Highlands of Phrygia: Sites and Monuments*. Princeton: Princeton University Press.
Higgins, R. A.		*Catalogue of the Terracotta Figurines in the Department of Greek and Roman Antiquities, British Museum*. London, British Museum.
	1954	Volume 1 (Greek: 730-330 B.C.).
	1959	Volume 2, Parts 1 and 2 (Plastic Vases of the Seventh and Sixth Centuries B.C.; Plastic Lekythoi of the Fourth Century B.C.).
	1961	"A Terracotta Hare." *BMQ* 24: 45-46.
	1963	*Greek Terracotta Figures*. London: British Museum.

	1967	*Greek Terracottas*. London: Methuen Co.
Hoffmann, H.	1962	*Attic Red-Figured Rhyta*. Mainz: Philipp von Zabern.
Holloway, R. R.	1957	*A Terracotta from Gordion and the Tradition of the Seated Kybele*. M.A. thesis, University of Pennsylvania.
Jacopi, G.	1931-39	*Clara Rhodos* IV: *Scavi nelle necropoli camiresi 1929-30*. Rhodes: Istituto Storico-Archeologico.
Johnston, R. H.	1970	*Pottery Practices during the 6th-8th Centuries B.C. at Gordion in Central Anatolia: An Analytical and Synthesizing Study*. Ph.D. dissertation, Pennsylvania State University.
Jones, R. E.	1986	*Greek and Cypriot Pottery: a review of scientific studies*. BSA—Fitch Laboratory Occasional Papers no. 1. Athens.
Karageorghis, V.	1976	"Chronique des fouilles et découvertes archéologiques à Chypre en 1975." *BCH* 100: 839-906.
Kleiner, G.	1942	*Tanagrafiguren*. *JdI* Ergänzungsheft 15. Berlin: Walter de Gruyter.
Körte, A., and G. Körte	1904	*Gordion: Ergebnisse der Ausgrabung im Jahre 1900*. *JdI* Supp. 1, V. 5. Berlin: Georg Reimer.
Kohler, E.	1980	"Cremations of the Middle Phrygian Period at Gordion." pp. 65-89 in K. DeVries, ed., *From Athens to Gordion*. Philadelphia: The University Museum, University of Pennsylvania.
	1995	*The Lesser Phrygian Tumuli: Inhumations*. GEFR II. Philadelphia: The University Museum, University of Pennsylvania.
	forthcoming	*The Lesser Phrygian Tumuli: Cremations*. GEFR II, 2. Philadelphia: The University Museum, University of Pennsylvania.
Koşay, H. Z. and M. Akok	1966	*Alaca Höyük Kazısı 1940-1948 Deki Çalismalara ve Kesiflere ait ilk Rapor*. Ankara: Türk Tarih Kurumu Basimevi.
Kübler, K.	1954	*Kerameikos* V,1: *Die Nekropole des 10. bis 8. Jahrhunderts*. Berlin: Walter de Gruyter.
Kühne, H.	1969	"Die Bestattungen der hellenistischen bis spätkaiserzeitlichen Periode." pp. 35-45 in K. Bittel *et al.*, *Boğazköy 4: Funde aus den Grabungen 1967 und 1968*. ADOG 14. Berlin: Gebr. Mann.
Kurtz, D. C., and J. Boardman	1971	*Greek Burial Customs*. Ithaca: Cornell University Press.
Lambrechts, P.; J. Strubbe; M. Waelkens; and G. Stoop	1972	"Les fouilles de Pessinonte: le temple." *AntCl* 41: 156-173.
Langlotz, E.	1932	*Griechische Vasen in Würzburg*. Munich: J. B. Obernetter.
Lantier, R.	1931	"Les grands champs de fouilles de l'Afrique du Nord (1915-1930)." *AA* 46: 461-575.
Laumonier, A.	1921	*Catalogue de terres cuites du Musée archéologique de Madrid*. Bordeaux: Feret et Fils; Paris: E. de Boccard.
	1956	*Exploration archéologique de Délos* XXIII: *Les figurines de terre cuite*. Paris: E. de Boccard.

Lazarides, D.	1960	*Pelina Eidolia Abderon.* Bibliotheke tes en Athenas Archaiologikes Hetaireas, 47. Athens.
Lehmann, K.	1975	*Samothrace: A Guide to the Excavations and the Museum.* 4th ed. Locust Valley, N.Y.: J. J. Augustin.
Lo Porto, F. G.	1962	"Tombe archaiche tarentine con terrecotte ioniche." *BdA* 47: 164-165.
Lordkipanidze, I.	1974	"La Géorgie et le monde grec." *BCH* 98: 943-948.
Mathiesen, H. E.	1982	*Ikaros, The Hellenistic Settlements* I: *The Terracotta Figurines.* Jutland Archaeological Society Publications XVI,1. Copenhagen: Nordisk Forlag.
Maximova, M. I.	1927	*Les vases plastiques dans l'antiquité* (époque archaïque). Paris: P. Geuthner.
Mellink, M. J.	1956	*A Hittite Cemetery at Gordion.* Philadelphia: The University Museum, University of Pennsylvania.
	1973	"Archaeology in Asia Minor: Eskişehir." *AJA* 77: 190.
	1981	"Conclusions." Pp. 263-272 in R. S. Young, *Three Great Early Tumuli*, GEFR I. University Museum Monograph 43. Philadelphia: The University Museum, University of Pennsylvania.
	1983	"Comments on a Cult Relief of Kybele from Gordion." Pp. 349-360 in *Beiträge zur Altertumskunde Kleinasiens: Festschrift für Kurt Bittel.* Mainz: Philipp von Zabern.
Mendel, G.	1908	*Catalogues des figurines grecques de terre cuite.* Constantinople: Ahmed Ihsan.
METU	1965	*Yassihüyük, A Village Study.* Ankara: Middle East Technical University.
Metzger, H.	1972	*Fouilles de Xanthos* IV: *Les céramiques archaïques et classiques de l'acropole lycienne.* Paris: Librairie C. Klincksieck.
Mitchell, S.	1974	"Blucium and Peium: The Galatian Forts of King Deiotarus." *AnatSt* 24: 61-75.
Mitten, D.	1978	"Terracotta Figurines from the Isthmian Sanctuary of Poseidon." Paper read at Annual Meeting of Archaeological Institute of America, Vancouver, B.C., 28 December 1978.
Mollard-Besques, S. (see also S. Besques)		*Catalogue raisonné des figurines et reliefs en terre cuite grecs, étrusques, et romains.* Paris: Musée National du Louvre.
	1954	Volume 1 (Époques préhellenique, géometrique, archaïque, et classique).
	1963	Volume 2 (Myrina).
	1972	Volume 3 (Époque hellénistique et romaine, Grèce et Asie mineure).
de Morant, H.	1956	*Musée Pincé: art grec, art romain.* Angers, France: Imp. de l'Anjou.
Moraux, P.	1957	"L'établissement des Galates en Asie mineure." *IstMitt* 7: 56-75.
Munsell	1975	*Munsell Soil Color Charts.* Baltimore: Kollmorgen Corporation.
Muscarella, O. W.	1967	*Phrygian Fibulae from Gordion.* London: Bernard Quaritch Ltd.
	1974	*Ancient Art—The Norbert Schimmel Collection.* Mainz: Philipp von Zabern.

Naumann, F.	1983	*Die Ikonographie der Kybele in der phrygischen und der griechischen Kunst. IstMitt* Beiheft 28. Tübingen: Ernst Wasmuth.
Naumann, R.	1967	"Das Heiligtum der Meter Steunene bei Aezani." *IstMitt* 17: 218-247.
Nicholls, R. V.	1952	"Type, Group and Series: A Reconsideration of Some Coroplastic Fundamentals." *BSA* 47: 217-226.
	1970	"Greek Votive Statuettes and Religious Continuity, c. 1200-700 B.C." Pp. 1-37 in B. F. Harris, ed., *Auckland Classical Essays Presented to E. M. Blaiklock*. Auckland: Auckland University Press; Wellington: Oxford University Press.
	1984	"La fabrication des terres cuites." *Les dossiers, histoire et archéologie* 81: 24-31.
Nohlen, K., and W. Radt	1978	*Kapikaya: ein Felsheiligtum bei Pergamon*. AVP XII. Berlin: Walter de Gruyter.
Orsi, P.	1906	"Gela." *MonAnt* 17: entire volume.
von der Osten, H. H.	1937	*The Alishar Hüyük: Season of 1930-32*, Part 2. OIP 29. Chicago: University of Chicago Press.
von der Osten, H. H., and E. F. Schmidt	1932	*The Alishar Hüyük: Season of 1927*, Part 2. OIP 8. Chicago: University of Chicago Press.
Özgüç, T.	1971	*Demir Devrinde Kültepe ve Civari; Kültepe and Its Vicinity in the Iron Age*. Ankara: Türk Tarih Kurumu Basimevi.
Özgüç, T., and M. Akok	1947	"Die Ausgrabungen an zwei Tumuli auf dem Mausoleumhügel bei Ankara." *Belleten* 11: 57-85.
Pagenstecher, R.	1909	*Die calenische Reliefkeramik. JdI* Ergänzungsheft 8. Berlin: Reimer.
Parke, H. W.	1977	*Festivals of the Athenians*. Ithaca: Cornell University Press.
Perdrizet, P.	1897	"Voyage dans la Macédoine première." *BCH* 21: 514-543.
Peredolskaja, A. A.	1964	*Attische Tonfiguren aus einem südrussischen Grab*. (Beiheft 2). Halbjahresschrift Antike Kunst Herausgegeben von der Vereinigung der Freunde Antike Kunst, Beiheft 2. Switzerland: Urs Graf-Verlag.
Piotrovsky, B. B.	1969	*The Ancient Civilization of Urartu*. New York: Cowles Book Co., Inc.
Powell, T. G. E.	1960	*The Celts*. New York: Praeger.
Prayon, F.	1987	*Phrygische Plastik: die früheisenzeitliche Bildkunst Zentral-Anatoliens und ihre Beziehungen zu Griechenland und zum Alten Orient*. Tübingen: Ernst Wasmuth.
Radt, W.	1973	"Pergamon Grabungskampagne im Herbst 1972." *AA* 88: 260-269.
	1978	"Pergamon: Vorbericht über die Kampagne 1977." *AA* 93: 407-432.
Richter, G. M. A.	1926	*Ancient Furniture: A History of Greek, Etruscan, and Roman Furniture*. Oxford: Clarendon Press.
	1954	*Catalogue of Greek Sculptures* (Metropolitan Museum of Art, New York). Cambridge, Mass.: Harvard University Press.
	1958	"Ancient Plaster Casts of Greek Metalware." *AJA* 62: 369-377.

Ridgway, B. S.	1977	*The Archaic Style in Greek Sculpture*. Princeton: Princeton University Press.
Robinson, D. M.	1933	*Excavations at Olynthos* VII: *The Terracottas of Olynthos*. Baltimore: The Johns Hopkins Press.
	1952	*Excavations at Olynthos* XIV: *Terracottas, Lamps, and Coins Found in 1934 and 1938*. Baltimore: The Johns Hopkins Press.
von Rohden, H.	1884	"Rappresentazione identica sopra una cassetta di terracotta canosina e sopra uno specchio a libretto di Corneto." *Annali dell'Istituto di corrispondenza archeologica* 56: 30-49.
Rollas, A. N.	1960	"La collection de terres cuites du Musée." *Annual of the Archaeological Museums of Istanbul* 9: 77-79.
Roller, L. E.	1983	"The Legend of Midas." *CA* 2: 299-313.
	1986	"A Hellenistic Statuette from Gordion: Kybele among the Muses." Abstract of paper delivered at Annual Meeting of Archaeological Institute of America, Washington, D.C., 29 December 1985. *AJA* 90: 209.
	1987a	*Non-Verbal Graffiti, Dipinti and Stamps*. GSS I. Philadelphia: The University Museum, University of Pennsylvania.
	1987b	"Hellenistic Epigraphic Texts from Gordion." *AnatSt* 37: 103-133.
	1988	"Phrygian Myth and Cult." *Source* 7(3/4): 43-50.
Rouse, W. H. D.	1975	*Greek Votive Offerings*. Cambridge, England: The University Press, 1902; repr. New York: Arno Press.
Russayayeva, A. S.	1982	*Antichnye Terrakoty Severo-Zapadnogo Prichernomorya* (VI-I VW do n.e.) Kiev: Naukova Dumka.
SAI	1970-1974	*Svod Archeologicheskih Istochnikov (Archeologiya SSSR)* vol. G1-11, pts. 1-4. Moscow: Instituta Arkheologii Naka. Akademii Nauk SSR.
von Salis, A.	1913	"Die Göttermutter des Agorakritos." *JdI* 28: 1-26.
Sams, G. K.	1971	*The Phrygian Painted Pottery of Early Iron Age Gordion and Its Anatolian Setting*. Ph.D. dissertation, University of Pennsylvania.
	1979a	"Imports at Gordion: Lydian and Persian Periods." *Expedition* 21: 6-17.
	1979b	"Patterns of Trade in First Millennium Gordion." *ArchNews* 2/3: 45-53.
	1994	*The Early Phrygian Pottery*. GEFR IV. Philadelphia: The University Museum, University of Pennsylvania.
Schafer, J.	1968	*Hellenistische Keramik aus Pergamon*. Pergamenische Forschungen Bd. 2. Berlin: Walter de Gruyter.
Schede, M.	1964	*Die Ruinen von Priene*. Berlin: Walter de Gruyter.
Scheurleer, C. W. L.	1922	"Neuerwerbungen der Sammlung C. W. Lunsingh Scheurleer im Haag." *AA* 37: 202-238.
Schirmer, W.	1969	*Die Bebauung am Unteren Büyükkale-Nordwesthang in Boğazköy: Ergebnisse der Untersuchungen der Grabungscampagnen 1960-63*. Berlin: Gebr. Mann.
Sieveking, J.	1916	*Die Terrakotten der Sammlung Loeb*, II. Munich: A. Buchholz.

Skia, A. N.	1898	"Panarxaia Eleusiniake Nekropolis." *ArchEph* 1898: 29-122.
	1912	"Neoterai Anaskaphai en te Panarchaia Eleusiniake Nekropolei." *ArchEph* 1912: 1-39.
Smith, A. H.	1900	*A Catalogue of Sculpture in the Department of Greek and Roman Antiquities, British Museum*. London: British Museum.
Squarciapino, Floriani, M.	1962	*I culti orientali ad Ostia*. Études préliminaires aux religions orientales dans l'Empire romain, Vol. 3. Leiden: E. J. Brill.
Stoop, J. M.	1960	*Floral Figurines from South Italy*. Leiden: Van Gorcum and Co.
Stroud, R. S.	1965	"The Sanctuary of Demeter and Kore on Acrocorinth Preliminary Report I: 1961-1962." *Hesperia* 34: 1-24.
	1968	"The Sanctuary of Demeter and Kore on Acrocorinth, Preliminary Report II: 1964-1965." *Hesperia* 37: 299-330.
von Sybel, L.	1881	*Katalog der Skulpturen zu Athen*. Marburg: N. G. Elwert.
Sztetyllo, Z.	1976	*Mirmeki*. Warsaw: Panstwowe Wydawnictwo Naukowe.
Tezcan, B.	1964	*Yalincak Village Excavation in 1962-1963*. Ankara: Middle East Technical University.
Themelis, P.	1979	"Ausgrabungen in Kallipolis (Ost-Aetolien) 1977-1978." *AAA* 12: 245-279.
Thompson, D. B. (see also D. Burr)	1949	"Ostrakina Toreumata." *Hesperia* Supp. 8: 365-372.
	1950	"A Bronze Dancer from Alexandria." *AJA* 54: 371-385.
	1962	"Three Centuries of Hellenistic Terracottas, IIC: The Satyr Cistern." *Hesperia* 31: 244-262.
	1963a	*The Terracotta Figurines of the Hellenistic Period*. Troy Supp. III. Princeton: Princeton University Press.
	1963b	"Three Centuries of Hellenistic Terracottas, III: The Late Third Century B.C." *Hesperia* 32: 276-292.
	1963c	"Three Centuries of Hellenistic Terracottas: The Second Century B.C." *Hesperia* 32: 301-317.
	1966a	"Three Centuries of Hellenistic Terracottas, VII: The Early First Century B.C.: A. The Kybele Cistern." *Hesperia* 35: 1-19.
	1966b	"Three Centuries of Hellenistic Terracottas, VII: The Early First Century B.C.: B. The Mask Cistern. VIII: The Late First Century B.C." *Hesperia* 35: 252-267.
	1973	*Ptolemaic Oinochoai and Portraits in Faience: Aspects of the Ruler Cult*. Oxford: Clarendon Press.
Thompson, H. A.	1948a	"Archaeological News: Agora." *AJA* 52: 523-526.
	1948b	"Excavations of the Athenian Agora, 1947." *Hesperia* 17: 149-196.
Töpperwein, E.	1976	*Terrakotten von Pergamon*. Pergamenische Forschungen, Bd. 3. Berlin: Walter de Gruyter.

Töpperwein-Hoffmann, E.	1971	"Terrakotten von Priene." *IstMitt* 21: 125-160.
	1978	"Exkurs: die Terrakotten von Mamurtkale." Pp. 77-89 in K. Nolan and W. Radt, *Kapikaya*. AvP XII. Berlin: Walter de Gruyter.
Touratsoglou, I.	1968	"Mia 'Arethousa' kai Alla Pelina Eidolia ap' te Xalkidike sto Mouseio tes Thessalonikes." *BCH* 92: 37-71.
Trumpf-Lyritzaki, M.	1969	*Griechische Figurenvasen*. Abhandlungen zur Kunst-, Musik-, und Literaturwissenschaft Bd. 73. Bonn: H. Bouvier.
Tuchelt, K.	1962	*Tiergefässe in Kopf- und Protomengestalt*. Istanbuler Forschungen, Bd. 22. Berlin: Gebr. Mann.
Vermaseren, M. J.	1977a	*Corpus Cultus Cybelae Attisque* III: *Italia-Latium*. Études préliminaires aux religions orientales dans l'Empire romain. Vol. 50. Leiden: E. J. Brill.
	1977b	*Cybele and Attis: The Myth and the Cult*, tr. A. M. H. Lemmers. London: Thames and Hudson.
	1987	*Corpus Cultus Cybelae Attisque* I: *Asia Minor*. Leiden: E. J. Brill.
Virgilio, B.	1981	*Il "tempio stato" di Pessinonte fra Pergama e Roma nel II-I secole A.C.* Pisa: Giardini.
Voigt, M. M.	1983	*Hajji Firuz Tepe, Iran: The Neolithic Settlement*. Hasanlu Excavation Report I, gen. ed. R. H. Dyson, Jr. Philadelphia: The University Museum, University of Pennsylvania.
Waelkens, M.	1985	"An Early Imperial Sanctuary of the Emperor Cult at Pessinus (Galatia)." Abstract of paper delivered at Annual Meeting of Archaeological Institute of America, Toronto, Ont., December 1984. *AJA* 89: 355.
	1986	"The Imperial Sanctuary at Pessinus: Archaeological, Epigraphical, and Numismatic Evidence for Its Date and Identification." Pp. 37-72 in E. Akurgal *et al.*, eds., *Epigraphica Anatolica Zeitschrift für Epigraphik und historische Geographie Anatoliens*. Bonn: Rudolph Habelt.
Webb, V.	1978	*Archaic Greek Faience*. Warminster, England: Aris and Phillips, Ltd.
Webster, T. B. L.	1950	*Greek Terracottas*. London: Penguin Books.
	1960	"Greek Dramatic Monuments from the Athenian Agora and Pnyx." *Hesperia* 29: 254-284.
	1965	"On the Dramatic Terracottas of Lipari." Pp. 319-328. In L. Bèrnarbo Brea and M. Cavalier, *Meligunis-Lipara* II: *La necropoli greca e romana nella Contrada Diana*. Palermo: S.F. Flaccovio.
	1969	*Monuments Illustrating Old and Middle Comedy*. 2d ed. *BICS* Supp. 23. London.
Webster, T. B. L. and J. R. Green	1978	*Monuments Illustrating Old and Middle Comedy*. 3d rev. ed. *BICS* Supp. 39. London.
Welles, C. B.	1934	*Royal Correspondence of the Hellenistic Period*. New Haven: Yale University Press.
Wiegand, T, and Schrader, H.	1904	*Priene, Ergebnisse der Ausgrabungen und Untersuchungen in den Jahren 1895-1898*. Berlin: Georg Reimer.

Williams, C. K., II	1977	"Corinth 1976: Forum Southwest." *Hesperia* 46: 40-81.
	1978	"Corinth 1977, Forum Southwest." *Hesperia* 47: 1-39.
Williams, C. K., II; J. MacIntosh; and J. E. Fisher	1973	"Excavations at Corinth, 1973." *Hesperia* 43: 1-76.
Williams, E. R.	1978	"Figurine Vases from the Athenian Agora." *Hesperia* 47: 356-401.
Williams, E. T.; G. Cadet; N. A. Guardala; E. Huang; and F. A. Winter	1987	"Analysis of Pottery by PIXE: Late Classical and Hellenistic Imports to Gordion." *Nuclear Instruments and Methods in Physics Research* B22: 430-432.
Winnefeld, H.	1910	*Die Friese des grozsen Altars*. AvP III,2. Berlin: Georg Reimer.
Winter, F.	1893	"Ubersicht über die auf der athenischen Akropolis gemachten Funde von Terrakotten." *AA* 8: 140-147.
	1903	*Die Typen der figurlichen Terrakotten* 1 and 2. Berlin and Stuttgart: W. Spemann.
	1908	*Die Skulpturen*. AvP VII,1. Berlin: Georg Reimer.
Winter, F. A.	1977	"An Historically Derived Model for the Dorian Invasion." Pp. 60-71 in *Symposium on the Dark Ages in Greece*. E. N. Davis, ed. New York: Hunter College.
	1984	*Late Classical and Hellenistic Pottery from Gordion: The Imported Black Glazed Wares*. Ph.D. dissertation, University of Pennsylvania.
	1988	"Phrygian Gordion in the Hellenistic Period. *Source* 7(3/4): 60-71.
	forthcoming	Late Classical and Hellenistic Pottery. GEFR. Philadelphia: The University Museum, University of Pennsylvania.
Young, J. H. and S. H. Young	1955	*Terracotta Figurines from Kourion in Cyprus*. Philadelphia: The University Museum, University of Pennsylvania.
Young, R. S.	1949	"An Early Geometric Grave near the Athenian Agora." *Hesperia* 18: 275-297.
	1950	"Excavations at Yassıhöyük-Gordion." *Archaeology* 3: 196-201.
	1951a	"Archaeological Research in Turkey, 1949-50: Gordion." *AnatSt* 1: 11-14.
	1951b	"Gordion—1950." *UPMB* 16: 3-19.
	1952	"Archaeological Work in Turkey, 1951, Gordion." *AnatSt* 2: 20-22.
	1953	"Progress at Gordion." *UPMB* 17: 3-39.
	1955	"Gordion: Preliminary Report, 1953." *AJA* 59: 1-18.
	1956	"The Campaign of 1955 at Gordion: Preliminary Report." *AJA* 60: 249-266.
	1957	"Gordion 1956: Preliminary Report." *AJA* 61: 319-331.
	1962	"The 1961 Campaign at Gordion." *AJA* 66: 153-168.
	1966	"The Gordion Campaign of 1965." *AJA* 70: 267-278.

	1968	"The Gordion Campaign of 1967." *AJA* 72: 231-241.
	1975	*Gordion: A Guide to the Excavations and Museum.* rev. ed. Ankara: Türk Tarih Kurumu Basimevi.
	1981	*Three Great Early Tumuli.* GEFR I. University Museum Monograph 43. Philadelphia: The University Museum, University of Pennsylvania.
Züchner, W.	1942	*Griechische Klappspiegel.* Berlin: Walter de Gruyter.

Introduction

The 171 terracotta figurines and related figural vessels included in this volume are all those which were excavated by The University Museum of the University of Pennsylvania in the Gordion campaigns between 1950 and 1973. Included as a part of this study are all moldmade and handmade terracotta representations of humans, divinities, other supernatural creatures, and animals; models or non-vessel miniatures; masks; medallions; molds for figurines or vessels; objects other than vessels; and figural vessels either moldmade or hand-modeled, but linked by technique to terracotta figurines. A group of handmade animal figurines which *may* be vessel attachments are included in the animal-vessel category. Other plastic attachments for vessels or spouts in the form of animal heads do not form a part of this corpus except as comparanda or when the function is uncertain.

Despite the fact that some of the objects in this corpus are or will be published in other Gordion volumes—e.g., the Hittite-period animal figurines in a volume together with the Bronze Age pottery (Gunter 1991), or the archaic Greek plastic vessels in a volume on the pre-Hellenistic Greek pottery (DeVries, forthcoming)—these have also been included in this study to allow as comprehensive a picture as possible of the coroplastic objects used throughout the history of Gordion.

All of the terracotta figurines excavated at Gordion are in Turkey. The majority are in a storage depot at Gordion, while a few are on display in the local museum at Gordion; others are on exhibit in the Museum of Anatolian Civilizations in Ankara and some, especially those excavated during the 1950 and 1951 seasons, are in a storage facility at the Archaeological Museum in Ankara.

Excavation History

As is indicated in the Conclusions (p. 71), our view of the local coroplastic industry and the pattern of imported products is affected greatly by the history of archaeological excavation at Gordion. Although archaeologists from The University Museum excavated for sixteen seasons at Gordion between 1950 and 1973, the site is enormous and has been by no means exploited to its fullest potential for revealing the history of Gordion and Central Anatolia. The goals of those American excavations were largely focused on the Phrygians, specifically the Early and Middle Phrygian periods, and on revealing information about a culture and people otherwise relatively unknown in the archaeological record. Further excavations will fill out the stratigraphic picture especially of the Late Phrygian/Hellenistic and Roman periods and will shed more light on the coroplastic assemblage at Gordion.

Gordion: Setting, Brief History and General Chronology
Fig. 1.

The large settlement mound at Gordion (ca. 500 x 350 m. at its widest points and ca. 15 m. at its maximum height), called the City Mound (used throughout to indicate the settlement site), is encircled by fortification systems of the Early and Middle Phrygian periods which enclose a palatial area of these same periods comprising a series of free-standing megara and service areas to one side (see Figs. 2-3). To the southwest of the City Mound is a smaller mound, known as the Küçük Hüyük, joined to the City Mound by low spur walls (Küçük Hüyük is used throughout). The Küçük Hüyük is actually a tumulus of clay heaped over a mudbrick fortification system of the 7th century B.C. On the spurs of the hills which run down to the floodplain of the Sangarius and in other low-lying areas of the plain are the cemeteries of Gordion, most notably clusters of large and small burial tumuli of the

Early and Middle Phrygian periods (tumulus/tumuli is used throughout to designate burial mound[s]). Less elaborate burials of various periods, including a major Hittite-period cemetery, also occur along the ridges running to the floodplain.

Gordion's history is largely known from the excavations conducted by the Austrian Körte brothers in 1900 (Körte and Körte 1904) and from the extensive archaeological work carried out by The University Museum of the University of Pennsylvania under the direction of Rodney S. Young from 1950 to 1973. Assyrian records and Greek and Roman literary accounts help to supplement Gordion's history from the later 8th century B.C. to the Roman period (for main references see *ibid*.: pp. 3-5).

Gordion was inhabited from Early Bronze Age times (later 3d millennium), though as yet we don't know how continuous occupation was into the Middle Bronze Age. The Early Bronze Age settlement was a small mound which rises to a considerable height in the northeastern part of the City Mound and was partially leveled to accommodate the Phrygian settlement. On the outer slopes of this mound, Middle and Late Bronze Age levels can be detected. A substantial settlement of the Hittite period, recognized thus far from two deep soundings (Megs. 10 and 12) and scattered Hittite ceramics on the City Mound, existed at Gordion during the Hittite Old Kingdom and Empire periods, 1650-1200 B.C. (for summary of information regarding Bronze Age settlements see especially Gunter 1991: 103-105).

The heyday of Gordion, as the capital of the Phrygian Kingdom, is the 8th century B.C., and it is this period and the following ones of Lydian and Persian domination (7th-4th centuries B.C.) that are best known archaeologically. The Phrygians, who spoke an Indo-European language and wrote in an alphabet akin to that of the Greeks, arrived in Asia Minor sometime before the 8th century B.C., though how early we can only speculate. The identification of archaeological strata corresponding to the earliest Phrygian period is still limited, although buildings which might belong to this pre-8th-century phase have been tentatively identified (Sams 1994). See Fig. 2 for plan of Early Phrygian City Mound.

The annals of Sargon II of Assyria (722-705 B.C.) record that a certain Mita of Mushki, now identified as King Midas of Gordion, came into conflict with and was defeated by the Assyrians. Midas was not the first king of the Phrygians but he was certainly the most famous, for it is he whose wealth and greed became the subject of Greek fables (see Roller 1983). Midas, according to ancient sources, committed suicide (Strabo 1,3,21 and Roller 1983: 301, n. 15 for myth) during the Kimmerian invasion of the early 7th century (see Mellink in R. S. Young 1981: 272 and Sams 1994). In the late 7th or early 6th century B.C. the inhabitants of Gordion laid a two-and-a-half- to four-meter-thick layer of clay over the burned Phrygian city in order to rebuild the settlement at a higher level along the lines of the earlier megara service areas and citadel walls. See Fig. 3 for Middle Phrygian City Mound. The Küçük Hüyük was built up in this same period with a fortification system which joined the City Mound. The building of this satellite citadel probably corresponded to the period of Lydian control of Gordion beginning under Alyattes (615-560 B.C.) or Kroisos (560-546 B.C.), who we know from historical sources (Herodotos I, 72-73) subjected Asia Minor as far east as the Halys River (modern Kizil Irmak). The burning of the massive fortification system of the Küçük Hüyük and the creation of a central tumulus of clay over it probably coincided with the advance of Persian forces under Cyrus through Asia Minor against the Lydians under King Kroisos in 547-546 B.C. From this time Gordion and Asia Minor were under the control of the Persian Empire until Alexander the Great "freed" Asia Minor of the yoke of Persian rule in the late 4th century B.C. A major earthquake of the early 4th century in which at least some of the Middle Phrygian buildings on the City Mound collapsed may mark the end of that phase in Gordion's history (Roller 1987b: 103-104, n. 3; DeVries 1990: 399-400).

Alexander and part of his army may have wintered at Gordion in 334/3 B.C. After his death, Alexander's vast empire was split into kingdoms, with Asia Minor secured by the Seleucids. Powerful rival kingdoms grew up in Asia Minor at Pergamon, in the Pontus and in Bithynia. We hear nothing about Gordion and little about Phrygia in this period until 278 B.C., when King Nikomedes of Bithynia imported Celtic tribes into Asia Minor to serve as mercenary soldiers in his war against his brother for control of Bithynia. Sometime afterwards (Moraux 1957: 56-75) three of these Celtic tribes were granted permission, probably by Mithradates II of Pontus (R. E. Allen 1983: 138-141), to settle in Central Anatolia. These Celts were known to the Greeks as Keltoi or Galatai and the region in which they settled became known as Galatia (the name given to the Roman province established in 25 B.C.). The three Celtic tribes distributed themselves over this newly acquired territory and staked out specific portions for themselves; the Tolistoagii held the Phrygian region around Gordion and Pessinus, while the Trocmi held the area further to the east around the old Hittite centers; the Tectosages settled in the central region around Ankara. (For sources see F. A. Winter 1977: 61-62).

After a brief period (ca. 275-240 B.C.) following the influx of Celts, during which foreign contacts probably suffered and Gordion may have been depopulated (F. A. Winter 1984: 34, 254), the cultural life at Gordion became enriched by the presence of these Celts. There is little which can be identified in the way of specifically Celtic cultural material from this period of Celtic domination at Gordion (F. A. Winter 1977: 62-66; 1988), but Celtic-type names written in Greek script provide testimonia of the presence of these Celts at Gordion (Roller

1987b: 129, nos. 56, 57). The population mix of native Phrygians, Celts, Greeks (see Conclusions, p. 79) and possibly some lingering Persians (Cook 1983: 180) created a thriving community where trade and commerce with regions outside Phrygia can be documented. (For a summary of the evidence for the ethnic character of Gordion in this period see DeVries 1990: 402-405.) Gordion was using Greek pottery styles, speaking (in some degree) the Greek language, and by the mid-3d century B.C. writing in exclusively Greek script (Roller 1987b: 106-108) and maintaining many cultural ways of the Greeks. One may say that the population of Gordion in this period was Hellenized to a great degree. It is also during this phase of Celtic domination of Gordion that we have evidence for substantial Attalid interest in Phrygia. The Attalids of Pergamon, in fact, made attempts to control or curb Celtic activities in Asia Minor both by mounting a series of military campaigns against them and by forming alliances with them (R. E. Allen 1983: 136-144; see also Conclusions, p. 79). Pessinus, where an important shrine to Kybele is located just sixty kilometers from Gordion, was a focus of Attalid interest (Devreker and Waelkens 1984: 14-17). See Fig. 4 for plan of Late Phrygian/Hellenistic Gordion.

The last event in Gordion's history as we know it from literary sources (Livy 38, 18) was the campaign launched by the Roman Senate in 189 B.C. commanded by Manlius Vulso and assisted by the Pergamene Attalos II, with the purpose of finally bringing the Celts under control. Livy says of this expedition that when Manlius Vulso arrived at Gordion the inhabitants had all fled to the nearby mountains, leaving Gordion deserted. Archaeological evidence has corroborated Livy's statement. The City Mound at Gordion was left largely abandoned until sometime in the Roman Imperial period, when resettlement in specific zones (especially on the southwest side of the City Mound) has been detected (see Fig. 4 for Late Phrygian/Hellenistic plan). Further archaeological exploration of Gordion in Roman-period levels will allow us to evaluate the validity of Strabo's statement (12, 5, 3) that Gordion was in his day (64/3 B.C.-A.D. 21) nothing more than a village; or Livy's remark (38, 18) that Gordion was an emporium in his day (59 B.C.-A.D. 17). A substantial road, which is probably Roman but was identified as a portion of the Persian Royal Road (R. S. Young 1957: 319), is evidence that Gordion was not isolated in this period but was no doubt linked to other nearby and important Roman centers such as Ankyra (modern Ankara). Finally, there is no stratigraphic evidence for medieval occupation of Gordion other than the occasional stray sherd or figurine.

The terms Early Phrygian period, Middle Phrygian period and Late Phrygian/Hellenistic period are used throughout this volume to indicate the following:

Early Phrygian (EP): the post-Hittite period from the arrival of the Phrygians (9th century B.C.?) to the destruction of Gordion by the Kimmerians in the early 7th century B.C. (see Mellink in R. S. Young 1981: 272; Sams 1994 for specific date for the Kimmerian invasion); see Fig. 2 for plan of site in this period;

Middle Phrygian (MP): the phase after the Kimmerian destruction to the arrival of Alexander the Great and his army at Gordion in 334/3 B.C.; see Fig. 3 for plan of site in this period;

Late Phrygian/Hellenistic (LP/H): the period after the arrival of Alexander (334/3 B.C.) to the abandonment of the site in 189 B.C.; see Fig. 4 for plan of site in this period.

While there is no disagreement among Gordion scholars over the terminology and *terminus* of the Early Phrygian period, the later periods present a more complicated picture. In the course of a recent study of the Gordion stratigraphy, scholars have begun to point to an earthquake destruction of the early 4th century B.C. as the end of the MP period (most thoroughly explained by DeVries 1990: 399-400). The ensuing period, from the early 4th century to the arrival of Alexander in 334/3 B.C., thus has been called the Late Phrygian period, a period marked architecturally on the City Mound by shabby buildings and small cellars dug into the floors of the Middle Phrygian buildings (see Roller 1987b: 103-4, n. 3; DeVries 1990: 400). The period from 334/3 B.C. to just after the coming of the Celts (ca. 275 B.C.) represents a phase of renewed architectural activity and significant contact with the Hellenized world (Roller 1987b: 107). This phase has been labeled the "Early Hellenistic" period by DeVries (1990: 400-401). The interruption in the pottery sequence at Gordion from 275 to 240 forms another phase in this complex period (F. A. Winter 1988: 64, 70, n. 26). Lastly, the period from 240 to the abandonment of the site in 189 B.C. represents the final phase in this sequence and has been commonly called "the Desertion Level" (throughout R. S. Young's preliminary reports) or the Final Hellenistic Period by DeVries (1990: 401-405). Thus, one could divide this author's simplified EP, MP, LP/H system into the following six-period system:

EP: coming of Phrygians to early 7th century B.C.
MP: early 7th century-early 4th century
LP: early 4th century-334/3 B.C.
Early Hellenistic: 334/3-275 B.C.
Interim Period: 275-240 B.C.
Final Hellenistic Period: 240-189 B.C.

It is not in many cases possible to identify the Late Phrygian/Hellenistic figurines in this corpus with these precise chronological phases. It is clear only that the majority of the Late Phrygian/Hellenistic figurines come from the Desertion Level. Thus, this author has maintained the simplified nomenclature for the periods, outlined above.

I

Catalogue

Introduction to Catalogue

The Catalogue has been ordered in a quasi-typological fashion. Standing at the head of the Catalogue are three groups of figural vessels: Central Anatolian-manufactured animal vessels (and possible vessel fragments or attachments in the form of animals); Greek or Greek-inspired plastic (i.e., moldmade) vessels; and locally manufactured bust-flower thymiateria. Within each grouping the items are arranged in a general chronological order, as far as possible given the archaeological data.

In the next section, Kybele and Related Types, the Central Anatolian products are arranged first with the imported types following. This practice of separating the Phrygian (or generally Central Anatolian) from foreign products is used throughout the Catalogue where relevant. Other female types follow next in the Catalogue with standing (including dancing) and seated figures, female heads and other fragments linked together. Within each subgrouping, the figurines are arranged in a general chronological order, with the local and Central Anatolian products at the front of each section. Male figures, divine, semi-divine and human, follow next with a small category of unidentifiable—i.e., sexless—humans as the next group. Miniature masks follow, arranged in general chronological order.

A large category of animal figurines is first subdivided into Central Anatolian versus Non-Central Anatolian products, with the vast majority being manufactured in Central Anatolia. A small group of Bronze Age figurines is distinguishable, while the remaining animals are subdivided by animal type. The quadrupeds are further divided into groups by size and special characteristics.

The last major category is a miscellaneous one with miniature vehicles and wheels, boots or shoes and other miscellaneous items listed separately.

Sections of the Catalogue relating to a single subject, e.g., Kybele or animals, are headed by a general discussion of the group, usually including discussions of chronology, technique, provenience, style, scale, typology and function.

Each entry is headed by a Catalogue Number for this volume, followed by the number assigned to the object in the course of excavation prefixed by a letter, e.g., "T" for Terracotta or "P" for Pottery. See p. 182 for a Concordance giving Gordion field numbers and the corresponding Catalogue Numbers.

Each catalogue entry includes the context in which the figurine was excavated, cited by the tumulus, trench or building designation and level or stratum as described in the excavation notebooks (NB) and following the conventions of the Gordion excavations. If the figurine or vessel is part of a larger deposit, the Terracotta Deposit number is given and the reader referred to the full discussion of these deposits on pp. 65-70. Discussion of the context and its date, where relevant and possible, is given below each entry in the commentary.

The dimensions are given in the metric system using the following abbreviations:

H. = Height
L. = Length
W. = Width
D. = Diameter
Th. = Thickness
Est. = Estimated
Max. = Maximum

P. preceding the above abbreviations indicates the preserved dimension rather than the dimension of an intact figurine, e.g., P.H. = preserved height. In each case the preserved dimensions are the maximum dimensions unless otherwise noted, e.g., P.W. shoulder. Bibliographic references to previous publications of the figurines follow the dimensions. Braces { } are used to denote item numbers within a plate or figure, e.g., pls. 3{2,4}, 5{12a}. Pl., Fig. (with uppercase) are used to denote illustrative material within this volume while pl., fig., ill. (with lowercase) denote a reference within another author's work.

The catalogue description begins in each case with a discussion of the figurine's state of preservation. Next is a description of the figurine's form—front, back and interior; and a comment on the technique by which the figurine was made—moldmade or handmade, in sections, with hand-tooling, etc. Here and elsewhere in the discussion of the manufacturing techniques of terracotta figurines, a certain terminology is used which follows fundamental articles by R. V. Nicholls (1952: 217 ff.; 1984: 24-31).

Following the discussion of technique for each catalogue entry is a description of the decoration, whether glazed, painted, slipped or burnished/polished. The following terminology is used to describe these decorative techniques:

polish/burnish: solid or sporadic strokes created by rubbing a tool over the figurine's surface;

groundcoat: white or buff engobe or slip over which darker colors are applied;

slip: a suspension of clay in water applied before firing;

paint: clay with mineral pigments which provide color;

glaze: clay with sufficient siliceous material and fluxes to produce vitrification and a glossy appearance;

"glaze": as in Greek black-glazed; clay with black iron pigment which sinters in firing to produce a lustrous surface.

Next is a description of the clay fabric of the figurine including the color (as described by the author), the size and amount of particles mixed into the clay, the texture and a Munsell number. For the latter the standard tables in *Munsell Soil Color Charts* (1975) have been used to match, in most cases, against broken interior surfaces of the figurines. Where surface readings are taken, these are so indicated. All readings have been taken in natural daylight and the author is aware of the unreliability of the readings produced by this method, which is dependent on the strength of the light and the eye of the examiner, to name only two factors. The author's own color names and the Munsell color names do not always coincide but have been left unaltered to alert the reader to the subjectivity of color descriptions.

Last is a statement regarding the manufacturing source of the figurine, based on fabric, style, decoration or comparanda. The term "locally manufactured" is reserved for figurines which one has good evidence to believe were manufactured at Gordion itself. "Central Anatolian-manufactured" indicates that the probable source is the region of Phrygia. Greek imports are labeled as such.

Following the catalogue description is the commentary on the individual figurine which may include comparanda, specific conclusions about chronology, provenience, function and context. With regard to chronology, a distinction is made between the suggested date for the level or fill in which the figurine was found and the actual date of the figurine, recognizing that at Gordion—as at most sites with long periods of occupation—materials can be transported from their original place of deposition to later strata in fills used to level areas for rebuilding or to build up tumuli. Gordion has, in addition, great numbers of pits dug in the Phrygian period into earlier levels, thus disturbing the material from these periods and often bringing earlier material up to Late Phrygian/Hellenistic-period contexts. The contexts do, however, provide *termini ante quem* for the materials contained within.

Animal Vessels: Central Anatolian (1-18)

Phrygian or generally Central Anatolian animal vessels (and possible animal-vessel fragments or attachments) form a significant corpus among the Gordion terracottas, as distinct from figurines in the form of animals (see below, **115-155**). The fragmentary nature of many of these animals precludes positive identification as vessels, yet based on form, technique and size, there is a likelihood that all the objects included in this category are vessels or vessel parts. The chronological spread and typological variation of these animal vessels are striking. Five, all from Tumulus P, belong to the Early Phrygian period (**1-5**) while one (**6**) can probably be placed in the Early or Middle Phrygian period. Six vessels fall chronologically, by virtue of the decorative techniques or context, in the Middle Phrygian period (e.g., **7**, **8-11**, **17**). That the manufacture of animal vessels continued into the Late Phrygian/Hellenistic period is shown by **12**, **13**, **15** and probably **14**. Probable animal attachments for vessels—e.g., **16**, **18**—also span the Middle and Late Phrygian/Hellenistic periods.

The difficulty of assigning very specific dates for these animal vessels, with the exception of **1-5** and **8**, renders an assessment of the general cultural inspiration for the vessel types problematic. It is clear, however, that the Early Phrygian examples are locally derived, possibly with echoes of Bronze Age forms (especially in **4** and **5**). At least **14** and **15**, probably Late Phrygian/Hellenistic animal vessels, show affinities to Achaemenid rhyta in their form. Certainly Greek animal vessels or plastic vases, in general, seem unrelated to most of these Phrygian types, with the exception of **8**, a mid-6th-century B.C. lion or dog vessel. It is probable that the majority of these animal vessels are inspired by a local Central Anatolian tradition and that it is only a minority which imitate foreign forms, either Achaemenid or Greek. For discussion of other Phrygian animal vessels see Tuchelt 1962: 64-68.

1   Animal Vessel: Goose
P 1411   Terracotta Deposit 1 (see p. 65)
H. 0.37; L. 0.305; D. 0.215 m.
Pl. 1
R. S. Young 1957: 327, pl. 93, fig. 24; 1981: 33, TumP 49, pl. 15 C-E.

Complete with mend at base of neck; surface worn and pitted.

Vessel in form of a goose with hollow stem flaring at bottom with raised rib halfway up. Rounded body with opening on back with flat raised rim around. Wedge-shaped tail with squared ends. Long neck and broad-billed head with bill slightly open as pouring spout; pierced nostrils. Wheelmade body with wheel-turned rim. Separately modeled head and neck, tail, added pedestal.

Dark brown paint on buff ground, burnished; matte reddish yellow paint over burnish on stem and bill. Foot and stem solidly painted matte reddish yellow. Bottom of body at front decorated with parallel wavy lines; at sides and back with parallel concave lines. Chest has feather pattern composed of scales with dots. Wings outlined by broad reserved bands bordered by fine dot rows between parallel lines; each wing bisected by columns of chevrons. Wings and tail have laddered herringbone pattern. Neck has herringbone pattern. Top of head decorated with dotted scale. Dot eyes inside double almond-shaped outlines. Bill has matte reddish yellow paint; opening indicated by incised lines at sides. Upper face of rim alternately painted and reserved. Inside unpainted.

Fine buff clay. No Munsell reading.
Central Anatolian-manufactured.

The burial in Tumulus P is dated just prior to the time of the Kimmerian invasion, ca. 700 B.C. For a complete discussion of the tumulus and its contents see R. S. Young 1981: 1-77; also Terracotta Deposit 1.

2 is a match for this vessel.

2 Animal Vessel: Goose
P 1412   Terracotta Deposit 1 (see p. 65)
H. 0.335; L. 0.37; D. 0.22 m.
Pl. 1
R. S. Young 1957: 327; 1981: 33, TumP 50, pl. 16A, B.

Broken and mended with small slivers missing from underside of tail. Surface pitted.

Vessel in form of goose. See description of **1**, which matches this vessel. Differences are deeper body and forward-inclined neck of this vessel; lower pedestal without raised rib. Round eyes.

Same decorative scheme as **1** except stem and base reserved. Eyes are dots within double rings; bill reserved and decorated with bands and dotted triangle pendent between nostril openings.

Fine buff clay. No Munsell reading.
Central Anatolian-manufactured.

See **1** for matching vessel.

3 Animal Vessel: Ram Jug
P 1403   Terracotta Deposit 1 (see p. 65)
H. 0.191; L. 0.252 m.
Pl. 2
R. S. Young 1957: 328, pl. 94, fig. 27; 1981: 36, TumP 58, pl. 17G.

Broken and mended with small fragments missing from neck and lower body at right side.

Jug in shape of ram. Elongated body with four small round feet. Center of back has filling hole surrounded by high collar. Tail is turned and arched over back, attached to base of neck for basket-like handle (squarish in section). At front is roughly modeled neck and head of ram with snout pierced for pouring. Horns looped into complete circle with ends overlapping. Probably wheelmade body with added feet, head and handle.

Decoration in matte black paint on reserved red surface. Borders around body with bands and wavy lines. Between borders on one side are rows of latticed squares with small checkers at corners; on other side, large zone of plain checkerboard with small checks. At each side of chest and neck is circular ladder pattern, dotted at center. Bands bordered by wavy lines at top of neck and around top of collar around filling hole.

Fine red clay. No Munsell reading.
Central Anatolian-manufactured.

See discussion of Terracotta Deposit 1.

4 Animal Vessel: Goat Jug
P 1424   Terracotta Deposit 1 (see p. 65)
H. 0.15; L. 0.21; W. 0.12 m.
Pl. 2
R. S. Young 1957: 328, pl. 94, fig. 28; 1981: 38, TumP 62, pl. 18A,B.

Complete and undamaged.

Jug in shape of stylized ram. Askoid body with four short peg-feet. At center of back is small filling hole surrounded by low raised rim. Tail curves up at rear to back to form loop handle; at front horns join together and attach at shoulders. Small ears are added beside horns. Square snout is pierced by small pouring hole. Eyes are stamped rings. Around neck is collar of double row of stamped rings. Probably wheelmade body with added head, horns, handle and feet.

Well polished.
Fine clay with black mica-film surface. No Munsell reading.
Central Anatolian-manufactured.

See Terracotta Deposit 1 for discussion.

5 Animal Vessel: Deer or Bull Jug
P 1425   Terracotta Deposit 1 (see p. 65)
H. 0.135; L. 0.155; D. 0.11 m.
Pl. 2
R. S. Young 1957: 327; 1981: 38, TumP 63, pl. 18C, D.

Missing part of handle, two feet and several chips.

Jug in shape of stylized animal, deer or bull. Ellipsoidal body with square peg-feet, circular filling hole in center of back surrounded by low raised rim. Neck has low raised collar. Horns curl up to side from top of head. Square basket handle joins behind horns to rear of body. Muzzle is squared and pierced with round hole for pouring. Eyes are stamped rings. Wheelmade body with attached horns, handle, feet and modeled head.

Polished to high black luster.
Medium-fine, light brown clay. No Munsell reading.
Central Anatolian-manufactured.

See Terracotta Deposit 1 for discussion.

6 Animal Vessel: Bull-Headed
P 2576   Trench NCT-W1/3, pit into clay from beneath Floor 6
P.L. 0.125; W. ears 0.133 m.
Pl. 3
R. S. Young 1962: 155, pl. 41, fig. 2.

Lacking bottom half completely. Top half preserves part of eyes, forehead, horns and ears to rim. Rim much broken away.

Fragment of bull-headed vessel. Short, erect horns, curving inward; ears short, erect, attached to horns at base. Plain, slightly flattened rim. Hand-modeled.

Incised details. Outlined triangle on forehead with two small holes bored through, possibly for insets. Eyes elliptical with three framing grooves. On side of neck and head, mane and hair indicated by tiers of overlapping vertical zigzag lines. Excellent polish over exterior before incision.

Heavy gray fabric with few inclusions, polished to dark gray.

Central Anatolian-manufactured.

Context indicates a date for the vessel in the Early or Middle Phrygian period, but probably no later than the 5th century B.C.

7 Animal Vessel?: Lion's Head
MC 119   Trench NCT-A11, Layer 6, upper fill, N. section
P.W. 0.06 m.
Pl. 3

Single fragment preserving upper part of head.

Lion's head, possibly plastic vessel. Crudely modeled by hand with heavy incised lines for features including brow wrinkles.

Thin red slip over exterior.

Soft red clay. Munsell: slip 10R 5/6 (red); core 10YR 6/6 (reddish yellow).

Probably Central Anatolian-manufactured.

This fragment comes from a context as late as the 5th century B.C.

8 Animal Vessel?: Lion or Dog?
T 2   Tumulus C, "second rock complex" and partially in pit with join from looters' back-dirt
P.H. 0.108; P.L. 0.116; W. at rump 0.065; Th. walls 0.005-0.007 m.
Pl. 3
Kohler 1995: 30, pl. 15c, D.

Joined from eight fragments preserving left hind leg, most of rump, all of tail and half of right side. Trace of carbon (or black paint) on right flank, tail and body. Small amount of white lime incrustation on exterior surface.

Sejant quadruped, possibly lion or dog, probably used as vessel. Rear paws with incisions to mark claws; large haunches, thick coil for tail curled against right haunch. Tubular body rises steeply at 50-60 ° angle. Interior walls smoothed with fingers and spatula. Foot of animal is solid. Probably wheelmade body, hand-modeled with additions and finishing.

Exterior is polished to orangish brown.

Orangish clay with small amount of tiny gold mica particles, fired gray at core. Small black speckles just below surface. Munsell: beneath surface where chipped 5YR 7/8 (reddish yellow); surface burnish 5YR 5/6 (yellowish red).

Central Anatolian-manufactured or possibly Lydian import.

The carefully prepared interior and uniformly thin walls suggest a vessel. The orangish-brown polished surface and gold mica might indicate a Lydian origin for this animal vessel, although a Central Anatolian locale is not ruled out. **9** is a closely comparable animal paw, in both the clay and the style. The animal may be a lion or a dog. The vessel's form and size may suggest an affinity with the archaic East Greek plastic animal vessels like **19**.

The vessel was found among the contents of the ruined timber chamber and stone packing (called "second rock complex") of Tumulus C, probably for a child's burial. Found with the vessel in the completely disturbed fill of rotted beams and stone were fragments of lydia, black-on-red bowl sherds, plain gray- and red-ware sherds, alabastron fragments and knucklebones. The lydia and other pottery date Tumulus C to between 550 and 540 B.C. (See Kohler, 1995: 25-34 for full description of Tumulus C and contents. For preliminary publication of tumulus see R. S. Young 1951a: 11-12; 1952: 20).

9 Animal Vessel Fragment?: Lion's or Dog's (?) Paw
P 2248   Trench WML-4S, clay under Wall F
P.H. 0.0225; P.L. 0.036; W. 0.018 m.
Pl. 3

Single fragment preserving front of paw, broken at diagonal at top.

Animal paw, possibly of lion or dog, with three incised grooves for claws. Interior is solid. Handmade.

Surface is polished or burnished.

Fine pinkish orange clay polished to pinkish brown on exterior. Small amount of mica, possibly gold mica. Munsell: below surface 10R 6/8 (light red); surface burnish 5YR 6/6 (reddish yellow).

Central Anatolian-manufactured or possibly Lydian import.

See **8** for a better-preserved example of a similar animal vessel (?), dating no later than around the mid-6th century B.C.

10 Animal Rhyton: Lion
P 2497   Trench PN, Cellar A, fill in corner
P.L. 0.133; Max.W. head 0.035 m.
Pl. 4
R. S. Young 1962: 155, pl. 41, fig. 3.

Rim broken away; tube mouth chipped; some paint rubbed off polished portions.

Slim, curved tubular rhyton ending in lion's head which rises above short tubular spout under chin. Ears are flat ovals defined by ridges; eyes are round bumps; muzzle is square and arched in behind front teeth; lower jaw is open, flat and square. Raised ridge forms bottom of mane. Hand-modeled head with wheel-turned body.

Bichrome decoration. Down back over a matte cream slip is red and black herringbone pattern between red and black lines. On ridge of ears is red; down back of head is red stripe between two black stripes; from eye to neck is ladder pattern in red. Jeweled line runs around jaws and over muzzle. Eyes are dotted black. Mane outlined in stripe of red around top of ridge. Rest of vessel is red polished. Cream slip remains matte.

Fine clay, fired buff. No mica.

Central Anatolian-manufactured.

This animal rhyton comes from a probably 5th- or

4th-century B.C. context, and its bichrome style indicates a Middle Phrygian date.

11 Animal Vessel?: Deer?
T 103   Trench WS 5-6, N, Level 5
P.H. 0.061; P.W. 0.028; P.Th. 0.036; Th. walls 0.005 m.
Pl. 4

Single fragment of head and neck, broken at turn to back on left side. Missing right ear and antler. Glaze mostly flaked off.

Possible animal vessel in form of finely modeled deer with rounded head; small pointed ears; antlers rising from top of head; rounded snout ending in flat surface; neck flaring out from head with flat sides. Interior of neck is hollow. Probably wheelmade body with hand-modeled head.

Head and front and sides of neck are covered with white groundcoat. Back of head and neck, and tip of snout, are undecorated. Over white, preserved in small sections, is orange-brown paint polished to glassy finish. On back of neck paint is applied in patches and is unpolished. Traces of black paint on forehead between antlers, on antlers, at right eye and right jawline.

Lightly micaceous reddish orange clay with many small, light inclusions, fired gray at core. Munsell: 2.5YR 5/8 (red).

Probably Central Anatolian-manufactured.

The pottery from this level includes black-glazed wares of 4th-century B.C. type as well as black polished sherds, but the painted decoration indicates an earlier date for the deer.

12 Animal Vessel?: Stag's Head
T 42   Trench ET-S, SW corner, under Floor B
P.H. 0.140; P.W. 0.067; P.Depth 0.097; Th. walls 0.004-0.006 m.
Pl. 4

Joined from four fragments preserving left side of head and neck. Muzzle intact. Lacking right side of head from above eye, right ear and right side of antlers. Surface chipped and discolored green, red and black. Four other non-joining body fragments.

Stag's head with upright ears and antlers. Well modeled with erect head facing forward. Between ears, tiers of antlers rise from thick roll above forehead. Inward-curving forehead; conical muzzle; shallow depression for nostrils. Left eye is deep depression. Back of head and neck arches down and is treated less carefully. Additional piece of clay over neck near break forms small pocket. Interior is hollow with smooth walls. Probably hand-modeled with body probably wheelmade.

Exterior surface is completely covered with ivory-white groundcoat except at back of head. Red paint over white on interior of ear and upper part of antlers; black paint in line above forehead; black on throat and on left side of head and neck in short, vertical strokes to represent individual hairs; black on lower neck just above break. Surface is polished.

Light red, lightly micaceous, hard-fired, compact clay with small amount of dark inclusions. Munsell: 2.5YR 6/6 (light red).

Probably Central Anatolian-manufactured.

The size, hollow interior and general character of this stag's head indicate that it probably served as a vessel.

This animal head comes from a deposit sealed below a floor including pottery datable to after ca. 325 B.C. Material above this floor included a coin dating after 316 B.C. This piece is probably late 4th-century B.C. or Late Phrygian/Hellenistic in date.

13 Animal Vessel?: Goat
T 65   Trench MN-W, Layer 3 fill, above House 3
P.H. 0.092; P.W. lower break 0.055; P.Th. 0.065; Th. walls 0.005-0.007 m.
Pl. 4

Single fragment preserving head and neck of animal, missing right ear and horn (?) and tip of left horn (?). Broken at lower neck. Paint has worn off most of surface.

Head of animal, probably goat, hollowed out for possible use as vessel. Long and pointed head; short, erect ears with gouged triangle for inner ear; antlers or horns set inside ears; at center of forehead is raised knob. Eyes are large and bulging, nostrils are pierced; mouth is broad, deep groove. Neck is wide, flaring cylinder. Interior hollow with well-smoothed interior walls. Handmade head with neck and probably missing body turned on wheel.

Exterior has traces of yellowish buff groundcoat over which is purple-red paint on left eyeball, on band beneath eyes, between ears, beneath chin on neck, on other parts of neck, in band around neck at lower break, on right and left back sides.

Lightly micaceous reddish brown clay, fired gray at core. Very fine clay with tiny light inclusions. Munsell: 2.5YR 6/6 (light red).

Central Anatolian-manufactured.

Layer 3 fill must be dated after the mid-3d century B.C. (coin: C 651: Seleukos II [246-220 B.C.], Antioch). From the same trench and sequence come **65**, a standing female; **86**, a female head; and **103**, Eros head.

14 Animal Vessel: Deer?
P 2583   Trench NCT-W1/3, under Hellenistic House B, clay just over burned fill
P.L. 0.11; P.W. at hoof 0.045; D. spout 0.045 m.
Pl. 5
Sams 1979a: 13, fig. 11 left.

Underbody and one leg preserved. Surface worn.

From short cylindrical spout, body of deer (?) extends. Animal has leg with cloven hoof close to chest. Hollow interior. Modeled by hand with wheel-turned cylindrical body.

Fine polishing to black.

Fine clay with gritty inclusions, fired gray.

Central Anatolian-manufactured.

Cf. **15**: both are imitations of Achaemenid-type rhyta.

This vessel may come from a disturbance into the clay, indicating a possibly Late Phrygian/Hellenistic date.

15 Animal Vessel: Goat
P 666   Terracotta Deposit 4 (see p. 67)
P.H. 0.126; P.L. 0.081; P.W. 0.04 m.
Pl. 5
Sams 1979a: 13, fig. 11 right.

Mended from several fragments, preserving head, neck and right foreparts. Broken off behind right front shoulder and missing horns, snout and left foreleg.

Animal vessel in form of couchant goat with forelegs tucked beneath body. Arching neck and small triangular head with erect ears. Incisions mark horns and split hoof. Interior hollow with smooth walls. Well modeled by hand, probably once attached to wheelmade body.

Polished exterior surface.

Fine clay fired gray at core and black on surface. No Munsell reading.

Central Anatolian-manufactured.

The gray fabric and black polish are typical of Phrygian pottery from Gordion, and the type imitates Achaemenid rhyta (cf. Muscarella 1974: nos. 135, 162-163). For other locally manufactured rhyta see R. S. Young 1962: pl. 41, figs. 2-3. This example is almost certainly Late Phrygian/Hellenistic in date. See discussion of Terracotta Deposit 4.

16 Vessel Attachment?: Bull's Head?
T 105   Trench WS 5-6, S2, Layer 6 or 7
P.H. 0.06; P.L. head 0.039; W. head 0.027 m.
Pl. 5

Single fragment preserving head and neck of animal, lacking horns and chip from front of neck. Paint and groundcoat well preserved except on muzzle.

Stylized animal's head, possibly of bull, probably plastic attachment for vessel. Neck is long cylinder with thick walls and drilled-out inside (D. 0.01 m.). Face is flattened triangle with blunt squarish snout. At top of head are stumps of two large horns, oval in section. Handmade.

Most of exterior covered with thick white groundcoat over which are painted stripes of red and black. Down center of face is red stripe and framing face to right and left and top are black lines forming triangle. Red vertical strokes on right and left sides of face indicate eyes. Down length of neck are diagonal stripes, alternately black and red, radiating from two red lines. Red and black stripes are burnished, while groundcoat is left unburnished.

Compact, lightly micaceous yellowish brown clay with small light and dark inclusions. Munsell: 7.5YR 6/4 (light brown)-6/6 (reddish yellow).

Central Anatolian-manufactured.

The layer below that in which this animal head was found contained ample pottery for dating and coins of the late 4th-century B.C. (C 1229, C 1230). The layer from which this head comes is late 4th century B.C. or later. The painting technique, however, is typical of Middle Phrygian bichrome pottery and the animal head may well be an earlier remnant in this layer.

17 Animal Vessel or Attachment: Bird
T 104   Trench TB8-S1, Level 5
P.H. 0.047; P.W. 0.055; P.Th. 0.04; Th. walls 0.005-0.008 m.
Pl. 5

Single fragment preserving breast and front of right and left wings. Broken off at back and bottom, missing head and lower body. Surface chipped and scarred.

Well-modeled bird, possibly hawk, seated with wings tucked against sides of body. Body is full and chest is high convex surface. Interior is hollow with roughly smoothed walls, possibly for use as vessel or vessel attachment. Handmade.

Surface is polished to dull sheen.

Micaceous brown clay with many light inclusions, hard-fired to slate gray on surface. Munsell: interior 7.5YR N4/ (dark gray).

Central Anatolian-manufactured.

The pottery in the level with this bird included Late Phrygian/Hellenistic sherds and the level above contained pottery of the latest occupation period at Gordion (prior to 189 B.C.), but this gray polished bird may well belong to an earlier period.

18 Vessel Attachment?: Duck's Head
P 486   Trench ET, N Ext. 4, Level 4
P.L. 0.046; W. head 0.012; W. neck 0.015 m.
Pl. 5

Single fragment preserving neck and head, broken cleanly across neck. Small chips from right edge of bill and tip, left side of neck.

Head of duck, possibly plastic attachment or handle. Neck is arching in smooth convex curve, turning and narrowing to beak or bill; right eye is raised dot surrounded by groove; left eye is squarish depression. Incised line running from inside right eye to center of forehead, turning down left side in front of left eye. Mouth is defined by curving incisions on right and left sides. Solid. Handmade.

Red paint added over lightly polished surface on top and back of head. Red band on right side and top behind right eye and behind left eye; two curving red bands beside incision for mouth.

Light orange, lightly micaceous clay with tiny light inclusions. Munsell: 7.5YR 8/6 (reddish yellow).

Central Anatolian-manufactured.

A Phrygian painted pot with a handle in the form of a duck (P 389), not included in this corpus, is comparable.

Pottery indicates a date early in the Late Phrygian/Hellenistic period for the context.

Plastic Vessels: Greek or Greek-Inspired (19-34)

The eleven 6th-century molded vessels in this corpus represent for the most part products of East Greek workshops. The two exceptions, **19** and **28**, are possibly imitations of the East Greek type vessels, from Lydia (?) and from Anatolia (?), respectively. Rhodes is often cited as the East Greek island which produced the majority of these archaic plastic vessels because so many were recovered from excavations there (Higgins 1959: 9 ff.), but clay analyses and further excavation at East Greek sites indicate that other East Greek centers probably also manufactured these vessels, most notably Miletos (Jones 1986: 671-673). Boardman suggests a South Ionian origin (now certainly Miletos) for some of these molded vessels found at Tocra (Boardman and Hayes 1966: 66; Jones 1986: 671-673), and one kore vessel from Gordion might be assigned to a South Ionian (Milesian) workshop (**27**).

It is commonly accepted that these special ceramic containers were produced as unguent bottles and that perfumed oils were being marketed by East Greek centers for export. Later Greek vase-painting scenes show boys or young men carrying aryballoi, the later standard variety of such perfumed oil flasks, by cords around their wrists to or from gymnasia. The plastic vessel in the form of a dead hare (**21**) is especially suited for this method of carrying since the suggestion would be that a real hare had been hunted, killed and displayed en route to the gymnasium for others to see. The high rim of the pomegranate vessels makes these suitable also for the attachment of a cord and the suspension of the flask from the wrist. Since they have no means of resting upright by themselves they would have to be suspended. The standing kore vessel (**27**), the kore bust (**28**) and the Anatolian (?) animal (**19**) are free-standing vessels and could either be carried or rest by themselves on their flat bases. The hedgehog (**20**) was probably meant to rest on its peg-like legs.

Although plastic vessels were manufactured at East Greek centers (Higgins 1959: 11, no. 1601) in the second half of the 7th century, the earliest examples from Gordion date to the first half of the 6th century, with the hedgehog (**20**), pomegranate and hare types (**21**, **24**, **25**, **26**) among the earliest. The ram's head (**22**), dove (**23**), kore head (**29**) and kore bust (**28**) all fall around the middle or third quarter of the 6th century and the standing kore (**27**) around the decade 540-530 B.C.

Within this molded-vessel category are also three probably Attic or Attic-inspired products, including a lion mold which may have been used to produce an Attic-type vessel (**31**). Not included in this corpus because we are lacking most of the molded portions are fragments of two or three molded red-figure rhyta (P 55, P 380, P 3356, P 4688, P 5086), probably from the Sotades Shop, one of which is probably an Amazon Rider type (Sams 1979a: 10, fig. 4). Other types of Attic vessels of this period exist at Gordion (see DeVries, forthcoming).

The latest of the Greek or Greek-inspired vessels or vessel parts are two representing females, a probable vessel handle in the form of a Nike (**33**) and a vessel in the form of a Greek deity, probably Tyche (**34**). Both can be assigned a late 3d- or early 2d-century B.C. date, although the former is certainly locally manufactured, while the latter is a Greek import.

19 Plastic Vessel: Couchant Quadruped
   P 1153   Terracotta Deposit 2 (see pp. 65-66)
   H. 0.050; L. 0.111; W. rump 0.06; D. rim 0.022 m.
   Pl. 6

Complete except forelegs and chips. Head and neck repaired from many small fragments. Surface badly flaking and much worn. Small round hole pierced through rump may not be original to vessel.

Vessel in shape of couchant quadruped with head turned back along left flank and hind legs tucked beneath rump. Haunches of hind legs project from rump on both sides. Neck is very long; head is long and pointed with small round ears or horns set on either side of head. Orifice is raised tube with flat, overhanging rim set behind neck on back of animal. Probably hollow-molded with wheelmade orifice.

No painted decoration, other than traces of white on exterior. Exterior surface is polished to moderately glossy pinkish brown, especially well preserved on right flank.

Clay is very slightly micaceous, ranging in color from pinkish brown on exterior to light gray beneath surface. Munsell: burnished exterior 5YR 6/3 (light reddish brown); beneath surface 7.5YR 5/4 (brown).

Probably Anatolian-manufactured.

This polished animal vessel is probably an Anatolian imitation of popular Greek animal vessels. It is not clear if the quadruped is a feline, sheep or deer. Vessels in the form of sheep (e.g., Berlin, Antiquarium 8738, from Aegina: Ducat 1966: 152; Boehlau 1898: 156, fig. 71; Maximova 1927: pl. 13{52}); and deer (Maximova 1927: Corneto, pl. 40{151}) are not very common. The head turned back along the flank may be meant to represent an animal in grooming pose. This specific type is not known in the repertoire of Greek animal plastic vessels, and that together with the polished rather than glazed surface suggests an Anatolian manufacturing site.

The date of this vessel must depend on the chronology of the deposit in which it was found (see discussion of Terracotta Deposit 2, p. **xx**). The vessel probably dates to the 6th century B.C., but because of the broad range of material in the deposit in which it was found, it is not possible to be more precise about its date from the context. If the animal vessel is an Anatolian imitation of East Greek vessels, it should probably be placed towards the end of the 6th century B.C.

20 Plastic Vessel: Hedgehog
   P 1157   Terracotta Deposit 2 (see pp. 65-66)
   H. 0.049; L. 0.095; W. 0.052; D. rim 0.007 m.
   Pl. 6

Intact. Snout slightly chipped, surface and paint worn. Orange-brown stain on bottom.

Plastic vessel in form of hedgehog with small head, pointed snout, ovoid body, and four low round peg-like feet. Slightly raised orifice attached at middle of back. Hollow-molded body with applied orifice.

Tiny black-brown glazed dots cover back. Ears are glazed black-brown, eyes are ringed by black-brown; mouth is reddish brown.

Fine white-yellow clay, tending toward very pale green. No trace of mica. Munsell: 2.5Y 8/2 (white).
Probably East Greek-manufactured.

The closest parallels for the Gordion hedgehog are the following: Corinth CP 3039 (unpublished); Higgins 1959: 26, no. 1641, pl. 16 (from Kamiros); CVA France XII (Louvre VIII), pl. 5{14,16} (from Sardis); CVA Poland I (Goluchow: Musée Czartoryski), pl 7{3} (from private collection); CVA Italy XIX (Museo Civico di Genoa-Pegli I), pl. 902{8}; Istanbul Museum inv. 9967 (from Çandarlı, unpublished; see Pl. 39.)

The difference between the Gordion hedgehog and these examples is the orifice. The Gordion example has only a very slightly raised rim around the orifice (a feature of the "Etruscan" hedgehog from Würzburg: Langlotz 1932: 22, no. 157, pl. 18), while the others have regular aryballos-type raised spouts with flat ledge rims. This orifice type may be an East Greek feature.

Ducat has divided all the Greek hedgehog plastic vessels into two major groups according to the form of the body and the decoration (1966: 125 ff.). The groupings are not well rationalized since the Gordion example is close to molded vessels from both groups. Higgins (1959: 26) believes the British Museum example is Rhodian, and Ducat (1966: 125 ff.) labels both of his main groups Rhodian. The color of the clay of the Gordion hedgehog is slightly greener than that of the pomegranates (**24-26**) and is close to that of the Gordion dead-hare molded vessel (**21**) (though there are traces of mica in the hare which are not visible in the hedgehog).

Given the nature of Terracotta Deposit 2, there is no archaeological evidence from Gordion to help with the dating of this hedgehog type. Ducat assigns his Type A and Type B hedgehogs to two larger groups (Group Grenade IA and Group Grenade III) based on stylistic criteria and dates them respectively ca. 570-560 and ca. 580 (1966: 125 ff., 165). It is probably safer to simply assign the hedgehog to the first half of the 6th century B.C.

21 Plastic Vessel: Hare
   P 2234   Trench TBT-12, Level 5 pit
   H. 0.067; L. 0.077; D. rim 0.008 m.
   Pl. 6

Joined from two fragments, lacking ears, front paws and small chips.

Plastic vessel in form of dead hare, with head and ears laid against back. Round orifice applied to chest. Rear paws are long narrow bars. Probably meant to be suspended by cord around orifice. Probably hollow-molded body with attached wheelmade orifice.

Dark brown dots glazed over fine buff slip on body. Details of eyes, ears, mouth and tail in dark brown.

Very fine buff-white clay with greenish tinge. Slight traces of micaceous particles. Munsell: 2.5Y 8/2 (white).

Probably East Greek-manufactured.

There are no precise parallels for this dead-hare vessel. The type of the dead hare is common among plastic vessels (Ducat 1966: 128-131), but a feature appearing on most of these examples, though not on the one from Gordion, is the outstretched fore and hind legs. Among the types of "live" crouching hares there are closer parallels for the tucked leg position (e.g., Higgins 1959: no. 1647, pl. 18 from Nola; Maximova 1927: pl. 22{87}=Lausanne 4017; C. K. Williams et al. 1973: 17, no. 17, pl. 4, Corinth C-73-187 [cf. also C-62-260]). One East Greek hare vessel in the Vathy Museum, Samos (no inv. no.) has the same tucked leg position as this one and an orifice between the extended forepaws.

Plastic vessels in the form of hares were popular in the 6th century and were made in Etruria (Ducat 1966: 131 f.), Corinth (two examples above) and East Greece (usually said to be "Rhodian").

The clay and glazed-dot decoration of this hare vessel are identical to those of the hedgehog **20** and, thus, should have the same manufacturing site. Although the Gordion hare is closer in the pose of the legs to the two examples found at Corinth than to East Greek examples, and the clay of both the hare and hedgehog has a greenish tinge associated with buff-white Corinthian clay, the hollow-molded body is an East Greek rather than a Corinthian feature.

There are no good pegs by which to establish a chronology for the dead-hare vessels. Higgins suggests a date of ca. 575-550 for the British Museum example from Nola (Higgins 1959: 28, no. 1647, pl. 18; 1961: 46 n. 5) based on evidence from Rhodes.

22 Plastic Vessel: Ram's Head
   P 4437   Trench CC-3C, ashy layer under W wall of Building U
   P.H. 0.03; P.W. 0.032; P.Th. 0.041; D. rim 0.008 m.
   Pl. 6

Single fragment preserving head, broken off at neck and across left side of head. Surface worn. Right side of muzzle and top of head chipped. Incrustation on left side of head.

Plastic vessel in form of ram's head with orifice on top of head. Probably moldmade.

Shiny purple-red paint preserved on horns, and dark brown on lower back part of horns. Black-brown paint on inside of right ear, inner corner of right eye. Traces of red-orange around groove of right eye.

Clay is very fine, yellow-buff at core, buff-white on exterior. Slight traces of mica visible. Munsell: 10YR 8/4 (very pale brown)-8/6 (yellow).

East Greek-manufactured.

The ashy level in which this vessel was found dates to the early 4th century B.C., although it contains a considerable amount of material going back to the 6th century B.C.

The closest parallel for this plastic vessel is one from Kamiros in the British Museum (B 289; Higgins 1954: 58, no. 96, pl. 19), which Higgins dates to after ca. 530

B.C. Ducat does not accept such a late date and believes that ram's head vessels of this variety could be as early as ca. 560-550 B.C. (1966: 95 ff., esp. 99 and 100).

23   Plastic Vessel?: Dove?
T 109   Trench PPB2, Floor 2
P.H. 0.032; D. neck 0.017; W. head 0.013 m.
Pl. 6

Single fragment of neck and head with bottom of neck finished. Surface worn and chips missing from edge of neck.

Bird's head, probably of a dove, with concave surface at base of neck for joining to body. Neck arches in continuous contour; sides of head are flat; top is smooth convex curve; beak is long, arching downward slightly and narrowing to tip. Handmade head, probably attached to hollow-molded vessel.

Traces of white paint (?) on right side of head, area of left eye and left side of neck.

Fine reddish brown clay with no mica. Munsell: 2.5YR 6/6 (light red).

Probably East Greek-manufactured.

According to the excavator, the level in which the bird was found contained 4th-century or Late Phrygian/Hellenistic ceramic material.

Comparable birds' heads from Erythrai, Miletos, Pitane, Corinth and Xanthos indicate a 6th-century date for the animal and the likelihood that the goose belongs to a 6th century unguentarium: from Erythrai; Bayburtluoğlu 1977: 117 f., nos. 71 and 72, pl. 40; from Miletos, on display in Izmir Museum (no inv. no.); from Pitane (Çandarlı) in Istanbul Archaeological Museum (inv. no. 10269; see Pl. 39); in Corinth MF 77-62 from Hero Shrine (C. K. Williams 1978: 35, pl. 2{16}, 6th century, down to second half; from Xanthos, Metzger 1972: 80, no. 148, pl. 32, "Rhodian."

24   Plastic Vessel: Pomegranate
P 3229   Trench O-Q1, North Cellar, in dismantling walls of cellar, through Floor 3
P.H. 0.053; D. body 0.074; D. opening 0.009; Th. walls 0.002-0.004 m.
Pl. 7

Joined from thirteen fragments, lacking bottom center, top center and around one-sixth of body. Surface chips missing from top, shoulder and body. Walls laminating. Paint chipping. Interior incrusted with white.

Plastic vessel in shape of pomegranate with lower body divided into lobes produced by pinching sides. Probably wheelmade body.

Exterior covered with smooth buff-yellow slip. At juncture of body and shoulder is zone of incised tongues glazed alternately maroon and black. On shoulder is large zone composed of long petals with incised triangles between (lotus pattern). Petals are painted matte maroon, while triangles and background are painted black. Incision is sloppy.

Clay is fine, slightly micaceous and fired yellowish buff on surface. Munsell: core 10YR 8/2 (white); exterior slip 10YR 8/3 (very pale brown).

East Greek-manufactured.

See **21** for discussion.

An East Greek lydion (P 3245) found together with the pomegranate can be placed around the second quarter of the 6th century B.C. (see Greenewalt 1966: 71, Type EG1), while the catalogued Phrygian fibula from the same level (B 1550 = Type XII, 14) is probably much earlier (Muscarella 1967: 24-26; cf. Caner 1983: no. 898, before late 8th/early 7th century B.C.).

25   Plastic Vessel: Pomegranate
P 2555   Terracotta Deposit 2. (see pp. 65-66)
P.H. 0.072; D. body 0.068; D. rim 0.014; Th. walls 0.002 m.
Pl. 7
Sams 1979b: 48-49, fig. 6.

Joined from six fragments, lacking fragments of body, shoulder, and rim and surface chips. Paint is peeling and surface worn.

Plastic vessel in form of pomegranate with lower body divided into six lobes. At bottom center is conical blossom with hole in tip. Spout attached at top. Probably wheelmade body and spout.

Exterior is covered with yellow-buff slip. Shoulder zone and spout decorated with incised and painted pattern. At base of shoulder is border zone composed of incised meander pattern painted black. Above, on shoulder, is zone of incised petals alternating with elongated triangles. Petals are painted alternately matte maroon and black. Triangles and sides of spout painted black. Incision work sloppy.

Clay is yellowish buff with slight traces of mica. Munsell: 2.5Y 8/2 (white)-8/4 (pale yellow).

East Greek-manufactured.

26 for discussion.

26   Plastic Vessel: Pomegranate
P 1154   Terracotta Deposit 2 (see pp. 65-66)
H. 0.07; D. body 0.075; D. opening 0.01 m.
Pl. 7
Sams 1979b: 48-49, fig. 6.

Mended from four fragments. Complete except cracks and surface chips. Surface worn. Paint peeling.

Plastic vessel in shape of pomegranate with lower body divided into six lobes. At bottom is blossom composed of conical tip with six incised lines and hole at bottom. Spout at top is composed of two superimposed rings. Probably wheelmade body and spout.

Exterior is covered with smooth buff-yellow slip. On shoulder is painted and incised pattern of petals alternating with triangles with zone of tongues below. Petals are glazed purple-red, while triangles and background are black.

Clay is fine, yellowish buff with slight traces of micaceous particles. Munsell: core 10YR 8/4 (very pale brown).

East Greek-manufactured.

The three plastic pomegranate plastic vessels from Gordion are similar in clay and decorative style. **24** and **26** are very nearly identical in shape and decoration, while **25** displays slight differences. **25** is, for example, squat with a steeply sloping shoulder and a long spout. It is decorated with a meander in the lower zone while in the lower zones of the other two is a tongue pattern.

Ducat (1966: 144) dates all pomegranate vessels to between 590 and 570 B.C. He bases the high date on an example found at Gela in a tomb with a Corinthian aryballos "of the pointed type" (cf. Orsi 1906: 59, fig. 32, "a Corinthian lekythos, heart-shaped with a checker-board zone"; cf. Maximova [1927: 173], who says the lekythos found with the pomegranate at Gela is Proto-corinthian). If the aryballos in question is the Early Corinthian pointed type, then it is certainly justifiable to date the beginning of the production of the pomegranate vessels to at least the early 6th century. Higgins agrees with this dating and assigns three examples in the British Museum to the early 6th century (1959: 30-31, nos. 1652-1654). The evidence from Gordion is not decisive for the dating of this vessel type and indicates only that the pomegranate vessels were manufactured by the second quarter of the 6th century B.C.

The distribution of these decorated pomegranate vessels is widespread (e.g., Gela, Eleon in Thrace, Sardis, Rhodes, Samos, Naukratis), but East Greek centers produce the majority of them. Although Higgins (1959: 10-11, 30-31) and Ducat (1966: 142 ff.) identify this type as Rhodian, the composition of the clay is not typically Rhodian. Based on the white-buff clay and decoration, it is wiser to identify East Greece in general as the source for this pomegranate type of plastic vessel.

27 Plastic Vessel: Kore
  T 1 Tumulus A, in deposit in pit cut through floor of tumulus
  H. 0.269; L. base 0.056; W. base 0.072; W. shoulder 0.067 m.
  Pl. 8
  R. S. Young 1950: 199; 1951b: 17-19; 1952: 20; Kohler 1980: 68, fig. 28; Prayon 1987: 194, pl. 45 a-b.

Joined from ca. twelve fragments. Complete except chips from right and left sides of head, right side below elbows and back. Small cracks on face. Traces of carbon on tip of nose, left side of head, left elbow and right front of base. Left front of head burned. Rust discoloration on right arm.

Plastic vessel in form of standing kore holding bird (facing to proper right) in both hands. Kore stands with left foot in advance of right on low rectangular base. She is dressed in headband, transverse himation and chiton with narrow raised panel extending length of front. Crowning head is short spout with flat ledge rim. Narrow (D. 0.009 m.) opening through length of interior. Hollow-molded with front and back molds, with wheelmade spout and plinth added. Base probably made from third mold. Both front and back molds are worn.

Traces of white paint (?) adhere to hair, face, neck and himation, between toes and around feet. Spout is painted matte brown-red, and brown-red dots appear on front of chiton and himation. Chiton appears to be darker than rest of figure and was probably painted.

Hard-fired red-orange clay with many large lime inclusions, and some small dark inclusions and spalls. Some silver micaceous particles. Munsell: exterior 2.5YR 5/6 (red).

East Greek-manufactured, probably South Ionian (Miletos).

Tumulus A, the first tumulus excavated at Gordion by the University Museum team, contained a cremation burial and rich burial gifts. In a small pit, cut through the floor of the tumulus and part of the single deposit, were white clay, bone chips, the teeth of a young person and a large array of burned and unburned objects including this kore vessel near the top of the deposit. Based on the large number of pieces of gold and electrum jewelry, spindle whorls, an ivory statuette of a kore holding a hare (BI 3) and this kore among the burial gifts in Tumulus A, it is likely that this was the burial place of a young woman.

A close chronology for the burial in Tumulus A depends largely on the date of this vessel. There are numerous examples of the standing kore type of plastic vessel. The canonical type of kore vessel (with matte-painted decoration, wearing chiton and transverse himation, holding a dove against the chest with one hand, pulling the himation to the side with the other), of which this is a variation, evolved by around the mid-6th century B.C. (Higgins 1967: 32: "Aphrodite Group").

General chronological limits for this canonical group of kore vessels are provided by stylistic comparisons with sculpture in the round, but more precise and reliable indicators are provided by tomb groups containing plastic vessels, Attic and Corinthian pottery (Ducat 1966: 85 f.). A kore vessel of this canonical type was found in a tomb in Taranto with a Late Corinthian pyxis (570-560), a Late Corinthian lekythos (ca. mid-6th century) and an Attic black-figure Siana kylix (ca. 550) (Lo Porto 1962: 164-165, fig. 20d). A kore vessel pulling her chiton with her right hand and holding a bird in the left was found in Grave 64 at Gela with an Early (?) Corinthian powder pyxis (Orsi 1907: col. 52, fig. 25) which Diehl dates to the third quarter of the 6th century (540-520) (1964: cols. 526-530, no. 15). A kore vessel of the same type was found in a tomb at Thera with Early and Middle Corinthian vases (Dragendorf 1903: 19 ff., 25, fig. 60).

A relative chronology for kore vessels holding a bird in both hands, such as the Gordion example, is only partially clear. This hand position is derivative of the pose with one hand pulling aside the skirt and the other holding a dove. The arm position with both hands holding a bird may well have been in vogue by the beginning of the third quarter of the 6th century, when the general type of kore plastic vessel became canonical.

There are only five other published examples of the rarer type of kore vessel holding a dove with both hands: (1) Athens NM 5668 = Polytechnion 363, from the Acropolis (F. Winter 1903: 41, fig. 3; 1893: 147, fig. 28); (2) N.Y. Metropolitan Museum of Art 30.11.6, from Palermo, a janiform kore vessel (Alexander 1930: 242, no. 10, figs. 1-4; Albizzati 1928: 1-4, figs. 1-5); (3) Paris, Musée du Louvre no. 61, "from Phoenicia" (Maximova 1927: no. 64, pl. 16); (4) Budapest, no. A24 (Ducat 1966: 65, no. b4); (5) Ludwig Collection (Berger 1982: 14 ff., no. 81). In none of these cases is information on specific contexts or chronology available.

The head of the Gordion example is close to two fragments from Samos (Diehl 1964: cols. 523, 526-530, fig. 15 {15,16}, Sa 120 and Sa 124), both of which Diehl dates to ca. 540-520. Comparisons of other stylistic details of these terracotta figures (e.g., protruding buttocks with himation arching above, stepped folds with rounded contours of himation and central panel of chiton) with large-scale sculpture can be used to support a date around the decade 540-530 B.C. for the Gordion example (Ridgway 1977: 95-97).

Ducat believes that all the kore plastic vessels wearing transverse himatia ending in stepped folds over the abdomen originate in Rhodes (1966: 72). Higgins (1967: 30) is convinced that the later groups (i.e., the canonical types after 550, like the Gordion example) are Samian or Milesian in origin. R. E. Jones has recently shown from ceramic analysis that Miletos is the probable manufacturing site for this type of plastic vessel (Jones 1986: 671-673).

28 Plastic Vessel: Kore bust
P 1160   Terracotta Deposit 2 (see pp. 65-66)
H. 0.092; W. base 0.065; Th. 0.045 m.
Pl. 9
R. S. Young 1975: 55.

Complete except for two chips at rim of spout. Surface is worn and laminating, especially at lower left front. Dark incrustation on back and white and green incrustation on left side. Nose is very worn. Paint much faded and flaking.

Plastic vessel in form of female bust. Spout with flat ledge rim is attached to top of head. Two braided tresses composed of beaded sections fall over each shoulder. Round pellets for earrings are attached to earlobes. Torso spreads from neck to flat base, oval in contour. Interior hollow. Front made from single mold; back hand-modeled; spout wheelmade.

Fine buff slip is applied over face, neck and front of body, now worn off eyebrows, eyelids, nose and chin. Spout is painted black. Hair, back of head and lower front of bust have traces of streaky black glaze.

Orange clay with many gold and silver particles and few inclusions. Clay has soft texture. Munsell: 5YR 6/6-6/8 (reddish yellow).

Possibly Lydian or East Greek-manufactured.

Like the series of standing kore plastic vessels which divide into two groups on the basis of chronology—an earlier group characterized by brightly colored glazed surfaces (e.g., Ducat 1966: pls. 4-6) and a later group distinguished by matte-painted decoration—the kore busts follow the same pattern. It is to the later group that this bust is related (e.g., Higgins 1954: 49, no. 59). The Gordion bust, however, differs from most examples of this group in its lack of shoulders and undefined short torso. Of the published examples of bust vessels only three are very close to the Gordion example with its the short unmodeled torso: Rome Musée Kircher no. 620, provenience unknown (Maximova 1927: 130, fig. 24); an example from Lindos (Blinkenberg 1931: no. 2118, pl. 95; Mendel 1908: no. 280 pl. 2{4}; Istanbul inv. 2821); and an example from Cuma (Gabrici 1913: 71{7}, col. 542).

The facial features of the kore bust from Gordion are unlike those on any of the known examples of kore vessels.

The clay of **28** matches closely that of Lydian pottery from Gordion (e.g., P 1042, P 2593) in the orange color, gold and silver particles and laminated surface deterioration, although there are East Greek clays which closely resemble Lydian clay. Streaky black glaze is characteristic of Lydian painted decoration, as well as, e.g., Clazomenian decoration. The kore bust may well be a Lydian imitation of a common East Greek type or a deceptive East Greek vessel.

It is reasonable to assume that the chronology of the matte-painted East Greek kore bust vessels would closely follow that of the matte-painted standing kore vessels (i.e., beginning close to ca. 550 B.C.). Only one tomb group provides any corroborating evidence for a date. The Macri Langoni tomb 178 from Kamiros on Rhodes produced three plastic vessels: a kore bust of the glazed type, a kore bust of the matte-painted type, and a ram's-head type, along with a large amount of Corinthian pottery, mostly Late Corinthian with some Early and Middle Corinthian pieces (Jacopi 1931-39: 314, figs. 346, 349; CVA Italy X (Rhodes II), pl. 493; see Ducat 1966: 44). The chronological range of material suggests only that the kore bust could coincide with the latest Late Corinthian pottery in the tomb. If the Gordion example is indeed a Lydian imitation of an East Greek unglazed type of kore vessel it should not be any earlier than the mid-6th century. The button earring, characteristic of the earlier glazed type of kore vessel (e.g., Ducat 1966: pls. 4-6), might suggest a connection with the glazed type of bust which begins, according to Ducat (*ibid.*: 45 ff.), around 590-580 B.C. and continues down to the mid-century. Though a date generally in the third quarter of the 6th century is safe to assume, a more tentative guess would put the kore bust close to 550 B.C.

29 Plastic Vessels: Kore
T 40   Trench ET-O4, ashy earth layer above Late Phrygian house floors
P.H. 0.053; P.W. 0.046; Th. at neck 0.006 m.
Pl. 9

Single fragment preserving face, right ear. Broken across forehead and left hairline and below chin. Chip from left side of neck and left side of nose. Breaks are well worn. Exterior discolored green. Black line on forehead at break. Shallow scratch over right eye and upper cheek.

Female face is full and fleshy with almond-shaped eyes, large nose and heavy jutting chin. Right ear turns at ca. 45° angle from face. Interior is hollow. Moldmade.

Slight traces of white paint on lips and neck. Pupil of left eye is painted reddish brown and center of pupil of right eye is reddish brown dot. Lips are painted reddish brown. Along right side and front of neck is row of reddish brown dots. Bottom of ear and area below ear are painted reddish orange.

Fine pinkish orange clay with few lime inclusions and no trace of mica.

East Greek-manufactured.

This archaic female head almost certainly comes from a plastic vessel. The only clue to the specific type of plastic vessel is the painted line of dots, representing a necklace, at the top of the neck, a feature not seen on standing kore vessels, but very common on the female bust variety (e.g., Higgins 1959: nos. 1608-1614, pls. 5-8; Ducat 1966: pls. 4{3}, 5{1-3}, 6{2-3}).

The Gordion example differs in style and painting technique (i.e., it is matte-painted rather than glazed) from female bust vessels which wear necklaces. The Gordion example is more closely related to the matte-painted variety of kore busts (e.g., **28**) although these are not known to have painted necklaces.

The stylistic features of the head are close to those of the standing kore vessel (**27**) from Tumulus A and therefore might be similarly dated to around the third quarter of the 6th century B.C.

30   Plastic Vessel: Female Head Kantharos
P 2347   Trench TBT-4/3 shoveling platform, Layers 3-4
P.D. 0.052 m.
Pl. 9

Single fragment preserving forehead and hair of upper part of kantharos.

Kantharos in form of female head, possibly of maenad. Hair rises steeply from forehead with tiny raised dots covering hair. Thin walls with open interior. Moldmade.

Thin black glaze on interior, slightly smeared behind face, thick and of good quality on interior of rim. Face is painted white and hair is bright red.

Fine orange-buff clay.
Attic-manufactured.

This vessel belongs to a class of Greek late 6th- and 5th-century kantharoi, mugs, aryballoi or oinochoai composed of single or janiform heads with black glaze and/or red-figure decoration on the neck, rim or handle portions (Beazley 1963: 1529-1552; 1929: 38-78). The clue to the identification of this head as that of a female is the white face, a consistent convention for Greek females. The raised-dot hair is typical of rendering of hair on head vases of Dionysos, Negroes, Herakles and Silenoi, as well as for women (e.g., for latter see *ibid*.: 57, nos. 3-4, figs.10-11 on p. 59, p. 62, nos. 30-33, fig. 15 on p. 64).

31   Mold: Lion's Head
T 46   Trench NCT-A6, central section, layer 2
P.H. 0.132; P.W. 0.096; Th. 0.012-0.025 m.
Pl. 10

Single fragment preserving finished edge at top and at left side of mane. Broken around three other edges. Many small chips, nicks and cracks on surface. Back surface preserved. Parts darkened from burning. Green stain below eye. Some incrustation.

Baked mold fragment with concave interior, roughly convex exterior and irregularly finished edges. Half of lion's face with high, wavy mane; horizontal eyebrow; deep-set prominent eye set off by series of concentric ridges and grooves inside which eyeball bulges; high-set, modeled cheek; deeply hollowed nostril; snarling mouth with one triangular incisor appearing at back. Intaglio retouching visible on surface.

Gritty, hard-fired clay, gray at core, gray-brown near surface.
Munsell: near surface 10YR 7/1 (light gray).
Locally manufactured?

The mold comes from a late 4th-century or Late Phrygian/Hellenistic context but one which cannot be more specifically dated.

The only specific parallel for this mold is a lion's-head mold from Olynthos dated to the 5th century B.C. (Robinson 1933: 92 f., no. 370, pl. 44).

This lion's-head mold may be derived from a 5th-century Attic animal-head vase (cf. Hoffmann 1962: 13-14, pl. 4), or more likely from a local archetype created in imitation of this type of vase.

32   Plastic Vessel: Satyr's Head
P 5138   Trench ST, Level 4
H. 0.046; W. 0.045; Th. 0.004-0.017 m.
Pl. 10

Single fragment broken all around. Glaze much worn and flaking.

Fragment of open vessel in form of satyr's head. Pointed right ear and right rear portion of head are preserved along with edge of face with end of incised eyebrow. Hair is grooved and head is topped by twisted garland or crown. Moldmade.

Lustrous black glaze on interior and exterior.
Fine, pale orange clay.
Attic-manufactured.

The satyr's head comes from a purely Late Phrygian/Hellenistic context and should date stylistically to the 4th century B.C.

For a rhyton in the form of a satyr's head, see E. R. Williams 1978: 378-379, no. 69, pl. 103 (ca. 360 B.C. from Athenian Agora). See also Trumpf-Lyritzaki 1969: FV 97, pl. 13; nos. FV 144 and FV 145, pl. 21; no. FV 219, pl. 26; no. FV 220, esp. pp. 69-70 for figure vases of satyrs.

33   Vessel Handle Attachment?: Nike Protome
P 648   Terracotta Deposit 4 (see p. 67)
P.H. 0.145; Max.W. 0.066; P.Depth 0.054 m.
Pl. 10 and Color Pl. I
F. A. Winter 1977: fig. 2; 1988: 64, 70, n. 32 (Romano catalogue number incorrectly cited as **28**).

Single fragment preserving upper body from head to backward turn of lower body, broken off at back of thighs in arching contour. Lacking both arms and wings except stumps. Chip on bun; nicks in forehead, on nose and right side of breast. Incrustation on face and neck. Facial features are worn but other details are sharp.

Vessel handle attachment (?) in form of winged Nike protome in frontal position. Nike is wearing sleeveless chiton with high-girded kolpos with ends of girdle hanging in front and pellet above belt at center. Neckline of chiton is broad V-shape, reinforced by hem along edge. Folds of chiton are rendered by shallow, sloppy gouges on breast and by incised lines on overfold. On right side near lower edge of kolpos is partially preserved "bolster" pierced through center from front. No "bolster" appears on left side. Head is turned slightly to left.

Hair is drawn up in flattened, disk-like bun at back of head. She wears fillet around head and pellets for earrings. Wings are attached behind shoulders and begin to flare out at diagonal. Interior of body is hollow. On interior small hole is pierced at join of head to body. Back of torso is roughly finished, applied by hand. Moldmade front with incised details for hair and drapery.

White groundcoat adheres to face, neck, chest, shoulders, back of right arm at break, grooves of drapery. Red-pink paint, powdery to touch, is applied to fillet, to strap at neckline and along break of arms, belt, pellet at waist, sides of "bolster." White necklace composed of narrow line and two oval elements joined at center is painted on neck. When piece was excavated pink paint was adhering to face and stumps of wings; yellow to wings. Front of chiton, "bolster" and left side of body are polished.

Fine, lightly micaceous brown clay fired charcoal gray on surface with few inclusions. No Munsell reading.

Central Anatolian-manufactured.

The fabric of this vessel handle (?) immediately recalls the typical fabric of Phrygian/Central Anatolian reduced wares. There can be no doubt that the manufacturing source of this Nike is the local region.

F. A. Winter (1977: 60ff., fig. 2) has pointed to the painted necklace on this figure (and to the necklace on **108**) as one of the few surviving traces of Galatian culture at Gordion. Winter identifies the necklace as a torque, a rolled metal ring with knobs at the open ends. The necklace worn by Nike is composed of a single band which ends at the throat in two egg-shaped knobs. There is no space between the two knobs and the painting is sufficiently sloppy to allow for some uncertainty about its identification as a torque.

The identification of the figure as Nike seems indisputable, and thus this one terracotta vessel bears witness to the odd mix of cultures in Phrygia in the Late Phrygian period: a figurine of a Greek deity, wearing possibly a Celtic ornament, produced in a Phrygian ceramic technique.

A date in the late 3d to early 2d century for this figurine vessel fragment is suggested by the context (see Terracotta Deposit 4), and this date reconfirms the general chronology established by D. B. Thompson partially on stylistic grounds for Troy figurines. The hairdo with deep incisions at the front and stiff bun at the back of the head is a style which begins according to Thompson at the end of the 3d century B.C. (1963a: 40-41, 93). The dull facial features of this figure can be paralleled by the features of figurines from Troy of the 2d century B.C. (e.g., *ibid.*: 135, no. 259).

34 Vessel: Tyche?
P 1664   Terracotta Deposit 5 (see pp. 67-69)
P.H. 0.076; P.W. 0.100; Depth 0.0435; P.L. "cornucopia" 0.079 m.
Pl. 10

Single fragment preserving upper torso of woman holding "cornucopia." Lacking head and neck, lower right arm, tip of "cornucopia" and fragments of its rim. Broken off at bottom of front at around height of hips. Spout in back of right shoulder is broken off. Surface of figure is well preserved. "Cornucopia" is worn. On chest are two small holes where gritty inclusions have pierced surface. Slip and traces of paint preserved.

Vessel in form of female figure standing in frontal position and holding long, tapering object horizontally just below waist. Woman is draped in chiton and himation. Sleeveless chiton has deep V-shaped neckline and is cinched above waist. Himation has slipped down and falls across arms at elbow height. Tubular object, probably cornucopia, tapers from wide open end at female's left side to closed pointed end at right side. On surface of "cornucopia" are tightly packed grooves running its length. "Cornucopia" is hollow. Back of upper body is flat surface. At back of right shoulder is opening 0.042 m. in diameter. Interior of upper body is hollow. Front of body and "cornucopia" are moldmade. Upper back is applied by hand. Neck is scored on upper surface with three deep incisions for attachment of separately molded head.

White groundcoat is preserved on front of female figure, on "cornucopia" and in traces on back of upper body. Only surviving trace of paint is golden yellow on upper surface of "cornucopia."

Light red-brown clay fired gray at core. Compact clay with small light inclusions and no micaceous particles. Munsell: exterior 5YR 6/4 (light reddish brown); below surface 2.5YR 6/8 (light red).

Greek-manufactured.

The identification of this female figure is problematical and is based on the identification of the long object held by the figure. That the object is a torch (and the figure, therefore, Artemis) seems unlikely based on its position, size and shape. Although cornucopias are normally held in a more upright position, the tapering form, striations on the surface and hollow core do suggest affinities with the horn of plenty.

Although Kybele is occasionally associated with the cornucopia (Vermaseren 1977a: 85-86, no. 314, pls. 180-181, 2d century A.D.), it is Tyche who commonly carries one (Allègre 1889: 222 ff.). For the association of the cornucopia with the Ptolemaic queens of Egypt see D. B. Thompson 1973: 31-35. In terracotta figurines of the Hellenistic period (e.g., Laumonier 1956: 118 f., pl. 31{301}; Mollard-Besques 1963: pl. 109d-f; nos. MYR 208, MYR 207, Myrina 1586 from Myrina), Tyche carries the cornucopia in her left hand, while in a relief from the Athenian Acropolis she holds a cornucopia in both hands (von Sybel 1881: 294-295, no. 4016; von Duhn 1877: 163-164).

There are, however, no exact parallels for this particular terracotta type and the origin of the figurine is unknown.

The use of a female figure as a vessel is paralleled by one other terracotta from Gordion (**33**), a Central Anatolian-made vessel in the form of Nike. The upper part of this female figure (**34**) and the "cornucopia" are hollowed, suggesting that it was intended to hold some liquid. The hole in the back of the right shoulder might have served as the filling hole while the wide end of the "cornucopia" might have been the pouring spout.

The context of this figurine vessel suggests a Late Phrygian/Hellenistic date and stylistically this vessel may be dated to the period from the last quarter of the 3d century B.C. to 189 B.C. The deep neckline and high-girded chiton are characteristic of this period (D. B. Thompson 1963a: 35-36).

Evidence of the presence of the cult of Tyche at Gordion, at least in private worship, comes from a completely preserved stone base for a statuette bearing the Greek inscription ΑΓΑΘΗΣ ΤΥΧΗΣ (I74; Roller 1987b: 110-111, no. 3). Agathe Tyche was associated with the Greek cult of Kybele and may also have been in Late Phrygian/Hellenistic Gordion (see Roller 1987b: 110, n. 35).

Ill. 1. Reconstruction of a bust-flower thymiaterion.

Bust-Flower Thymiateria: Locally Manufactured (35-51)

It is clear from the various fragments and parts of moldmade busts and flowers from Gordion that these otherwise incongruous elements belong together to form thymiateria. The holes cut through the tops of the heads of the human figures served to hold a cup in the form of a flower which was probably used to burn incense (see Ill. 1 for reconstructed thymiaterion). These bust-flower thymiateria were locally manufactured at Gordion, as shown by **44-48**—fragments found in the Late Phrygian/Hellenistic kiln establishment (Terracotta Deposit 5)—and by **39**, a terracotta head made in the black polished technique common in the ceramic production of Gordion. All of the Gordion examples probably date to the last phase of activity before the abandonment of the site in 189 B.C.

Female busts with incense receptacles or other containers on their heads are known from various locations and in various periods: e.g., a late 5th-century example from

Halikarnassos (Higgins 1954: 128, pl. 62{444}); Punic busts of Demeter (?) from Carthage (Lantier 1931: col. 482, fig. 9; Breitenstein 1941: pl. 90{758}); a "Demeter" bust thymiaterion from Olbia dated to the first half of the 3d c. B.C. (Russyayeva 1982: 60, no. 24; *SAI* 1970: 41, no. 22, pl. 13, 2); and late 3d-2d-century examples from Failaka Island (Ikaros) in Kuwait (Mathiesen 1982: 41-42, nos. 72 and 73). The best-known series of thymiateria in the form of busts which support flower censers is that from Southern Italy and Sicily (see Stoop 1960; Bell 1981: 233-234, esp. no. 932). These range in date from the 4th to the 3d centuries B.C. (Stoop 1960: 3, 21-23).

Thymiateria composed of bust and flower are also found in mainland Greece, at Olynthos from the early 5th to the early 4th centuries B.C. (Robinson 1933: pl. 48{383-385}) and at Corinth in a 146 B.C. deposit (C. K. Williams 1977: 72, no. 27, pl. 25). The flower cup of the Corinthian example is set separately into a hole in the head, as in the case of the Gordion thymiateria. Closer to Gordion, a Kybele head from Troy wearing a hollow polos may be a thymiaterion (D. B. Thompson 1963a: 78, no. 47); a female bust from Amisos (Samsun) wearing a hollowed-out polos bearing a flower in relief with Erotes climbing up the shoulders of the bust (on display, Archaeological Museum, Istanbul, no inv. no.) may also be a thymiaterion; a female bust from near Balìkesir (in ancient Mysia, near the upper Atnos River) now in the Archaeological Museum in Istanbul (Rollas 1960: 77ff., no. 21) has a flower cup molded in one piece with the head, as does a female (?) figurine from Mirmeki on the north coast of the Black Sea (Sztetyllo 1976: 106, fig. 107). The so-called Demeter bust thymiaterion from Olbia has a plain cup attached to the head (Russayayeva 1982: 60). The bust-flower thymiateria which, stylistically and chronologically, seem closest to the Gordion examples are those from Failaka Island (Ikaros) in Kuwait. The pop-eyed look, massive features and hair style of the females are close. The Failaka examples are described as "Oriental" and are associated with such places as Seleucia on the Tigris and Egypt (Mathiesen 1982: 41-42). None of the comparable bust-flower thymiateria from Failaka or other sites is close enough, however, to the Gordion examples to suggest that they were exported from Gordion.

The Gordion examples seem to be unique local creations of a coroplastic workshop familiar with the traditions and types of thymiateria—a form found scattered around the Mediterranean but with origins or at least its most popular locale in Greek and Punic Southern Italy and Sicily.

The strong association of at least some of these bust-flower thymiateria with probable household shrines (e.g., **35**, **38**, **42**) indicates that their function was not simply decorative. The burning of incense at shrines and sanctuaries is well attested, at least in ancient Greece, with both funerary and cultic functions (Rouse 1975 [1902]: 22, at feasts for the dead; Parke 1977: 21-22; Burkert 1985: 62, 73, at sacrifices to deities). Incense can be directly linked to ritual associated with the worship of Kybele in the Roman period (Vermaseren 1977b: 100; Squarciapino 1962: 14). It is clear that the primary function of these busts was as incense burners; many of the busts as well as the flower fragments show traces of burning, but in none were found traces of incense.

35 Bust-Flower Thymiaterion: Satyr
  T 32   Terracotta Deposit 4 (see p. 67)
  P.H. 0.101; W. at lower edge 0.094; Depth at lower edge 0.045; Th. walls 0.005 m.
  Pl. 11
  R. S. Young 1953: 8, fig. 4; 1975: 12.

Once complete but now missing chip from nose, top of head, left cheek, left shoulder and base at back. This damage occurred during attempted theft at Gordion Museum in 1970s. Back right side burned. Surface cracks on face and neck.

Bust of long-eared, male figure wearing slender garland around head. Hidden behind garland is circular hole cut through top of head and penetrating to interior. High crown of hair rises to left above forehead, marked by slight incisions. Hairline recedes to right and left. Long, pointed ears are set to either side of forehead and bunches of hair hang below ears. Face is full and rectangular. Brow is furrowed with two deep grooves; eyebrows arch over deep-set, bulging, wide-open eyes. Cheeks are prominent orb-like surfaces; nose is wide and bulbous. Mouth is slightly open with full lips. Chin juts out prominently with extra fatty roll below. Neck is thick. Torso is naked, revealing full and fatty chest, rounded sloping shoulders and heavy upper arms. Beneath chest torso ends in finished resting surface. Back has large triangular vent hole reaching to back of head. Back of shoulders is smoothed. Interior is hollow and rough with much carbon and yellow and white incrustation. Moldmade front with separately added garland. Back of head possibly molded; back of torso worked by hand. Vent hole crudely cut through before firing.

Pink paint on hair, eyes, face, neck and torso. Brighter reddish pink paint adheres to furrow between head and garland at lower right back of head. Excavator noted black on hair which is no longer present.

Highly micaceous light reddish brown clay fired gray at core in places, with large and small dark inclusions. Munsell: surface 2.5YR 6/8 (light red).

Locally manufactured.

The pug-nosed, full face and pointed ears are typical of a Hellenistic satyr. Despite the earlier published references to this figure as Midas with ass's ears, the identification is difficult to support. Silenos bust thymiateria are common in Sicily (e.g., at Morgantina, see Bell 1981: 233-234, nos. 932, 933). In these two 3d-century examples the bald head, bushy beard and pointed ears are characteristic of Silenos. In the case of the Gordion example the figure is probably not an elderly Silenos but a more youthful satyr.

36 Bust-Flower Thymiaterion: Female
T 59   Terracotta Deposit 6 (see pp. 69-70)
P.H. 0.155; P.W. at lower edge 0.140; W. head 0.081; Depth head 0.088; Th. walls 0.002-0.007 m.
Pl. 11

Joined from fourteen fragments preserving head and shoulders. Missing fragments of left side of face, right side and back of head, chest and lower resting surface. Chip missing from right side of chin and jaw. Surface discolored black on back of head. Most of slip flaked off face and bust.

Frontal female bust has garland coiled with fillet encircling head. On top of head is circular hole cut through to interior but plugged with bottom portion of flower cup. Cup is surrounded by thick mass of ancient plaster. Hair is parted in center and drawn back to thickened roll. From behind ears hair falls in two long braided strands over front of shoulders. Face is well modeled with full, almost childlike features; wide horizontally set eyes with thin ridges for lids; short, turned-up nose with flaring nostrils; small mouth; full and fleshy jaw; full puffy cheeks. One small earring attached to right ear. Back of head is rounded orb with ends of garland ending above nape of neck. Behind neck and back large triangular vent hole is cut. Interior hollow. Moldmade front and separately applied back with joints masked by braids at shoulders and garland on top of head.

White groundcoat covering front of bust and garland, hair, face and shoulders. Painted decoration on garland (discolored black); hair (red-orange), face (pink on upper eyelid; red around right nostril and on lips). No paint on back of head and body.

Reddish yellow clay, lightly micaceous, very hard-fired with small light lime inclusions, fired gray at core in places. Munsell: surface 7.5YR 7/8 (reddish yellow).

Locally manufactured.

The garland around the head and the large triangular vent hole cut in the back are similar to the satyr bust-flower thymiaterion (**35**). **37** and **38** also wear garlands.

See restored bust-flower thymiaterion with **47** as the flower (Ill. 1).

37 Bust-Flower Thymiaterion: Female
T 60   Terracotta Deposit 6 (see pp. 69-70)
P.H. with flower cup 0.202; P.H. bust 0.155; W. 0.064; Depth front to back 0.068; Th. walls 0.01 m.
Pl. 11

Joined from twenty-one fragments preserving face (missing three small fragments), jaw, hair, one-third of back of head, and one small fragment with resting surface of bust. Other non-joining fragments belong to head and shoulders and single fragment to end of flower cup for resting on head. Interior partially broken away.

Frontal female bust wearing garland coiled with fillet around head. Hair is parted in middle and drawn off face to sides in thick rolls. Hair falls along left side of neck in thick braid. On left ear is round ball earring. Face is well modeled and triangular with low forehead, widely spaced wide-open eyes, up-turned nose, well modeled lips, rounded fatty chin. No modeling on bust. Back of head is convex orb with hole in top behind garland. Around hole are traces of plaster incrustation. Molded fluted flower-cup fragment rests in hole in head. Interior is hollow with smoothed walls. Moldmade face with applied back of head and bust (?).

Entire exterior surface is covered with white groundcoat, especially well preserved on face. Hair is painted black; diadem pink; flower cup pink; eyeball black; lips pink; other traces of pink on neck, forehead, below eyebrows, cheek, upper chin.

Poorly fired reddish yellow clay. Very dark at core, dark gray beneath surface. Lightly micaceous with light inclusions. Munsell: surface 7.5YR 7/6 (reddish yellow).

Locally manufactured.

38 Bust-Flower Thymiaterion: Female
T 33   Terracotta Deposit 4 (see p. 67)
P.H. 0.103; P.W. 0.08; P.Depth 0.079 m.
Pl. 12

Joined from eight fragments preserving portions of face and beginning of neck. Back of head is more fragmentary. Surface is missing on most of face and badly worn and flaking in other places. Head is burnt on right and left sides.

Frontal female head with full face, well-modeled cheeks, rounded heavy chin. Woman wears garland coiled with fillet around head with raised knob at center and gouges along surface. Hair is parted in center, drawn to sides in thick rolls and gathered above nape in chignon. Back of skull is domed and in top of skull behind fillet is large circular hole (W. 0.033 m.). Around hole and on interior is plaster incrustation. Interior is hollow. Head is molded in two pieces, front and back, and joined behind garland.

Faint traces of red paint on hair and fillet; traces of blue over white groundcoat on garland.

Reddish yellow, highly micaceous clay with small, dark inclusions; highly friable. Munsell: 7.5YR 7/8 (reddish yellow).

Locally manufactured.

39 Bust-Flower Thymiaterion: Female
T 83   Terracotta Deposit 5 (see pp. 67-69)
P.H. 0.07; P.W. 0.042; P.Th. 0.052 m.
Pl. 12

Single fragment of head preserving left side including edge of face. Rust-colored stains especially on interior.

Female head with large hole cut through top of head behind fillet or diadem. Hair is parted in center and drawn off face and rolled in sections around forehead. Interior is hollow with rough walls. Back is smooth orb. Moldmade front.

White powdery groundcoat adheres to forehead and grooves around hairline. Pink paint in narrow band on garland and above garland on head.

Very hard clay fired light gray throughout; lightly micaceous with few small inclusions. Munsell: 2.5Y N7/ (light gray).

Locally manufactured.

This head is intentionally fired gray, i.e., in a reducing atmosphere, like much of the local pottery. This is another indication of the local origin of these bust-flower thymiateria.

40 Bust-Flower Thymiaterion Fragment
 T 119 Uncertain context. See Terracotta Deposit 5 (pp. 67-69)
 P.H. 0.062; P.W. 0.071; Th. walls 0.007; D. hole 0.031 m.
 Pl. 12

Single fragment of back of head preserving half of hole in top of head and edge of section at left. Surface chipped and discolored on exterior at left; interior darkened, possibly from burning. Lime incrustation on interior.

Section of back of head from bust-flower thymiaterion. Large round hole in top of head once held conical flower cup or censer of thymiaterion. Back of head, off center to right, is uneven convex surface, perhaps to indicate bun or thickened section of hair. Along left finished edge is series of gouges. Interior is hollow with smooth walls. Probably hand-modeled with left edge being edge of back section, once attached to front molded section.

Slight traces of white groundcoat or plaster (?) on back right and left sides. Few traces of reddish brown paint on left edge and lower break, probably on hair.

Lightly micaceous, reddish yellow clay with many inclusions. Hard-fired, slightly grayish at core. Munsell: surface 7.5YR 7/6 (reddish yellow).

Locally manufactured.

41 Bust-Flower Thymiaterion: Female
 T 54 Trench NCT-A10, Layer 5, Pit G
 P.H. 0.051; W. 0.122; Depth 0.053; Th. walls 0.005-0.007 m.
 Pl. 12

Single fragment preserving bust, lacking neck and head. Surface chip from upper chest. Paint well preserved.

Draped female bust. Woman wears sleeveless chiton with scoop neckline. Thick plaits of hair fall diagonally along crest of shoulder. Back is smoothed and flattish. Circular vent hole (D. 0.025 m.) is cut in center of back. Bottom resting surface is flat. Interior is hollow, walls smoothed. Moldmade front. Moldmade or hand-modeled back joined to front at shoulders where join is visible on interior but is masked on exterior by plaits of hair.

Entire exterior surface, front and back, is covered with white groundcoat. Hair is painted dark red. Skin is buff-pink. Trace of red at edge of left arm and garment.

Lightly micaceous reddish yellow clay with small lime and some dark inclusions. Hard-fired, gray at core. Munsell: surface 7.5YR 7/6 (reddish yellow).

Locally manufactured.

Found in pit with bone pins, stylus and knife handle. Contents of pit date to Late Phrygian/Hellenistic period.

Form, style and size are characteristic of the bust-flower thymiaterion type.

42 Bust-Flower Thymiaterion: Artemis?
 T 25 Terracotta Deposit 5 (see pp. 67-69)
 P.H. 0.100; P.W. base 0.164; P.Depth 0.065; Th. walls 0.011-0.022 m.
 Pl. 12

Joined from five fragments preserving upper back from above waist to shoulders, missing neck, head and most of front of upper torso. Surface is much incrusted with plaster (?) and slightly burned. Colors are well preserved.

Draped female bust, probably Artemis with quiver. Figure wears sleeveless chiton buttoned at shoulders. Deep folds are indicated on back of bust. Tubular object, probably quiver, is secured over right shoulder and hangs at diagonal across back. Strap is indicated over right shoulder in front. High girdle is indicated on back by wide raised band. Bottom of fragment has finished flat resting surface. Interior is hollow. Walls well smoothed. Moldmade in two pieces, front and back. Head may have been separately molded. Quiver is added.

Exterior is covered with white groundcoat. Skin is pink; quiver and strap are red, as are buttons of chiton or peplos. On lower right side in front paint is discolored gray-black.

Very fine reddish yellow clay with few inclusions. Small amount of mica visible. Munsell: 7.5YR 7/6 (reddish yellow).

Locally manufactured.

Form, style and size are characteristic of the bust-flower thymiaterion type.

43 Bust-Flower Thymiaterion?: Female
 T 121 Trench SET-WC2-4 and NC1, Layers 1-1b
 P.H. 0.067; P.W. 0.052; Th. walls 0.005-0.01 m.
 Pl. 13

Single fragment preserving lower resting surface, breast and lower neck of female. Exterior surface burned. Incrustation of white lime (?) on interior and exterior.

Fragment of upper torso of draped female wearing chiton. Finished edge at bottom suggests that bust was intended. Back is concave, uneven surface with fold of clay at finished edge. Moldmade.

White groundcoat adheres to exterior on breast.

Micaceous reddish yellow clay fired gray at core. Small dark inclusions. Munsell: 7.5YR 7/6 (reddish yellow)-6/4 (light brown).

Locally manufactured.

The fragment comes from a context containing assorted Late Phrygian/Hellenistic pottery, including one possibly Roman bowl fragment. Nothing specific can be ascertained about the date of this fragment.

The possibility that this female bust belongs to the bust-flower thymiaterion group is suggested by the size, finished lower edge and clay. Not enough of the fragment, however, is preserved to be certain of the identification.

44 Thymiaterion Mold Fragment
 T 71 Trench ET-012, CD, Level 4. Terracotta Deposit 5 (see pp. 67-69)
 H. 0.154; D. rim 0.159; Th. walls 0.01-0.05 m.
 Pl. 13
 Edwards 1959a: 267, pl. 68, fig. 19; 1959b, fig. 9.

Intact except small chips from rim and surface chips on interior. Two fragments repaired with glue. Two long cracks run down length of mold from rim. Clay is very soft and probably only lightly baked. Darkened by contact with fire at top of cone and on one side near top. Various flaws visible including fingerprint on interior.

Clay mold for flower cup of thymiaterion. Mold is thick and cone-shaped with flat surface at apex of cone on exterior and rough exterior walls. Inside of cone is hollow and bears petals of flower in low relief. Petals are long ovals with rounded tips and central spines. Base of petals is at center of mold—a flattish, uneven round surface. Rim is composed of two steps: upper, uneven, slightly rounded surface and narrow, inset, right-angled ledge. Exterior walls are worked by hand. Interior much worn. See **45-48** for flower-cup fragments made from this mold.

Buff-brown clay, light gray on surface. White lime inclusions; small amount of small light grit and mica. Munsell: core 2.5Y 7/4 (pale yellow); exterior surface 10YR 7/2 (light gray).

Locally manufactured.

The association in one kiln of this mold and at least four fragments of flowers taken from this mold, as well as a female head (**39**) which can be shown by other parallels to be part of a bust which served as a thymiaterion, is evidence for local production of these bust-flower thymiateria.

The type of flower, a lily (?), is close to that on which Eros reclines in **99**.

45-49   **Thymiaterion Fragments: Flower Cups**
     T 74, T 116, T 117, T 123, T 130a,b
     45-48: Terracotta Deposit 5 (see pp. 67-69)
     45: P.H. 0.071; P.W. 0.06; Th. walls 0.008-0.009; Est.D. rim 0.130 m.
     46: P.H. 0.051; P.W. 0.073; Th. walls 0.003-0.006; Est.D. rim 0.110 m.
     47: P.H. 0.077; P.W. 0.055; Th. walls 0.004-0.006; Est.D. rim 0.130 m. Ill. 1
     48: P.H. 0.044; P.W. 0.064; Th. walls 0.005-0.009; Est.D. rim 0.140-0.150 m.
     49: (a) P.H. 0.031; P.W. 0.070; Th. walls 0.008-0.011; Est.D. rim 0.110 m.; (b) P.H. 0.031; P.W. 0.031; Th. walls 0.005-0.012 m.
     Pl. 13

Single fragments preserving rims of conical thymiaterion cups in shape of flowers. Rim is stepped with slightly flaring lip. Interior is hollow; walls are smoothed. On exterior are molded in low relief long rounded petals with narrow ridges defining outer contours and interior lines. Tips of petals are upturned as body of cup turns out to rim. Joining petals at their tips are raised curving ridges. All fragments have flaws, either fingerprints, overlapping petals or ridges within petals, and sloppily made rims. All may have been discards. **45** and **48** show traces of burning or contact with carbonized material. Moldmade.

Traces of white groundcoat on exterior and interior of some fragments of **45**, **47**. Tiny traces of red (?) paint on petals of **46**, **47**. Evidence of polish on **49**.

Fine, lightly micaceous reddish yellow clay fired dark red-gray to gray at core with few dark inclusions, leaving surface pockmarked. Friable and poorly fired clay. Munsell: 5YR 6/6 (reddish yellow)-7.5YR 7/6 (reddish yellow). Fine pink-buff slip added to exterior and interior surface of **46**, **48**. Slip on **49** was fired dark brown-gray; Munsell: core 10YR 6/4 (light yellowish brown)-5/2 (grayish-brown); surface 10YR 6/3 (pale brown)-5/1 (gray).

Locally manufactured.

The clue to the association of these flower fragments with bust-flower thymiateria comes from their discovery in the Pottery Establishment together with molds for a flower (**44**), a bust (**50**) and a female head with an opening in the top (**39**); from the fragmentary flower found with **37**; and from parallels outside of Gordion (see above, p. 18).

See restored drawing (Ill. 1) of bust-flower thymiaterion **36** with **47**.

50   **Mold: Female Bust**
     T 70   Terracotta Deposit 5 (see pp. 67-69)
     P.H. 0.218; W. at base 0.233; Depth 0.08; Est.H. head 0.117 m.
     Pl. 14
     Edwards 1959a: 267, pl. 68, fig. 20; 1959b: fig. 10.

Restored from ca. forty fragments preserving lower three-quarters of mold. Upper part of mold and many tiny fragments from front and larger fragments from back missing. Clay badly flaking and chipping due to lack of thorough firing. Many facial features unclear.

Large clay mold for front of female head and upper torso. Mold is triangular and composed of thick mass of clay with wide, flat lower edge and incurving sides. Back of mold is irregular flattish surface, built up of layers of clay.

Female head has oval face, large eyes with defined lids and eyeball, mouth set close to nose, thick lips and well-rounded chin. Hair is rendered by incisions on right side of face and by deep grooves at top and left side. Shallow V-shaped incision marks drapery between large orbs for breasts. To right and left sides of head are diagonal and vertical grooves and incisions, perhaps to indicate veil. Mold taken from archetype and further enhanced by incision work. Unbaked state of mold and sloppiness of many features indicate that mold may never have been used and may have been discarded in kiln.

Gray-buff, unbaked, sun-dried clay tending toward olive green. Many lime and some grit inclusions. Munsell: 5Y 7/2 (light gray).

Locally manufactured.

This mold was published by Edwards (1959a: 267, pl. 68, fig. 20) as a female mask or protome with one hand raised and holding tresses. Although the mold is in a very fragmentary state, it is hard to visualize the area to the left of the head as a hand. The mold was probably intended to produce busts for the bust-flower thymiaterion type.

51   **Mold: Female Head**
     T 95   Trench CC2, fill under Floor 3b
     H. 0.121; W. 0.077; Depth 0.057 m.
     Pl. 14

Intact. Flaws and cracks in right cheek, eye, side of mouth and neck.

Mold of front of female head. Mold is thick and heavy, built up of many layers of clay. Mold widens at bottom (neck); edge is finished with smooth rim. Other edges of mold are rounded and merge with back, which is convex, roughly finished surface. At top of head is wide channel. Face is long and rectangular. Features are heavy: large protruding oval eyes; wide nose, turned up at end; lips set close to nose; heavy double chin. Hair surrounds face like halo in random, wavy curls parted at center over forehead. Neck is thick, flaring from beneath chin. Mold is very fresh, producing crisp impression.

Baked yellowish pink clay; lightly micaceous with many dark, some large inclusions. Munsell: ca. 5YR 7/4 (pink) but no clean breaks for testing.

Locally manufactured.

It is possible that this mold is for the head of a bust-flower thymiaterion. The size is comparable to **37** and **38**, and the facial features are similar although this face is longer and more rectangular. The odd depression in the mold at the top of the head may suggest that the mold was taken from an existing model which had a hole in its head at this point, like the bust-flower thymiateria.

The context from which the mold comes cannot be more specifically dated than 4th-century or later. This is probably a derivative mold with some fresh intaglio retouching of the eye outlines.

Kybele and Related Types (52-64)

It is not surprising that Kybele is the deity most frequently represented among the terracotta figurines from Gordion, since Phrygia was the reputed home of Kybele. Stone sculptural representations of Kybele are also known from Gordion and date as early as the late 7th or early 6th century B.C. (e.g., Mellink 1983: esp. 359). There are seven definite terracotta examples (**52, 53, 57-61**), two possible examples (**62, 63**), one phiale (**54**) and two fragments of tympana (**55, 56**) which most probably belong to Kybele figurines. A female with tympanum (**64**) is probably a "temple girl," linked by iconography to Kybele. Two of the Kybele representations are presumed to be manufactured at Gordion or at least in the region of Central Anatolia (**52, 53**) as may be the group of unassigned attributes (**54**, possibly **55, 56**). The rest are taken to be Greek imports to the site. All date to the Late Phrygian/Hellenistic period.

The basic iconography of the terracotta representation of Kybele from Gordion follows the traditional Greek iconographical lines of representations from Asia Minor: enthroned with the tympanum, phiale and lion as her attributes (see also Pls. 40-41 for marble Kybele [S 81, Pl. 40] and alabaster Kybele [S 103, Pl. 41] from Gordion) and, in one case (**57**), wearing a crown and riding a lion while holding a tympanum and a phiale. The latter iconography suggests the image of Kybele as the goddess who tames the wild beasts and rides in a chariot drawn by lions (T. W. Allen 1952: 80, Hymn XIV; Vergil, *Aeneid* III, 102-20). According to D. B. Thompson (1966a: 4 ff.), sculptural representations of Kybele riding a lion did not appear until the Pergamenes created the type on the Great Altar in the early 2d century B.C., a date continually under scholarly discussion. The type of Kybele riding a lion is repeated on a frieze from the temple of Athena Polias in Priene, which was probably modeled after the frieze at Pergamon (British Museum, inv. no. 1170; Smith 1900: 159, no. 1170). For the most complete compendia of representations of Kybele see Vermaseren 1977a and 1987 and F. Naumann 1983; for a more popular work on Kybele in general see Vermaseren 1977b: esp. 24-37.

There are some variations in the iconography of the terracotta Kybele types from Gordion, especially with respect to the position of the lion. Kybele rides a lion in one case (**57**), while in four other figurines a lion appears in her lap (**58** and **59**: head to Kybele's right looking toward viewer; **61**: head to Kybele's left; **53**: head to Kybele's right looking out to viewer) (see D. B. Thompson 1963a: 77-78 n. 49 for representation of Kybele with lion in lap); and in one case the lion is on a footstool with Kybele's feet resting on its back (**60**) (see Schede 1964: 104, fig. 122 for statue of Kybele from Priene with lion as Kybele's footstool). In the large locally made terracotta Kybele statuette (**52**), a lion is absent except as a suggestion on the footstool with lion's-paw feet. In a locally manufactured alabaster statuette of Kybele from Gordion (S 103 on Pl. 41), Kybele has a lion standing at her left side, while in the marble Kybele statuette from Gordion the lion forms the right front of the throne (S 81 on Pl. 40; see Roller 1988: 43-50, esp. 47, fig. 5).

The sphinxes which rest on the arms of the throne of this same terracotta Kybele (**52**) may simply be a common throne decoration (e.g., Richter 1926: 9, 33, 40, 52), although, as Holloway points out (1957: 30), sphinxes appear with Kybele in two other key sculptural monuments, a marble statue of Kybele in Pergamon (F. Winter 1908: 69-71, pl. 12) and a Neo-Attic relief from the Piraeus, in Berlin (Holloway 1957: 36; von Salis 1913: 4-5, figs. 3-4). A sejant sphinx may be the support for Kybele's right arm on **60**.

The tympanum or tambourine which, according to Herodotos (IV, 76), was used in the celebration of nocturnal rituals in honor of Kybele is a common feature of Kybele representations in general. At Gordion, it appears at Kybele's side in four of the figurines (**52, 57, 58, 60**,) and two more tympana (**55, 56**) are preserved as fragments broken from the left sides of two other figurines. In one instance a temple girl or attendant holds a tympanum at her left side (**64**). In only one case (**52**) does Kybele rest her hand on the tympanum from above rather than support it from below, as on the great majority of Kybele figurines and statues (see Holloway 1957: 36-42). On **59** Kybele is without her tympanum.

The phiale, an attribute not specific to Kybele, often appears in Kybele's right hand, e.g. at Troy (D. B. Thompson 1963a, nos. 16, 19, 22); Pergamon (Töpperwein 1976: no. 190); Mamurtkale (Conze and Schazmann 1911: pls. 11{8}, pl. 12{3}); Priene (Wiegand and Schrader 1904: 330, fig. 367); it is an attribute of Kybele at Gordion in **52, 57, 59, 61**, probably **58, 60**, and possibly **54**, a single phiale detached from a statuette.

The costume Kybele wears is consistent among the

Gordion figurines. On her head is a crown or polos. On **57** is a tall crenelated crown (cf. Kybele from Priene: Wiegand and Schrader 1904: 330, fig. 368; from Mamurtkale: Conze and Schazmann 1911: pls. 11{1,2}, 12{9}; from Troy: D. B. Thompson 1963a: 83, no. 46, pl. 12; from Pergamon: Töpperwein 1976: no. 190), while on **52**, a locally made statuette, the crown is a low crenelated variety like that of a Kybele figurine from Pergamon (*ibid*.: no. 199). The poorly preserved crown on **62** may be a variation of the crenelated type or a flaring polos. On **58**, **59**, **63** Kybele wears a low pill box type of polos (cf. Kybele from Priene: Wiegand and Schrader 1904: 330, fig. 367; from Mamurtkale: Conze and Schazmann 1911: pl. 11{6}; from Pergamon: Töpperwein 1976: no. 201). A veil was probably worn under the crown or polos of one Kybele figurine (**60**). Kybele's temple attendant (**64**) wears a veil and/or a Phrygian cap.

Kybele wears a chiton and a himation in all of the Gordion examples, and in every instance, where enough of the figurine is preserved, the himation is seen coming from the right side, creating a bunch over Kybele's lap, falling down the left side and covering most of her legs (**52**, **53**, **57-60**). Only on **52** are Kybele's sandals detailed, indicating a high-soled, split sandal with perhaps a thong between the big toe and the rest of the toes. Ball earrings are detectable on two examples (**52** and **57**) and two rings are worn by Kybele in the large statuette (**52**).

The throne type, with two palmette finials forming the ends of the upper back of the throne, is consistent on both the local and imported Kybele figurines (e.g., **52**, **58**, **59-60**, **62**) (cf. from Priene: Wiegand and Schrader 1904: 330, fig. 367; from Mamurtkale: Conze and Schazmann 1911: pls. 11{8}, 12{2}; from Pergamon: Töpperwein 1976: pl. 30{188}).

PROVENIENCE

As in the case of all the Gordion figurines, since scientific analysis of the clays has not been made, it is extremely difficult to identify the figurines' sources of manufacture. It is possible, however, to isolate groups of figurines with clays that are close in color, texture and composition and indicate that a single provenience is likely for some.

With the representations of Kybele, at least two probably Central Anatolian products can be isolated, based largely on style. **52**, for example, the large statuette of Kybele, is so close to other known locally made terracottas (e.g., the female heads of the bust-flower thymiateria) in the style of the facial features and in workmanship (the handling of the drapery folds) that it is almost certainly is a product of local coroplasts. It is less certain, however, that **53** was made at Gordion. The handmade, crude technique and the very sloppy style make it likely that such a figurine would not have been imported from beyond the Central Anatolian region. While both are enthroned figures, a lion is held in Kybele's lap in **53** but is absent in **52**. Holloway (1957: 32 ff.) points to a Pergamene source for the iconographic inspiration of the large Gordion Kybele, a suggestion which would seem likely in view of other Pergamene links with Gordion (see below, pp. 79).

Three of the Kybele figurines probably derive from the same manufacturing source (**57-59**) (see Conclusions, Group I, pp. 78-79). The clays of all three are closely comparable, and the facial features and painting style are also similar. **58**, **59** are so close in size, type design and painted decoration that they might be from the same workshop. The tympanum at the left side of **58**, not seen on **59**, is the only indication that both were *not* made from the same mold.

The figurine of Kybele riding a lion (**57**) is very close to Kybele figurines from the Pergamene sanctuary of Kybele at Mamurtkale (Conze and Schazmann 1911: 40, pl. 12{3}, MK T 1594, MK T 1530); Töpperwein-Hoffmann, 1978: 81, pl. 36, MK 10). Although Töpperwein-Hoffmann (*ibid*.: 80-81) indicates that the clay of the Mamurtkale figurines is Aeolian like that at Larisa on the Hermos, the excavators of Pergamon have found ample numbers of figurines from the acropolis of Pergamon of the same type and in the same clay as the Mamurtkale finds. The excavators believe that the Mamurtkale figurines are Pergamene (W. Radt, personal communication, July 1981). From the author's examination of the figurines from both the acropolis of Pergamon and Mamurtkale, it is possible to confirm the excavator's viewpoint and further to suggest that the three Kybeles from Gordion (**57-59**) are all probably Pergamene. (See discussion on pp. 78-79 for other figurines belonging to this same group, probably from Pergamon.)

A second group of figurines closely allied to the group that includes the three Kybeles mentioned above can be isolated from among the Gordion corpus according to the composition and color of their clays (see Conclusions, Group II, pp. 79-80). One of these (**61**) is a fragmentary representation of Kybele. The specific manufacturing source is not known. Two Kybele figurines from Gordion find their closest typological and stylistic parallels at sites along the Black Sea; e.g., **60** has parallels from Amisos (Samsun) and from Myrmekion in the Crimea, and **63** is close to figurines from Callatis (Mangalia) on the western end of the Black Sea, and both may have been manufactured at some Black Sea site.

FUNCTION

The function of all of the Kybele figurines from Gordion is certainly religious. How these figurines—or, in the case of **52**, a statuette of Kybele—were used in the cult of Kybele at Gordion is a more interesting question.

The position of Kybele as the chief deity of the Phrygians, one with autochthonous origins in Anatolia, is unassailable (see Bittel 1963: 7-22; Mellink 1983: 349-360; Roller 1988: 43-50). There are monuments and shrines of various types dedicated to Kybele, Kubaba or Meter dating to pre-Hellenistic times in Phrygia, the most famous of which are the rock-cut facades, niches, altars and relief figures in the Phrygian highlands (Haspels 1971: 73-111). By the period of Alexander and his successors, worship of Kybele takes on a more Greek form in Phrygia and all of Asia Minor. The monumental rock-cut outdoor shrines grew fewer (*ibid*.: 147-162), probably replaced by temples in sanctuaries—as at Mamurtkale near Pergamon (Conze and Schazmann 1911: 14 ff.)—or small altars and shrines, including household ones. In the Late Phrygian/Hellenistic levels at Gordion no building which can be labeled a temple of Kybele was uncovered, although the finds, including the terracotta fragments from several buildings thought to be domestic establishments, suggest that shrines existed within. For example, there may have been a domestic shrine in the SET "Level 2 House" (see Terracotta Deposit 3), where two of the Kybele figurines were found. Although the complete plan of the SET-NW house was never recovered (see Terracotta Deposit 4), the presence of the large Kybele statuette (**52**) in addition to another enthroned Kybele figurine (**60**), a vessel handle in the form of Nike and two bust-flower thymiateria suggests a shrine in what seems otherwise from the finds to be a domestic structure. In a room (Room 1) in one building in the southeast area of the Late Phrygian/Hellenistic Pottery Establishment (see Terracotta Deposit 5) was constructed a small niche in one wall (see plan, Fig. 7). The small finds from the two rooms of this building, as well as Building 7, included many stone sculpture fragments, inscribed bases, figurines of Kybele and a tympanum possibly associated with Kybele (**56, 61, 63**), Artemis (**42**), Tyche (?) (**34**) and other females. At least one shrine must have been incorporated in this area.

The house in Q₂E₂ (Terracotta Deposit 6) contains terracottas appropriate as votives in a domestic shrine: Kybele (**58**), a large statuette of Attis (?) (**97**), Eros (**99**), a standing female (**73**), as well as two bust-flower thymiateria (**36, 37**). The presence of the large statuettes of Kybele and possibly Attis may indicate that devotion was shared by this duo. F. Naumann sees no evidence for a Phrygian cult of Kybele and Attis or that Attis was a part of Phrygian mythology (1983: 98-100), although they are certainly linked iconographically in Greece by the Hellenistic period. Greek iconography and legend could well have inspired the Late Phrygian/Hellenistic pair at Gordion. Another bit of evidence for a conflation of cults of Kybele and another deity at Gordion comes from a Late Phrygian/Hellenistic alabaster statuette of Kybele which bears a dedicatory inscription in Greek, "to the Muses" (S 103 on Pl. 41; Roller 1986).

We must presume that small terracotta images of Kybele or her temple attendants (**64**) were placed on altars or tables, whether in domestic or public shrines, as votive gifts to the deity. There is only one tentative bit of evidence for another special use of figurines, in nocturnal rituals in honor of Kybele. Herodotos (IV, 76) relates the story of a Scythian who, after visiting Kyzikos and seeing the rituals of the Kybele cult there, went back to his native land and practiced the same ritual by "carrying a tympanum and hanging on himself images" (*agalmata*). Herodotos does not specify that these *agalmata* are terracotta images but it would make sense that small, lightweight figurines were suspended. There are no suspension holes on any of the Kybele figurines from Gordion and we are uncertain if the cultic rituals for Kybele at Kyzikos and Gordion were identical.

52 Kybele
   T 35   Terracotta Deposit 4 (see p. 67)
   H. 0.524; W. throne 0.234; Max.Th. 0.250; L. face 0.058; D. tympanum 0.125 m.
   Pls. 15, 16 and Color Pl. I
   R. S. Young 1953: 6-8, fig. 3; Holloway 1957; F. Naumann 1983: 369, no. 626, pl. 47{4}; Vermaseren 1987: no. 52; F. A. Winter 1988: 70, n. 42 (Romano catalogue number incorrectly cited as **47**).

Joined from many fragments. Missing small fragments and one crosspiece at back of throne, right finial of throne, right elbow, left front corner of footstool. During attempted theft at Gordion Museum in 1976 this object was damaged and portions lost, including upper torso from above roll of himation, head, upper right arm and back of throne.

Large statuette of Kybele seated in frontal pose on throne with her feet resting on high footstool. She holds phiale in upturned right hand, which rests on sphinx at top of throne arm, and supports tympanum at side with left hand. In top of tympanum are deep vertical slit and two oval holes, possibly for attachment of some object. Kybele wears turreted polos or crown, small round earrings, high-girded chiton, himation, sandals, and two rings on left hand. Throne has high back with crosspiece at mid-back and two oval finials at left back. Sejant sphinxes decorate tops of arms of throne. Footstool projects from lower front of throne and is decorated at front right corner with sphinx whose feet become large lion's paws.

Probably mostly moldmade, composed of small separately molded sections, e.g., head; upper torso, lower torso, feet and stool; sphinxes of throne. Clay is built up in layers in mold with fine clay slip which forms surface. Phiale and tympanum probably wheelmade. Back is hand-modeled. Round firing hole in back of head. Interior is hollow with rough walls. Some details rendered by hand-modeling or incision. Thick white plaster, painted over, found sealing ancient breaks especially on throne and drapery.

Traces of white groundcoat survive over much of statuette. Red paint is used for polos, himation, soles of sandals, tympanum, footstool; light blue for band of himation, chiton, wings of sphinxes at arms of throne; black for bands of himation, bands on throne, edge of tympanum in herringbone pattern; pink for breasts of sphinxes at arms, pattern on outside face of tympanum, interior of phiale, left arm; yellow for left front of throne over plaster. Back is unpainted.

Clay is hard-fired, yellowish red on surface and gray at core. Lightly micaceous clay with few light inclusions. Munsell: surface

7.5YR 6/6 (reddish yellow). Color and texture of clay are close to those of **97**.

Locally manufactured.

R. Ross Holloway (1957: 32 ff.) proposed that this large terracotta statuette from Gordion is of a type which can be definitely traced to the cult image of Meter in the Metroön in Athens and which can be more directly linked to Pergamon and a large marble image of Kybele of the Hellenistic period (F. Winter 1908: 69-71, pl. 12). The evidence that this type can be traced to the 5th-century B.C. Athenian cult image, however, is inconclusive, as D. B. Thompson points out (1963: 78, n. 58).

The pose of the Gordion Kybele with the left hand supporting the tympanum from above, the absence of the lion, and the details of the throne e.g., the sphinxes at the arms are close to the Pergamene model and, as Holloway demonstrates, have little in common with other known representations of Kybele. Since at least one Pergamene type of Kybele is found at Gordion (**57**), and Pergamon had close political contacts with the nearby center of Kybele worship, Pessinus (Strabo 12, 5, 3), it is not surprising to find that this terracotta statuette at Gordion is based on a Pergamene model. For a Kybele from Troy based on sculptural models, see D. B. Thompson 1963a: 23-24, no. 44.

The workmanship and style of the statuette, however, indicate a local manufacturing source. The very full face and heavy features, generally seen on terracotta figurines of the end of the 3d century B.C. and 2d century B.C. from Pergamon (Töpperwein 1976: 183, 214, no. 194, pl. 32; D. B. Thompson 1963a: 32, 83-84, no. 47, pl. 12), are so close to those of the group of locally made bust-flower thymiateria (see **35-51**) that a local source for this Kybele seems undeniable. Many of the details of the figure, e.g., the handling of the drapery folds and the jewelry, match those on **97**, a large-scale statuette of Attis (?), of probably local provenience. A date in the late 3d or early 2d century B.C. (pre-189 B.C.) for this statuette is indicated by the context.

What role this large image of Kybele played in its context is not entirely certain, although one can easily imagine a statuette on this scale being used in a shrine as an object of veneration. The context in which it was found seems to be that of a house (see Terracotta Deposit 4) and thus the Kybele statuette might have been the cult image in the shrine of this household. It was obviously used for some length of time and considered of some value, to judge from the extensive repair work undertaken in antiquity. M. M. Voigt (1983: 186-203) defines a methodology using ethnographically documented models for assigning functions to terracotta figurines on the basis of material, size, shape, pose, find-spot and signs of use and wear. The Gordion Kybele meets many of the requirements for a cult figure: large size, attributes, superior technology and evidence of minor damage.

53 Kybele
(a) T 13   Trench SET, E of Wall E, Layer 5, mixed fill
(b) T 19 Trench SET-N, Cut N-3-C, Layer 2
(a) P.H. 0.100; W. 0.097; Max.Th. 0.038 m.
(b) P.L. 0.057; P.W. 0.055; Max.Th. 0.020 m.
Pl. 17

(a) Joined from five fragments preserving torso from below neck to turn of legs. Throne partially preserved to right and left of torso. Right hand, lower arm of figure and forelegs of lion are missing.
(b) Single fragment preserving lower right edge of figurine with right foot and horizontal folds of garment.

Seated Kybele holding couchant lion in profile to right on lap. Throne is wide with straight back. Over front of right and left shoulders are single locks of hair. Kybele wears chiton and himation. Left hand rests on side of lion. Lion turns head toward viewer. Back has "hood" of clay at top. At center of back is roughly finished surface. Moldmade but with right and left back sides of throne applied. Applications of pellets for eyes of lion and much use of incision (e.g., muzzle of lion, drapery of figure).

No trace of white groundcoat. Red paint faintly preserved on outside edges of throne back on both fragments.

Pinkish brown micaceous clay filled with large dark gritty particles and white lime inclusions. Fired gray at core. Munsell: exterior 5YR 6/4 (light reddish brown).

Central Anatolian- or locally manufactured.

The poorly executed molding technique and the amateurish, sloppy style indicate a Central Anatolian or local source of manufacture and make it unlikely that such an object would have had much export appeal. The type of enthroned Kybele holding a lion is common enough in imported examples found at Gordion that a local source of inspiration for the representation is not lacking.

The context dates to the late 4th or 3d century B.C.

54 Miniature Phiale
T 137   Trenches TBT-2, TBT-3, Level 4
H. 0.014; W. 0.033 m.
Pl. 17

Single fragment preserving phiale and much of hand on underside. Only small chips missing.

Mesomorphic phiale held by schematic hand with no articulation of fingers except single groove on underside of phiale. Handmade?

Light brown clay, gray at core. Highly micaceous with silver particles. Munsell: core 7.5YR 7/4 (pink); surface 7.5YR 6/4 (light brown)-7/4 (pink).

Probably locally manufactured.

This phiale is part of a large-scale statuette, perhaps of Kybele. The clay is very similar and the size appropriate for a statuette such as **52** or **97**.

55 Tympanum
T 47   Trench CC, Late Phrygian/Hellenistic fill
D. 0.05; Max.Th. 0.01 m.
Pl. 17

Single fragment preserving complete tympanum and left hand to wrist.

Tympanum and left hand of figure. Left hand holds tympanum from bottom with forefinger outstretched supporting

outer rim and other three fingers curled over lower edge. Edge of himation appears at wrist. Back is flat. Handmade?
No painted decoration.
Orange-brown, very hard-fired clay with few dark inclusions. Possibly Central Anatolian-manufactured.

This fragment is part of a large statuette of Kybele, who usually holds the tympanum at her left side with her hand supporting the musical instrument from below.

56 Tympanum?
T 143   See Terracotta Deposit 5 (see pp. 67-69). Found in excavation storage box with uncatalogued terracotta fragments.
P.H. 0.046; W. 0.045; Th. 0.01 m.
Pl. 17

Single fragment broken at one side. Slip peeling at edge on exterior.
Flat circular object with one side squared, possibly tympanum of Kybele. Straight edges; flat back. Handmade?
Slight traces of white groundcoat on side of tympanum over which is yellow-gold paint. Front has brown groundcoat with white and traces of red over top.
Hard-fired, compact, lightly micaceous yellow-orange clay. Munsell: slip 7.5YR 6/2 (pinkish gray); core 5YR 5/8 (yellowish red).
Possibly Central Anatolian-manufactured.

57 Kybele Riding Lion
T 7   Terracotta Deposit 3 (see p. 66)
H. 0.162; W. base 0.150; Th. 0.064 m.
Pl. 18
F. Naumann 1983: 368, no. 617, pl. 47{2}; Vermaseren 1987: no. 53.

Joined from two fragments at neck. Lacking small fragments from right side of polos, head and upper back. Paint well preserved. Head burned and much worn. Much lime incrustation on exterior.
Kybele seated on right side of lion, holding phiale in right hand and tympanum at left side against head of lion. Lion is moving to left on low plinth base and turns head to front. Kybele wears tall crenelated crown on head, one ball earring on right ear, high-girded chiton and himation across lap in thick roll, and shoes. Moldmade front with hand-modeled back. Head and polos made from one mold, separate from body. Impressions made from sharp, fresh molds. In center of back is square vent hole (W. 0.029 m.). Interior is hollow, roughly smoothed.
White groundcoat covers front of figurine and base. Details painted over groundcoat in red for parts of polos, mouth, shoe and tympanum; black for eyes; dark red-brown for hair; pink for white band down front of chiton and right arm; orange for lion.
Clay is hard-fired, fine and compact with small lime inclusions and no trace of micaceous particles. Color of clay is orangish or reddish tan. Munsell: 5YR 7/6 (reddish yellow). Clay is close to **58-59**, **66-68**.
Greek-manufactured, probably Pergamene. See Group I, pp. 79.

The sculptural type of Kybele riding a lion is best known from the Great Altar at Pergamon, where Kybele is riding a fully galloping, chariot-pulling lion. She is drawing a bow from her quiver case and her veil is swirling behind her (Winnefeld 1910: 2, pl. 2). The terracotta type is certainly much less dramatic and active than the Pergamene sculptural representation (F. Winter 1903: 175, nos. 5, 6; D. B. Thompson 1966a: 3 ff., no. 1, pl. 1; Töpperwein 1976: p. 49 ff.; Laumonier 1956: 136, 193-194, pls. 39{361-362}, 68{679}).

Close parallels for this Kybele figurine come from Mamurtkale, a sanctuary of Kybele near Pergamon (Conze and Schazmann 1911: 40, pl. 12{3}; MK T1594, MK T1530; Töpperwein-Hoffmann 1978: 81, pl. 36, MK 10). The Gordion example is, in fact, so close to these examples that one may postulate the same source of manufacture, very probably Pergamon.

There is evidence from the context in which the figurine was found for the dating of this Kybele figurine in the late 3d or early 2d century B.C. (see Terracotta Deposit 3, p. **xx**). If the Pergamenes did create the iconography of Kybele riding the lion in the early 2d century B.C., the figure's date of the manufacture might be put very close to the 189 B.C. abandonment of Gordion.

58 Enthroned Kybele
T 61a,b   Terracotta Deposit 6 (see pp. 69-70)
(a) P.H. torso fragment 0.095; W. torso fragment 0.105; Th.Walls 0.003-0.005 m.
(b) P.H. head 0.029; Th. 0.015 m.
Pl. 18

(a) Joined from seven fragments preserving upper torso, broken at neckline, most of lion, upper right leg, right arm, tympanum at left side.
(b) Non-joining fragment of head preserving polos and upper half of head to mouth. Nose worn. Surface of both fragments is friable, chipped with peeling paint. Dark discoloration on back. Traces of carbon on face.
Kybele seated on high-backed throne, resting bent right arm on arm of throne, with tympanum high at left side and couchant lion in lap, with head toward Kybele's right looking at viewer. Kybele wears polos, chiton and himation. Moldmade. Body and head probably made in separate molds. Polos attached separately. Back is hand-modeled.
Front of both fragments covered with white groundcoat. Skin reserved white. Over white, red and black are applied for details. Red is used for wide vertical band of chiton, himation, tympanum, molding of polos; black for floral details of throne finials, hair, facial details. Back is unpainted.
Red-orange, very slightly micaceous clay with few small, light gritty inclusions. Munsell: 5YR 6/6 (reddish yellow). Clay is close to that of **57**, **59**, **66-68**.
Greek-manufactured, probably Pergamene. See Group I, p. 79.

59 Enthroned Kybele
T 6   Terracotta Deposit 3 (see p. 66)
H. 0.142; W. at top of throne 0.101; Th. 0.056; H. head to top of polos 0.033 m.
Pl. 18 and Frontispiece
F. Naumann 1983: 357, no. 537, 39{3}; Vermaseren 1987: no. 54.

Joined from seven fragments preserving entire figure. Lacking chips from bottom of drapery, face of lion, front edge of drapery at lap, phiale, hair, right breast, right leg, left finial of throne, and right lower back of throne (the latter restored in plaster). Painted decoration is very well preserved.

Kybele seated on throne holding small couchant lion in lap, with head toward Kybele's right looking at viewer; goddess holds phiale in outstretched right hand and wears polos, chiton and himation. Throne has high back terminating at upper corners in two palmette finials. Raised rectangular footstool with moldings protrudes from lower edge of throne. Back of polos is hollow; back of head flat; upper back part of throne is composed of overfold of clay which ends at shoulder height. Rest of back is open and interior is smoothed with spatula and fingers. Body and throne are probably made from single mold and head from another. Polos is attached by clay at back. Molds appear to be sharp and fresh.

White paint covers front and sides except back left side of throne. Flesh is white, as are large areas of himation and chiton. Details are rendered in red for lower part of polos, mouth, borders of himation and stripes of chiton, mouth of lion, phiale, moldings of footstool, dots on palmette finials; black for dots on polos, hair, eyes, moldings of footstool, floral designs on palmette finials, bands on sides of throne. Back is unpainted.

Fine, compact orange clay with small lime inclusions and small amount of dark inclusions. Munsell: 5YR 6/6 (reddish yellow). Clay of **58** is closely comparable. Clay is slightly redder than that of **57**, **66-68**, but is close enough to be within range of variability of clays from one site.

Greek-manufactured, probably Pergamene. See Group I, pp. 78-79.

58 and **59** are closely comparable. **58** is less well preserved than **59** but seems to have been of same size, same type and design, and similar in its painted decoration. Only clue that suggests they were not made from identical molds is tympanum, which appears at left shoulder of **58** but not on **59**. Both figurines were surely made in same workshop.

The type of Kybele seated on a throne with palmette finials at upper back edges, holding a lion in her lap and a phiale in one hand, is common. The peculiar style of these two seated Kybele figurines with their somewhat pinched and vacuous faces (4th century B.C.-type) enlivened by crisp, precise painted detail is not easy to parallel. None of the published terracotta figurines from Asia Minor bear any specific resemblance to these, though a mold from Callatis (Rumania) (Canarache 1969: 30-31), a figurine from Priene (Wiegand and Schrader 1904: 330, fig. 367) and a "Tanagra type" from Aegina (Higgins 1967: 104, pl. 48d) display some of the features of these, especially of **58**.

The date of these two figurines comes from their find-spots in household deposits (see Terracotta Deposit 6). It is likely that both of the houses in which these figurines were found were abandoned in 189 B.C. at the arrival of the Roman army. The crisp, fresh quality of the impressions and the well-preserved painted details suggest a date of manufacture for both of these close to the time of the city's abandonment i.e., probably early 2d century B.C.

60 Enthroned Kybele
T 34   Terracotta Deposit 4 (see p. 67)
P.H. 0.161; Max.W. 0.110; Max.Th. 0.079 m.
Pl. 19

Joined from eleven fragments preserving most of figure and front of throne. Lacking head of Kybele, right arm from below elbow, left foot and tympanum, as well as fragments of throne and chips. Surface worn, especially on lower legs. Lime incrustation at some breaks. Some discoloration of surface from contact with carbon(?).

Kybele is seated on her throne with her feet resting on lion on footstool. She holds tympanum at left side, stretches right arm forward and probably once held phiale in right hand. She is wearing high-girded chiton and himation and probably wore polos over veil, since folds of a veil appear on back and sides of throne. Throne is high-backed with upper ends ornamented with two pointed "palmettes" at right angles to each other. Small sejant sphinx (?) sits on top throne's right arm. Animal on left arm is not preserved. In front of throne is low footstool on which is seated small couchant lion, with body in left profile and head toward viewer. Back of top of throne is flat. Moldmade front. Hand-applied back. Interior is hollow and roughly smoothed. Very thin walls.

White groundcoat is preserved on right arm, chiton and himation of Kybele, upper part of throne, especially "palmettes," footstool. Pink paint was used on himation, sections of chiton, veil, left side of throne (veil?), animals on arms of throne and footstool. Black paint appears on lower edge of himation, sections of chiton, veil, throne in clusters of dots on "palmettes," left side of throne, parts of small animal on arms of throne, legs of throne in vertical band. Back is unpainted.

Highly micaceous, hard-fired red clay with many lime inclusions and small black particles creating speckled effect on surface. Munsell: 2.5YR 5/6 (red).

Greek-manufactured, possibly Black Sea region. See Group II, pp. 79-80.

The style of this Kybele figurine with the lanky body and proliferation of sharp-edged folds is distinctive but not specifically identifiable in terms of a manufacturing source. The closest parallels are from the area around the Black Sea, e.g., a Kybele from Amisos (modern Samsun) (Breitenstein 1941: 55, no. 507, pl. 62) and one from Myrmekion in the Crimea with a lion at her feet, dated to the 2d/1st century B.C. (Daux 1958: 352, fig. 2).

61 Enthroned Kybele
(a) T 53 and (b) T 115   Terracotta Deposit 5 (see pp. 67-69)
(a) P.H. 0.122; P.W. 0.058; P.Th. 0.087 m.
(b) P.H. 0.025; P.W. 0.035; P.Th. 0.034 m.
Pl. 19

(a) Joined from two fragments preserving lower right side of throne from arm to resting surface at bottom, back right side, and lower right arm, hand and right leg of Kybele. Surface is badly chipped and worn, and burnt gray on exterior and interior.

(b) Single non-joining fragment preserving left foot and resting surface. Discoloration from burning on upper surface. Lime incrustation on interior.

Kybele is seated on throne holding phiale in upturned right hand and couchant lion in profile to left in lap. Back is open. Interior is hollow with roughly worked surface. Moldmade.

White groundcoat on Kybele, lion, throne sides and front. Only trace of paint is red vertical band at rear right edge of throne. Back has no slip or paint.

Micaceous, red-orange clay with few inclusions. Munsell: 2.5YR 5/6 (red)-5YR 6/6 (reddish yellow).

Greek-manufactured, possibly from Black Sea region. See Group II, pp. 79-80.

62 Kybele?
T 86 Trench PN, Layer 2
P.H. 0.093; P.W. 0.065; Depth 0.026; Th. Walls 0.004-0.006 m.
Pl. 19

Single fragment preserving torso and head of figure. Right and left forearms and tips of throne are missing. Facial features have been chipped away. Chips missing from polos, back of head and lower back edges of throne. Surface is worn, darkened by fire.

Female figure wearing polos is seated on throne. Throne has high back with upper right corner terminating in "palmette" finial. Polos is high in front with "wings" to sides and back, like three-cornered hat. Thick roll of hair surrounds face and falls in two long strands over front of shoulders. At left side is projection which may be tympanum. Back of throne is flat at top, hollowed out beneath and forms "hood" ending at height of mid-back. Interior has hollow, concave rough walls. Moldmade.

No painted decoration.

Soft, micaceous, yellowish red clay, fired gray at core. Munsell: 5YR 6/8 (reddish yellow).

Greek-manufactured.

The seated female figure, the crown or flaring polos, the throne with "palmette" finial (as in **52, 58-60**) and the possible tympanum at the left side all suggest the identification of this figure as Kybele. A three-cornered polos can be found on female figurines from Aizanoi (R. Naumann 1967: 241 f., pl. 29{1-2}) and Kapìkaya (Nohlen and Radt 1978: 65, pl. 26, T 12). The poor state of preservation of the Gordion example, however, makes it difficult to specifically identify the headdress. It may be a so-called Phrygian helmet, worn by Kybele on a figurine from Mamurtkale dated to the 1st century B.C. (Töpperwein-Hoffmann 1978: 81, pl. 36, MK 12); a poorly preserved example of a crenelated crown (like, e.g., Mendel 1908: no. 2084, from Priene; see Pl. 39); or simply a flaring polos.

Also from Layer 2 of this same trench came **155**, a dove, 3d century B.C. pottery and a coin of Alexander the Great. From the layer above in the same area came **79**, a female protome. Trench PN lies just north of the Pottery Establishment (see Terracotta Deposit 5), and the excavator comments that the Layer 2 fill lies above what appears to be a clay-stuccoed tank, possibly used in the Pottery Establishment.

63 Kybele (?) Fragment
T 28 Terracotta Deposit 5 (see pp. 67-69)
P.H. 0.050; Max.W. at height of forehead 0.071; Th. 0.025 m.
Pl. 19

Joined from two fragments preserving upper half of head broken at height of eyes. Surface well preserved.

Upper part of female wearing low polos, in relief against high background with rounded contour, possibly schematically rendered veil. Back of fragment is flat with "hood" at height of bottom of polos. Hollow interior. Moldmade front with back applied by hand. Mold has produced crisp impression.

Surface of front is covered with white groundcoat, especially well preserved on face and hair. No paint preserved.

Lightly micaceous, light red clay, fired gray at core. Tiny white and some dark inclusions producing pockmarked surface. Munsell: exterior 2.5YR 6/6 (light red).

Greek-manufactured.

It cannot be certainly demonstrated that this female wearing a polos is Kybele. Poloi are not restricted to Kybele or even to deities. However, most of the Kybele figurines at Gordion do have poloi or crowns, while the other figurines which represent goddesses are bareheaded.

Three figurines of female deities from Callatis (Rumania) on the Black Sea are similar (Canarache 1969: 53, 58, nos. 13, 15, 25) in the use of a medallion-like background around the head. The clay of the latter two is described as light brick red, as is the clay of the Gordion example. See also F. Winter 1903: 174, no. 5, from Smyrna (Izmir).

64 Female with Tympanum
T 78 Trench WML-4M, near Floor 3 level
P.H. 0.06; P.W. 0.067; Depth 0.027 m.
Pl. 19

Single fragment preserving head and shoulders of woman, and left edge of figurine. Broken surface to left of figure. Back preserved to chest height. Surfaces badly worn.

Female wearing veil (?) over Phrygian (?) cap, facing front and holding tympanum on left shoulder. Raised area at right shoulder with two finger-like projections may be object (or animal?) held in right hand. Veil falls down sides of figure, forming edges of figurine. Forehead high; eyes small in deep hollows; face rectangular; cheeks and chin full. Back of figure is irregular convex surface. Interior solid. Moldmade.

Front of cap, face, neck and veil covered with reddish orange paint. Slight traces of paint on top and upper back. No trace of white groundcoat.

Very hard-fired, slightly micaceous yellow-pink clay with dark inclusions and lime particles. Munsell: 5YR 6/6 (reddish yellow).

Greek-manufactured.

There are many examples of the "temple girl" with tympanum from the Kybele shrine at Mamurtkale near Pergamon (Töpperwein-Hoffmann 1978: pls. 35{MK 4, MK 5, MK 8}, 36{MK 19, MK 20}). The only element which suggests that the figure should be identified as a temple attendant rather than Kybele herself is the cap. Kybele more often wears a crown (see **52, 57, 62**).

Females (65-96)

After the animal category, the group of female figurines, including complete examples, bodies and detached heads, is the most numerous single category of terracotta figurines at Gordion. As at Troy (D. B. Thompson 1963a: 124-136) and Myrina (Mollard-Besques 1963: 93-118, 164-184, pls. 110-128, 199-220), standing draped females and detached female heads are in abundance. At Gordion there are ten examples of standing draped females, mostly in fragmentary condition, one dancer (**75**) and one group composition, probably of dancing females (**76**), two seated females (**77**, **78**), and one probable female protome (**79**). Three of the female heads are probably parts of plastic decoration for pottery (**80-82**). The rest of the representations of females are detached heads, an arm (**95**) and a drapery fragment (**96**).

PROVENIENCE

The vast majority of the female figurines from Gordion are imports manufactured at Greek sites, with the probable exceptions of **65** and **80-82** (all probable plastic attachments for vessels) and **83** and **84**, probably Central Anatolian products of the Roman period. Similarities in style and clay composition link certain of the imported female types. For example, **67** and **68** were probably made from the same mold. It is no coincidence that these were recovered from the same house (see Terracotta Deposit 3), along with **57**, **59** and **66**, the former two Kybele figurines which were also probably manufactured at the same site (see discussion of Group I, pp. 78-79). Other groups of figurines can be isolated including **70**, **73**, **74**, **92** and **96** (Group II, pp. 79-80). A Pergamene workshop can be tentatively suggested for Group I, and possibly a Black Sea site for Group II.

CHRONOLOGY

Most of the female figurines from Gordion date to the Late Phrygian/Hellenistic period and most can be securely dated to the late 3d or early 2d century B.C., close to the 189 B.C. abandonment of Gordion (see Terracotta Deposits 3, 5 and 6). Only a small number of the female types can be definitely dated prior to the Late Phrygian/Hellenistic period (e.g., **77**, **79**, **85**), and two may be local products of the Roman period (**83**, **84**).

STANDING DRAPED FEMALE TYPES

Among the standing, draped Hellenistic female figurines many different types (costume and pose) are represented:

- right arm akimbo, left leg drawn back, body twisted to right, head to right, body muffled in himation (**66**);
- body twisted to left, head to left, right arm across waist, right leg drawn back, body wrapped tightly in himation (**67**, **68**);
- frontal body, right leg drawn back, right arm lowered, left arm bent and elbow against hip. Himation wrapped around arms and body at waist height (**69** and probably **72**);
- frontal body, muffled in himation wrapped over right shoulder to left side (**71**);
- right arm bent, right leg drawn back (**70**);
- left leg bent, body turned to left, himation around upper arms and back (**73**);
- frontal body, left leg bent, muffled upper body (**65**).

All these types are ultimately related to "Tanagra types" and can be seen as stylistically modified versions of these original "Tanagras" of the 4th century B.C. (see D. B. Thompson 1963a: 22-28 for discussion of "Tanagra types" and the Asiatic tradition of "Tanagras"). **67** and **68** exhibit, in the rich plasticity of the drapery and elegant handling of the twisting body, affinities with an Asiatic style which Thompson links to Pergamon (*ibid.*: 24). Examination of the clay of these two figurines also indicates a possible Pergamene origin. **66**, although in the same fabric as **67** and **68**, is rendered in a much stiffer style resulting in a more rigid, block-like appearance. While the folds of the upper body have a kind of illogical plasticity, the lower body is treated as almost a single block with a few hollows at the lower legs. The only life in the figure is accomplished by the twisted pose and the now blurred but once wide-eyed facial features.

69 is a lifeless rendering of a "Tanagra type" which enters the repertoire late in its history (late 3d-2d century B.C.). The himation is draped so as to reveal the right hand beneath, while illogically bunching in voluminous folds over the left hand. The chiton folds around the legs are heavy and anchor the statue to its base. **70** and **74**, fragmentary standing females, bear affinities in the composition of their clay and painting technique and may have been manufactured at the same Black Sea (?) site (see Group II, pp. 79-80). Stylistically, both show a crispness of line and sparseness of volume with broad flat or curving expanses which is unlike the majority of the female figurines from Gordion. **73** seems close to these two in the composition of the clay and painted decoration, yet the style differs considerably, revealing a small figure in an elegant, mannered pose with the garment creating a rippling effect.

The handling of the drapery of **71** and **72** is similar to each other with many undulating surfaces and bunched-up folds. The one possibly locally manufactured standing female, **65**, exhibits a careless style and a lack of interest in the surface effects of drapery. The himation is treated as a broad heavy garment with a few diagonal folds and the chiton has lifeless vertical plaits mechanically tooled into the surface.

The group of females, possibly dancing (**76**), is among the more exceptional of the Gordion corpus, for both its composition and style. The figure with the long flowing golden hair strikes a dramatic pose with her arms thrown up and her body twisted to the left. The fine folds of her thin chiton sweep left as her arm strains in the same direction. Similarities in clay composition and painting style link this group of figures with **70**, **73** and **74**, standing females, and **99**, Eros in a flower. All may have been manufactured at the same site or workshop (see discussion of Group II, pp. 79-80).

FEMALE HEADS

The detached female heads of the Hellenistic period also present a great variety of facial types, coiffures and headdresses. D. B. Thompson defines the Hellenistic facial types for the Troy figurines (1963a: 31-33) and it is this terminology which is adopted here.

FACIAL TYPE

The facial types include a pseudo-classicizing type with large, deep-set pop-eyes, large nose and heavy chin (**68**) and, from the same source, a face of more rounded type also with large eyes (these not so deeply set), large nose and heavy chin. **86** exhibits some of these same features, e.g., the heavy, classicizing face and chin, the large nose and eyes. Here the eyes are widely set with less of a pop-eyed look. It is interesting to note the variety in the facial types within the figurines probably produced at the same site. For example, the Kybele figurines (**57-59**) probably belong to the same group as **67** and **68** (see discussion of Group I, pp. 78-79), yet the definition of the facial features of **57-59** comes almost entirely from the painted details creating a perky, alert look on round or angular faces.

A round, almost childlike facial type but with much-blurred features is **87**. **89** is also of the round facial type, here with heavy eyelids, bulbous nose and full lips. These same heavy eyelids producing a squint-eyed look are seen on another figurine with a round facial type (**91**), yet here the nose is small and pert and the mouth is small.

An angular, more elongated facial type is popular among the Hellenistic imports to Gordion from the 3d century B.C. on (e.g., **88**, **92**, **93**), while **94** combines an angular face with a wide nose and full chin. A locally manufactured female face (Nike vessel handle (?): **33**) exhibits the angular facial type with small eyes and nose and heavy chin.

COIFFURE

The varieties of Hellenistic hairdos are described by D. B. Thompson (1963a: 36-44). At Gordion, most of these coiffures are represented:
- Knidian coiffure (parted in middle, drawn up loosely to side and back in thick roll) (**66**, **86**, **92-94**);
- Knidian coiffure with bun at back (**33**);
- Knidian coiffure with braid at back (**68**);
- Bowknot coiffure (**88**);
- Melon coiffure with deep waves (**87**).

The hair of **83**, a probably locally manufactured figurine of Roman date, rises in strands to a peak above the forehead and frames the sides of the face and neck in a thick roll.

HEADDRESS

The varieties of headdresses include: a thick rolled wreath (**66**), which becomes more popular in the later 2d century B.C.; a veil (**87** and **92**); a flat fillet (**86**); a rolled fillet (**33** and **91**); a sakkos or kerchief (**89**); and a broad stephane (**94**).

FUNCTION

As is the case for most figurines with non-divine subjects, it is difficult to determine what functions these figurines had in their original contexts. All of the Gordion females come from the City Mound and are, therefore, from non-funerary contexts. Three of the females, probably locally manufactured, are probably plastic decorations for vessels (**80-82**). The groups of Hellenistic female figurines from deposits, such as **66-68**, **93** (from Terracotta Deposit 3); **69**, **70**, **74**, **91**, **92**, **96** (from Terracotta Deposit 5); and **73** (from Terracotta Deposit 6), may tentatively be assigned functions as votive figurines for private shrines dedicated to Kybele (in the case of Terracotta Deposits 3 and 5) or to Kybele and Attis (in the case of Terracotta Deposit 6). As votives these figurines would have been set on an altar or base or suspended and would have been meant to represent the dedicant or simply a pleasing object for the deity.

Little more regarding the function of the rest of these female figurines can be ascertained from their contexts. One female head (**87**) comes from the floor of a house and another (**86**) from a pit in a trench which also produced a standing female (**65**) and an Eros head (**103**). Although the primary function of the majority of the female figurines was probably religious, a purely secular function may possibly be ascribed to some of the female types.

The use of terracotta figurines as dolls or toys to dress up and use in imaginative play is usually assigned only to a specific type of figurine of the Classical period (Higgins 1967: 75, 83, pls. 30B, 31C, 35C; see also D. B. Thompson 1963a: 87 ff., n. 89). The essential features of these dolls are nudity and detachable or movable limbs. There is no specific evidence that draped female figurines were used as toys.

"Tanagra types" are found in great numbers in graves (e.g., at Myrina; see Burr 1934: 5-6), which would suggest that they were the personal possessions of the deceased (whether male *or* female we don't know) *or* that they were gifts offered to the deceased to provide escort or service in the afterlife, like Egyptian *ushabtis*. In Tumulus A at Gordion, a cremation burial of ca. 540-530 B.C., large numbers of pieces of jewelry, spindle whorls, an ivory kore and a kore unguentarium were among the burial gifts, suggesting that a female was buried within. At Olynthos, where figurines were found in only sixty-two of around six hundred tombs of the 5th and 4th centuries, figurines were more common in children's tombs than in adults' (Higgins 1967: 1). The latter might suggest that terracotta figurines of some kinds were used as dolls or toys.

The other possible use for these draped females might be purely ornamental, as bric-a-brac to decorate one's house or as souvenirs or mementos of travels or a special event, such as a wedding or festival day. The evidence is, again, scanty, but the existence of figurines at Gordion, especially of the draped female type, in domestic establishments may suggest a decorative function for some. Whatever the ultimate use, it is very unlikely that the coroplasts who made these draped female figurines had a single market in mind. They were probably sold for use in homes, sanctuaries, shrines and graves. The fact that none have been recovered from graves at Gordion reflects only the fact that few tombs of the Late Phrygian/Hellenistic period have been excavated at the site (R. S. Young 1956: 250-252).

STANDING FEMALES

65 Standing Female
T 68   Trench MN-W, Layer 5 fill, below level of House 3
P.H. 0.098; Max.W. 0.053; D. 0.032; Th. walls 0.006-0.011 m.
Pl. 20

Joined from three fragments preserving lower torso from abdomen to base and lower back. Missing left foot, chip off lower front of garment and lower edge next to right foot.

Female wearing chiton and himation in contrapposto stance with right leg straight, left leg bent at knee and drawn to side. Body is narrow from front to back and presents almost one-dimensional view. Himation covers upper part of fragment with thick bunch of material falling along right side and excess hanging over left elbow down left side. Chiton falls in closely packed fluted folds over lower legs in front and on sides. Right foot peeks out from beneath drapery. Lower border of skirt forms base for figurine. Back is smoothed and rounded with no modeling or working. Interior is hollow with roughly worked walls. Front half is moldmade; back handmade. Join between front and back halves visible on interior. Additional tooling of folds of chiton with burin.

Tiny flecks of white groundcoat on himation. No paint survives. Entire exterior surface of front and back is slipped with fine buff clay.

Slightly micaceous light reddish brown clay with small dark and light inclusions. Munsell: 5YR 6/4 (light reddish brown).

Central Anatolian or locally manufactured.

The figure is crudely made and obviously derivative of a type of standing female figure with left hand on hip known from Myrina (Mollard-Besques 1963: pls. 113-116) and Troy (D. B. Thompson 1963a: 126, no. 164, pl. 37, "Myrina style of 2nd century B.C.").

Along with earlier material, a coin (C 651) of Seleukos II (246-226 B.C.), minted in Antioch, was found in Layer 5 in the process of removing House 3. A date as late as the second half of the 3d century or even the early 2d century is thus likely for the context of this standing female. Also found in the same trench and sequence in layers above were **13**, goat rhyton; **86**, female head; **103**, Eros head.

66 Standing Female with Wreath
T 5   Terracotta Deposit 3 (see pp. 66-67)
H. 0.242; Max.W. base 0.072; Depth base 0.075; Th. walls 0.005-0.011; H. head 0.030 m.
Pl. 20 and Color Pl. I

Joined from ten fragments preserving head, upper torso and legs. Missing section of waist at front and left side; back of wreath; fragment of back left side; chips from front right corner of base, front of upper torso and around vent hole. Paint well preserved on lower body. Lime incrustation on interior. Exterior darkened by contact with soil and face has dark incrustation.

Female wearing heavy rolled wreath, chiton and himation, standing on low plinth with right arm akimbo and left leg drawn back to side of base. Head is turned to right. Face is triangular with full cheeks and high cheekbones. Eyes are wide open and deep set. Mouth is small, composed of two ridges, upper turned down over lower at left side. Upper torso is muffled in himation from neck to mid-calf. Himation falls in thick bunch and folds along left side and in back forming simple curve as it dips down to level of calves. Right arm, beneath himation, is bent and hand rests on hip. Chiton appears beneath himation only on lower legs and covering feet. It is defined by variegated surface of low ridges and grooves. Base is low square plinth narrowing toward back. Himation and chiton on back of figure are treated simply. In center of back at height of right elbow is small circular hole (D. 0.006 m.). On back at height of upper thighs is large rectangular vent hole (0.034 x 0.019 m.). Interior is hollow and roughly smoothed with spatula and fingers.

Made from approximately six molds: front of head; back of head; front of upper torso; front of lower torso; base; back. Point of juncture between front and back halves of upper and lower torso pieces is detectable on right and left sides of interior where extra layer of clay seals seams. Wreath was handmade and added to head.

White groundcoat on wreath, crown of head, hair, left side of face and chin, entire front of body. Thick brick-red paint adheres to hair all around. Himation is light blue (turned green in places) with black borders. Chiton has pink front panel with black lower borders and sides. Black could be underpainting for another color which has disappeared or discoloration of original paint (e.g., blue).

Fine, tan-orange clay with few lime inclusions and no micaceous particles. Munsell: 7.5YR 7/6 (reddish yellow).

Greek-manufactured, probably Pergamene. See Group I, pp. 78-79.

The clay, painted decoration and style match those of **67** and **68**. See Terracotta Deposit 3.

The type of the standing female muffled in himation with one arm akimbo is well known (e.g., Sieveking 1916: pl. 50; Mollard-Besques 1963: 94-96, esp. pl. 111d, Bo72, from Myrina; Burr 1934: pl. 32{82}, from Myrina, first half of 2d century B.C.; Laumonier 1956: pl. 27{273}, 3d century B.C. from Rhenia; Belin de Ballu 1972: pl. 63{3}) and can be documented from the 3d century B.C. to the 1st century B.C. A close parallel for the Gordion example was excavated on Cyprus (Karageorghis 1976: 849, fig. 16). Only the upper body is preserved, with wreathed head and muffled upper body. The hair, like the Gordion female's, is painted red.

The wreath, thick and rolled, is not popular until the later 2d century B.C., according to D. B. Thompson (1963a: 45 ff., 135ff., nos. 260 ff.), but appears on this figurine which cannot be later than 189 B.C. For figurines from Pergamon with similar wreaths see Töpperwein 1976: nos. 315, 321, 322, pls. 47-48. See also wreaths on figurines from Macedonia (Mendel 1908: 3068-3069; Pl. 41). For a similar though earlier female wearing a wreath from Kallipoli (Aetolia) see Themelis 1979: 253, 260, fig. 9b; that site was destroyed by Galatians in 279 B.C. And for females with wreaths from Middle Hellenistic units at Tarsus (i.e., later 3d-early 2d century B.C.) see Goldman 1950: 368-369, nos. 493, 494, 496, 498, 499.

67 Standing Female
T 10   Terracotta Deposit 3 (see pp. 66-67)
P.H. 0.198; P.W. 0.067; P.D. 0.063; Th. walls 0.0015-0.01 m.
Pl. 21

Joined from six fragments preserving body from neckline to above feet including left breast, right arm, right and left sides. Traces of burning appear on uppermost fragment of chest, break and lower edge of himation.

Standing female draped in chiton and himation. Body is twisted to left. Garments fit tightly over full chest. From left breast himation falls in short radiating folds toward right arm, which is hidden beneath himation and bent across waist. From below right arm folds fall diagonally to right in deep channels. Beneath hand over abdomen are three superimposed rounded U-shaped folds. On left side of body himation falls over hips in undulating ridges. Overhanging zigzag edge of himation appears at left side of fragment. At bottom of fragment below undulating lower edge of himation, chiton appears. Interior is hollow with walls smoothed by fingers and spatula. Moldmade. Made from same generation of mold as **68**.

White groundcoat survives on upper fragment, covering shoulders and breast, and on himation and chiton. Traces of black on himation at left edge. Chiton is painted brown-black at left, while central section at bottom of fragment is blue.

Tan-orange clay with tiny white inclusions and no traces of mica. Munsell: 7.5YR 7/6 (reddish yellow).

Greek-manufactured, probably Pergamene. See Group I, pp. 78-79.

See text for **68**.

68 Standing Female
T 8/T 9   Terracotta Deposit 3 (see pp. 66-67)
H. 0.256; H. head 0.043; W. head 0.034; Th. head 0.035; P.W. base 0.069; Th. body 0.005-0.009 m.
Pl. 21 and Color Pl. I

Joined from fourteen fragments preserving head, shoulders and right half of body to base. Chip missing from nose. Facial features worn. Traces of burning on interior of body and left side of face and hair. Orange stain on left side of hair and brownish yellow lines on left cheek. White incrustation on interior of body.

Draped female standing in frontal position with head turned to left. Narrow face framed by hair parted in center and drawn to sides in roll marked with haphazardly executed incisions. Thickening at nape of neck suggests braid. Top and back of head are roughly smoothed. Forehead is shallow; right eye better defined and more deeply set than left; eyebrow defined by ridge; nose widened at end and nostrils marked by grooves; mouth small with tightly pursed lips; lower lip full. Body is tightly wrapped in chiton and himation accentuating form beneath. Right arm, beneath himation, is bent across waist. Folds of himation fall from arm in deep grooves to knee area. Right knee is slightly bent and right leg drawn back to right. Folds of himation fan out to right below knee. Chiton, defined by broad vertical folds in concave curve, is revealed at bottom edge on lower plane than himation. Interior of body is concave and smoothed with fingers and spatula. Moldmade. Head and body molded separately. Layer of fine clay applied to exterior surface of head.

Entire exterior surface is covered with white groundcoat. Traces of brownish black paint on lower locks beside face. One speck of pink-red paint on upper lip. Himation has black border at bottom. Chiton is black (discolored?) with pink vertical band down center.

Tan-orange clay with small white inclusions fired gray at core. No mica visible. Munsell: 7.5YR 7/4 (pink)-7/6 (reddish yellow).

Greek-manufactured, probably Pergamene. See Group I, pp. 78-79.

67 and **68** have matching bodies. Both were made from the same generation mold. The fabric, painted decoration and manufacturing technique are the same. In addition, **57-59, 66** exhibit similarities of fabric, technique and decoration and all probably belong to the same workshop. It is hardly coincidental that all except one of these (**58**) came from the same household deposit (see Terracotta Deposit 3).

The general type of the draped female in this pose is easily paralleled: F. Winter 1903: 33, no. 5; Töpperwein 1976: 181, nos. 20, 201, pl. 4. (end of 3d century B.C.), pp. 18, 202, nos. 35 and 36, pl. 6 (from Pergamon, end of 3d-beginning of 2d century B.C.); Mollard-Besques 1963: pl. 117d, MYR 248 (from Myrina, after-mid 3d century B.C.); Laumonier 1956: no. 273, pl. 27 (from Rhenia, 3d century B.C.); Wiegand and Schrader 1904: 158, fig. 133 (from Priene).

A close parallel in terracotta for the head type is harder to find. The best parallels for the head are in stone sculpture, e.g., a female from Rhodes (Gualandi 1979: 45, no. 6, fig. 9) dated to the end of the 3d or beginning of the 2d century B.C.

69 Standing Female
T 55   Terracotta Deposit 5 (see pp. 67-69)
P.H. 0.198; Max.W. 0.110; Max.Th. 0.052; Th. walls 0.004-0.008 m.
Pl. 22

Body nearly complete, lacking head, lower left arm, fragments of front, lower right side of chiton, front left side of base and back of base. Surface gray from burning.

Draped female on low squarish base in contrapposto stance with weight on left leg. Upper body has pronounced backward tilt with hips thrust forward. Right arm is slightly bent and lowered on right upper thigh, while left arm is bent with elbow set against hip and forearm extended. Female wears short-sleeved chiton with V-neck, fastened by buttons at shoulders. Chiton dips in rounded V-shape at neckline, falling to base and covering feet. Himation is wrapped around body at waist height, covering right arm and with excess falling over left arm. Back of body is roughly smoothed, flat in upper area and rounded in lower body. At middle of back is large rectangular vent hole (0.038 x 0.0275 m.), above which is small round hole with irregular edges (D. 0.008 m.). Tiny hole appears above this, but since walls are very thin it is likely that this was not intentional. Interior is hollow with roughly finished walls. Front of body made from relatively fresh mold though slightly flawed (e.g., damage to outside of left breast). Back added by hand. Head and base moldmade and added separately. Buttons at shoulders handmade and applied to finished product.

Front and sides are covered with white groundcoat, now much faded. Painted decoration on himation and chiton badly discolored so that both appear to be black (possibly once blue). Black on upper part of chiton in V-shape between breasts and defining band below breasts. Lower border of chiton has wide black band. Thin black line at mid-calf height. Right and left sides of chiton are solid black. Himation has black border at top (bunched folds around abdomen) and bottom. Overhanging folds on left side are mostly black. Sleeves of chiton are defined by two thin red horizontal lines. Speck of red survives on neck just below break. Back is unpainted.

Very slightly micaceous yellow-orange clay with lime inclusions and other small grit inclusions. Hard-fired, possibly somewhat discolored at core (seen on break at neck and on base) from secondary burning. Munsell: 7.5YR 7/4 (pink)-7/8 (reddish yellow).

Greek-manufactured.

The type of the standing draped female with himation dropping across waist, right arm beneath himation grasping chiton and left arm bent and held out at diagonal probably originated sometime in the late 3d or early 2d century B.C. Assuming a pre-189 B.C. date for the Gordion example, it is among the earliest terracottas of the type. For later examples see Burr 1934: nos. 91-93 (from Myrina, later 1st century B.C., "following sculptural tradition of 2nd or early 1st century B.C."); F. Winter 1903: 72, no. 4 (early 1st century B.C.); Kleiner 1942: pl. 12 top left: (from Myrina); Mendel 1908: no. 2567, pl. 10[3]: (from Myrina). The Gordion example is quite lifeless; the V-shaped folds on the front of the himation are mechanically rendered and the drapery clings less to the body than in all of these later examples.

This type of thin rectangular base occurs on so-called "Tanagras" of the best period and is used commonly for the standing "Tanagra-type" females at Myrina (Burr 1934: 20; see also D. B. Thompson 1963a: 17). Rectangular vent holes are also common on figurines which derive from the so-called "Tanagra types"(*ibid.*: 18-19), e.g., at Priene and Myrina (Töpperwein-Hoffmann 1971: 132; Burr 1934: 20).

For a figurine from Athens of the late 3d or first half of the 2d century B.C. with a rectangular vent hole and additional holes above and below the main hole, see D. B. Thompson 1963b: 277, no. 20.

70 Standing Female
T 52   Terracotta Deposit 5 (see pp. 67-69)
P.H. 0.135; P.W. 0.08; P.Depth 0.051; Th. walls 0.003-0.007 m.
Pl. 22

Joined from two fragment preserving front of lower torso from below waist to shins. Fragment broken all around. Paint well preserved but discolored. Exterior and interior burned.

Draped female standing with right leg bent and right arm probably bent and held out to side. Himation spreads out from right side in single thick fold as if hanging from bent arm. Himation ends above knee in curving contour and chiton appears beneath, defined by closely packed folds. Folds of chiton begin to fan out toward bottom on right side as if right leg is drawn back or out to right. Only small section of back with thick bunch of himation on right side is preserved. Back is smoothed surface. Interior is hollow; interior of walls smoothed with fingers and spatula. Moldmade.

White groundcoat covers front exterior surface. White himation has wide lower border of pink with narrow band of white at top. Himation falling along left side is pink. Chiton is solid pink with thin horizontal white line at mid-calf. Back is unpainted.

Hard-fired, micaceous, red-orange clay with small light and dark inclusions. Munsell: 2.5YR 5/6 (red)-5YR 6/6 (reddish yellow).

Greek-manufactured, possibly Black Sea region. See Group II, pp. 79-80.

The pose of this draped female is probably close to that of **69**, although with arms reversed, and to that of a figurine from Myrina dating to the beginning of the 2d century B.C. (Mollard-Besques 1963: MYR 650, pl. 127).

The clay matches that of the seated Kybele from the same deposit (**61**) and both figurines, as well as those in Group II (p. **xx**), are likely to be from the same manufacturing source.

71 Standing Female
  T 15   Trench NCT, Level 1b, E Ext.
  P.H. 0.058; P.W. 0.036-0.038; Depth ca. 0.028; Th. walls 0.004-0.005 m.
  Pl. 22

Single fragment preserving left side of torso from base of neck to around waist. Lacking head and upper neck, right edge of torso and entire lower body. Back preserved at top left. Surface intact.

Standing female in frontal position covered up to neck in himation pulled across body and over left arm at diagonal. Back is not modeled but is smoothed. Interior is hollow and smoothed on lower part. Moldmade front with incision to delineate folds.

Slight traces of white groundcoat in incised folds of garment and on shoulder area.

Micaceous pink-brown clay fired light brown on exterior and gray at core. Hard-fired with sandy and lime inclusions. Tiny bead-like protuberances and pockmarks on surface. Munsell: exterior 7.5YR 6/4 (light brown); interior 2.5YR 6/4 (light reddish brown).

Greek-manufactured.

Same type as terracotta from Myrina (Istanbul inv. 130; Mendel 1908: no. 2451). Context pottery from level includes material that can be dated to first half of 3d century B.C.

72 Standing (?) Female
  T 136   Trench MN, Clay Cut C, Kilns B and E
  P.H. 0.055; P.W. 0.049; Th. walls 0.004-0.006 m.
  Pl. 22

Single fragment preserving part of upper and lower torso and stump of left arm.

Draped female figure with body bent at waist; upper torso bending forward; left arm raised. Moldmade.

No painted decoration.

Pale orange clay, heavily micaceous with silver particles, white inclusions. Munsell: core 5YR 6/6 (reddish yellow); surface 5YR 6/6-7/6 (reddish yellow).

Greek-manufactured.

73 Standing Female
  T 56   Terracotta Deposit 6 (see pp. 69-70)
  P.H. 0.129; W. 0.048; Th. 0.003-0.006 m.
  Pl. 22

Four joining fragments preserving body and part of base to resting surface and two non-joining fragments of base. Lacking head, fragments of right and left lower chiton edge and base, lower side from below left arm to left foot. Paint well preserved.

Female wearing chiton and himation in mannered contrapposto stance on high cylindrical base. Body is long and narrow. Left leg is bent with hips thrust forward and body turned slightly to left. Himation is wrapped around arms with excess falling in flattened mass along right side. Chiton has V-shaped neckline and is belted high beneath breasts, falling in fluted folds to cover legs. Right foot peeks from beneath chiton. High cylindrical base has convex upper molding and tapers slightly to narrower resting surface. Back of figurine is open with interior walls roughly worked. Moldmade in one piece with upper molding of base; rest of base added separately.

Entire front of figurine is covered with white groundcoat. Himation and upper part of chiton are white with no trace of paint. Lower part of chiton is pink with band of white above. Back is unpainted.

Very slightly micaceous red-brown clay with tiny dark and light inclusions, fired gray-black at core. Munsell: surface 5YR 6/4 (light reddish brown)-6/8 (reddish yellow).

Greek-manufactured, possibly Black Sea region. See Group II, pp. 79-80.

The clay and painted decoration of this figurine match closely those of **74** and **76**. All three figurines are likely to be from the same workshop.

The context from which this figurine comes seems clearly to date to the late 3d or early 2d century B.C. and to represent the final Late Phrygian/Hellenistic phase of Gordion, i.e., pre-189 B.C.

A close stylistic parallel for the Gordion example is Myrina inv. no. 354 in Istanbul (Mendel 1908: no. 2579). See Pl. 41.

74 Standing Female
  T 26   Terracotta Deposit 5 (see pp. 67-69)
  P.H. 0.06; P.W. 0.057; Th. walls 0.005; H. base 0.011 m.
  Pl. 23

Single fragment preserving front of base, left foot and lower garment of draped female. Back missing. Paint well preserved.

Draped female standing on low, round base. Leg is drawn slightly to left side. Garment with wide, sharp-edged folds covers lower leg, allowing only left foot to peek out from beneath. Left foot wears high-soled sandal with pointed toe. Base has torus molding at upper and lower edges. Bottom is flat. Interior surface is roughly smoothed. Moldmade.

Entire front of garment is covered with white groundcoat, over which pink paint leaves two broad horizontal bands across legs reserved white. Foot is white. Sole of sandal is painted red. Top of base is black, while front edge is white. Bottom is unpainted.

Lightly micaceous brick red-orange clay with small dark, gritty inclusions. Munsell: 5YR 6/4 (light reddish brown).

Greek-manufactured, possibly Black Sea region. See Group II, pp. 79-80.

The clay and painted decoration closely match **73**, **76** and **92**. **92** from the same deposit may be the head for this standing female.

This type of low profiled oval base is close to Mollard-Besques 1963: pl. 112b, MYR 221 (first half of 2d century B.C.), from Myrina. A later variant of the same type of base is D. B. Thompson 1963a: 106, no. 92 (late 2d century B.C.), from Troy, and Mollard-Besques 1963: pls. 111b,d,f, 112a, 131d.

CATALOGUE

75 Female Dancer?
   T 122 Trench NCT, Context Storage Bag 28 (Level 1C samples)
   P.H. 0.08; W. 0.03; Depth 0.02 m.
   Pl. 23

Single fragment, badly worn, lacking head and chips from front of lower torso, left leg, right side and back.

Draped female, possibly dancer with long, narrow body, tightly wrapped in himation. Figure is twisted to left with right leg thrust forward and foot pointed at right diagonal. Right arm is probably bent and held against body beneath himation. Left arm may be akimbo. Bottom of figure is flat. Down back is sharp ridge and at back left is roughly finished surface. Moldmade.

No painted decoration. Trace of white, possibly incrustation, on back.

Non-micaceous gritty light red clay. Munsell: 2.5YR 6/6 (light red).

Greek-manufactured.

The best-known of Hellenistic dancers in miniature is the so-called "Baker Dancer" from Alexandria (see D. B. Thompson 1950: 371-385, late 3d-early 2d century B.C.). The Gordion example is certainly not comparable in quality or material, but the dating of the two is probably close, if we can assign the Gordion figurine to the late 3d or early 2d century, before Gordion's abandonment in 189 B.C. The context pottery cannot narrow the date of this figurine beyond the Late Phrygian/Hellenistic period.

The mantle dancer is a type which spans several centuries, from the Classical period (e.g., from Corinth, unpublished, MF 71-11, dancer with tambourine, neg. 71-33-36, Lot 7079, third quarter 4th century B.C.) to the 1st century B.C. (D. B. Thompson 1963a: 106, no. 90, pl. 24). (See *ibid*.: 102-107 for Troy examples and discussion of type.)

A similar example in terracotta from the Kybele shrine at Mamurtkale near Pergamon is identified as a male "schauspieler" (Töpperwein-Hoffmann 1978: 84, 89, pl. 37, MK 27) and is dated to the last third of the 3d century B.C. A 1st-century B.C. female dancer from Pergamon (Töpperwein 1976: no. 164, pl. 25) strikes a twisted pose similar to the Gordion example's.

76 Group Composition: Dancing (?) Females
   T 87a,b,c Trench W2S3, just under Floor 2
   (a) P.H. 0.109; P.W. 0.058; P.Th. 0.045; Th. walls 0.002-0.004 m.
   (b) P.H. 0.114; P.W. 0.039; Th. walls 0.002-0.005 m.
   (c) P.H. 0.05; P.W. 0.029; Th. walls 0.004-0.006 m.
   Pl. 23 and Color Pl. I

(a) Joined from six fragments preserving back of figure from shoulders to back of upper thighs. Lacking right and lower left arm from elbow. Chips from hair and back. Finished edge at lower right side. Colors well preserved. Traces of carbon on chiton.

(b) Joined from six fragments preserving right side of back from right shoulder to upper thighs. Finished edge at right side probably where front and back halves joined. Curving finished edge at lower left side, probably vent hole. Colors well preserved.

(c) Single fragment of central area of lower edge of chiton and left foot. Colors well preserved. Other small non-joining drapery fragments.

Group of two, possibly three women. Curving finished edges on fragments a and b are both probably sides of vent opening, thus giving clue to alignment of figures (see Pl. 23). Figures a and b are probably locking arms and facing each other in three-quarter pose. Fragment c may belong to third female standing in frontal position. Body of figure a is bent forward and to left in exaggerated S-curve, with arms raised. Four long twisted locks fall over left shoulder and back. Figure wears chiton and mantle or cape, edge of which is probably held in left hand so that it forms thick roll beside left arm and fans out beneath arm. Right side is rendered with little modeling and side of buttocks is flat. At lower right edge is section of circular vent hole. Figure b is standing in pronounced S-curve with right shoulder sloping down sharply, waist bent in on right side and back forming concavity as if hips are thrust forward. Figure wears chiton with sleeves bunched on upper arm. At lower left is one-third of circular vent hole. Figure c, perhaps from third figure or from figure b, has preserved lower edge of central part of chiton and left foot peeking out from beneath folds. Other small non-joining fragments from same group represent drapery. Interior of all figures in group is hollow with roughly finished walls. Moldmade in sections, fronts and backs. Hair of a is hand-tooled and added separately.

Exterior surfaces of fragments a, b and c are covered with white groundcoat except sections which might have been at back of group composition, e.g., right side of a, center back of b. Over white groundcoat are profuse, thickly painted details in two shades of pink, blue, gold, yellow and red.

On figure a, chiton is light pink with very thin yellow-orange lines corresponding to vertical modeled folds. Across buttocks is wide, light pink horizontal band with two horizontal lines at bottom edge of band in darker, thicker pink paint. Below pink lines are yellow-orange lines. Hair is gold. Arms are white. Mantle or cape is solid dark pink with pink lines for straps attaching at shoulders and around chest. At upper right break is thin vertical line of red. On figure b, chiton is white with overpainting of pink at front of shoulder. Below shoulder are two shades of pink, lighter pink covering right half and band of darker pink toward middle of back. Left side is unpainted. On fragment c, central vertical panel of chiton is pastel blue. To left and below blue panel is dark pink. Foot is painted red. Non-joining fragments of drapery are painted pink with thin yellow lines.

Hard-fired, non-micaceous, red-yellow clay, fired gray at core in thicker sections, with small dark inclusions. Munsell: 2.5YR 6/8 (light red).

Greek-manufactured, possibly Black Sea region. See Group II, pp. 79-80.

It is not clear exactly how these fragments relate to one another but it is certain from the context, size, clay, technique and painted decoration that they belong to a single group composition. As much as it is possible to reconstruct the group, two figures appear to be facing each other and a third (?) is in a frontal position. It is likely that the two or three female figures are dancing. The very dramatic figure with the long flowing golden hair suggests a maenad or a Muse.

The possibility of a three-figure composition leads one to consider the three Graces or three nymphs as an identification. No published parallels for this exact type of group composition exist, although there are, of course, terracotta groups of figures playing (e.g., plastic vase of two boys and girl playing ephedrismos: Robinson 1952: 204-208, nos. 265, 265A) or individuals dancing (e.g., F. Winter 1903: 158, no. 7 = Istanbul Museum 687 = Mendel 1908: 490, no. 3153) or women together in various poses (Mollard-Besques 1963: pls. 134-137, from Myrina).

The clay and painted decoration are very close to those of **70**, **73**, **74** and **99** and are likely to be from the same workshop. See Group II, pp. 79-80 for figurines probably from the same manufacturing site.

For a description of the context and imported black-glazed pottery see F. A. Winter 1984: 316. From the ceramics, a date in the second half of the 3d or early 2d century B.C. is possible for this context.

SEATED FEMALES

77 Seated Female
T 96   Trench PPP-N, Floor 5, robbed wall
P.H. 0.107; P.W. 0.03; P.Depth 0.058; Th. walls 0.002-0.005 m.
Pl. 24

Joined from three fragments preserving lower right side and right front of seated figure from lower torso to lower legs. Broken at bottom. Finished surface at back of chair leg. Worn. Surfaces discolored and slightly blackened from contact with fire.

Draped female wearing peplos with deep kolpos, seated on chair with right hand on right thigh. Fingers are positioned as if holding small object or plucking at drapery. Only back of right chair leg is shown. Interior is hollow with walls smoothed by spatula and fingers. Moldmade.

Traces of white groundcoat on exterior. No paint visible.

Very lightly micaceous pinkish tan clay fired gray at core with small dark and light inclusions. Munsell: 5YR 6/6 (reddish yellow).

Greek-manufactured, Attic?

Context allows a 5th-century B.C. date for this figurine and stylistically it might be dated to ca. 470 B.C. Although no attributes survive to identify the female, the suggestion that she may be a Kybele or Mother of the Gods type is not unreasonable.

78 Seated (?) Female
T 100   Trench WS 7, from digging platform, probably from Floor 5
P.H. 0.043; P.W. 0.065; Depth 0.029; W. resting surface 0.007-0.01; Th. walls 0.003-0.005 m.
Pl. 24

Single fragment preserving front and back of upper torso. Lacking front of head from mouth and entire back of head, right shoulder. Chips from left edge. Finished lower edge is worn smooth. White incrustation on breaks and interior.

Female figure, possibly seated against throne. Body is twisted slightly left, head tilted left. Head is small with narrow chin and long neck. Breasts are full and chest projects. At sides of head are thick wavy masses of hair flowing over shoulders. On right side upper arm is against breast. On left side is flat plane of mantle (?). Back is smoothed convex surface. Interior is hollow. Moldmade in two halves, front and back. Join of two halves is visible on exterior where sides are pinched together. Finished edge at bottom may be point of joining with another molded section of torso.

White groundcoat preserved in spots on exterior on face, neck, body, hair and mantle. Yellow paint is preserved on lower right side, beside right arm on throne (?). Traces of red paint on hair to right of head and near break at left.

Yellow-orange micaceous clay, gray at core with small light inclusions. Munsell: 5YR 7/6-6/6 (reddish yellow).

Greek-manufactured.

Context pottery indicates a date no earlier than the 4th century B.C. Stylistically the figure probably dates to the 4th century B.C.

FEMALE PROTOME

79 Female Protome Fragment
T 84   Trench PN, Layer 1b
P.L. 0.132; P.W. 0.085; Th. walls 0.003-0.008 m.
Pl. 24

Single fragment preserving left upper arm and left side of torso. Finished edge at left and bottom. Surface and paint well preserved.

Female protome with right arm bent at elbow. Woman is draped with himation looped over arm. Back has concave, smoothed walls with finished edge turning slightly from front to form lip. Molded in single section.

Exterior is coated with white groundcoat, especially thick at left edge. Over white is pink on arm and drapery. Faint traces of pastel blue on drapery. Back is unpainted with some traces of white slip on upper part.

Very fine, hard-fired, micaceous orange-red clay with fine dark "veins" running across back. Core is red-pink. Munsell: back 5YR 6/6 (reddish yellow); core: 10R 5/6 (red).

Greek-manufactured.

For comparable female protomes from Olynthos see Robinson 1952: 87, 89 ff., 93, 101-102, nos. 25, 31, 39, 62, 65, pls. 17, 20, 24, 31, 32; and from Lindos, see Blinkenberg 1931: 730-731 ff., pls. 146{3110, 3111}, 147{3119, 3120}, 148{3140, 3141}.

See also **62** and **155**, found in the layer below this protome in the same trench with a coin of Alexander the Great. The layer from which the protome comes probably dates in or after the last quarter of the 4th century B.C. and stylistically the protome dates to around the early 4th century B.C.

FEMALE HEADS

80 Female Head
P 810   Trench NCT-A1, fill beneath Floor 1
P.H. 0.089; Max.P.W. 0.068; W. at neck 0.04; Th. at lower break 0.016-0.02 m.
Pl. 24

Single fragment preserving head and neck with adjoining surface above. Broken at top center, proper right edge and bottom. Surface on exterior is chipped at right upper part of head and adjoining surface, right upper quadrant of face, neck at lower break. Preserved surfaces much worn. Incrustation on back and left side.

Female in frontal position with rounded projecting upper sections of adjoining surface to left and right. Hair frames face and is defined as roll with radiating ridges. Hair continues as shoulder locks to sides of neck to lower break. Face is heart-shaped; eyes set high and wide; mouth set close to nose; jawline sharp; chin flat on underside. No other details of facial features are discernible. Back of figure is flat except small strip of clay at lower left break. Moldmade.

No slip or painted decoration discernable.

Very coarse, gritty, non-micaceous clay. Brick red-orange on surface, fired gray at core. Munsell: surface 2.5YR 5/6-5/8 (red).

Central Anatolian-manufactured.

The pottery and other finds from the same context can be dated after 316 B.C. (coin: C 419). Stylistically the head can be placed in the 4th century B.C.

81 Plastic Attachment (?): Female Head
P 1694   Trench MN-W, Dump, Layers 1-5
P.H. 0.047; P.W. 0.03; P.Th. 0.026 m.
Pl. 24
F. A. Winter 1988: 64, 70, n. 34.

Preserves head and bit of adjoining surface around head. Much worn.

Female head in partial relief. Hair is parted above forehead and drawn to sides, framing face with roll on right and left sides. Wavy hair around forehead is tooled with incisions. Face is narrow with prominent cheekbones. Eyes are hollows; nose widens at tip; mouth is small. Back of head is smooth. Moldmade?

No decoration.

Slightly micaceous gray ware.

Central Anatolian-manufactured.

This piece is probably plastic decoration for a vessel such as P 709 or P 3972 (not included in this catalogue), with a female head in relief set below the vessel's rim or forming a handle. Although F. A. Winter (1988: 64) sees Celtic inspiration for this coiffure, it is more likely a general characteristic of Central Anatolian figurine style.

82 Medallion: Medusa's Head?
T 16   Trench SWT, Section A, Cut 4, Level 5
P.H. 0.061; W. 0.052; Depth 0.020 m.
Pl. 25

Intact with chips missing from edge. Relief badly worn.

Roughly oval medallion with probable Medusa's head in high relief. Surrounding relief is frame of deep flaring form, slightly upturned at back. Thick sections of hair surround head. Thickening beneath chin could be lion's paws or snakes tied together. Back is low convex surface, smoothed but with irregularities. Thin incisions at top left and at right side on back. Moldmade?

No painted decoration. Edge of frame burnished black.

Hard-fired brown-gray clay fired gray on surface. Highly micaceous with silver particles and with tiny grit inclusions. Munsell: back surface 10YR 6/1 (gray).

Central Anatolian-manufactured.

Cf. **98** for comparable medallion of Herakles (?).

This medallion was recovered from the only excavated area of the City Mound where there is evidence of rehabitation in the Roman period. A Latin inscription (I 29) was found in the same level and it is possible that the medallion dates as late as the Roman period, although its style still echoes that of the 4th century B.C.

Possibly meant to be used as plastic attachment for exterior or interior wall of vessel such as P 2562, black-glazed bowl with relief of male head on floor of interior. No evidence of attachment to vessel survives. For locally manufactured lentoid guttus with relief of Medusa on upper surface, see P 3255.

For medallions see also Laumonier 1956: 272 ff., esp. no. 1297 (from Delos), a Gorgon's head. For a comparable medallion of a Silenos see Canarache 1969: 73, no. 60 (from Callatis in Rumania).

83 Female Head
T 36   Trench ET-C1, loose fill
P.H. 0.076; P.W. 0.048; Th. 0.049 m.
Pl. 25

Single fragment preserving head to base of neck. Left ear missing. Surface chipped on left cheek, left side of hair, back of head, top of hair. Lower break is partially blackened from contact with fire and surfaces of face, neck and back of head are discolored gray.

Female head inclined sharply backward. Hair rising in peak above forehead and framing face and neck in thick roll. Deep incisions define individual hairs. Round face with high forehead; very large, widely set eyes with prominent lids; large straight nose with flaring nostrils; mouth set close to nose; lips large; upper lip bow-shaped and turning down at ends; jutting chin; long neck with sharp convexity from side to side. Large squarish right ear set low and at right angles to head. Attached to right and left sides of head below ears are flat triangular earrings. Back of head is smoothed and rounded. Back of neck is thick and flaring at lower break. Interior solid. Probably moldmade face. Hair is hand-modeled with incised details. Earrings handmade. Back of head and neck modeled by hand.

Slight traces of white groundcoat on hair. No painted decoration preserved.

Very hard-fired, slightly micaceous red-brown clay with small sandy inclusions. Fired gray at core. Munsell: 5YR 6/4 (light reddish brown).

Central Anatolian- or locally manufactured.

The context indicates a date no earlier than the Late Phrygian/Hellenistic period but it is likely from the stylistic features that this female head belongs to the Roman period. Parallels for this style (treatment of the eyes and hair especially) occur in limestone and marble at Pessinus and other Central Anatolian sites.

84 Female Head
   T 64   Trench MW, Layer 4, N end
   P.H. 0.043; P.W. at neck 0.03; P.Th. 0.036 m.
   Pl. 26

Single fragment preserving head and neck. Surface badly corroded, cracked and flaking. Facial features badly worn, especially left side of face. Nose broken off at tip, right eye corroded. White surface incrustation on back and face as result of acid bath. Yellow stain on broken surface on left side of face and red stain on right side of head.

Female head with hair in bun at back of head. Head is squarish with domed skull. Hair is rendered as ridge with "widow's peak" above low forehead. Narrow, shallow incisions from forehead to bun define individual strands. Flat bun with raised rim projects from back of skull. Large rounded ears project at right angles from hairline. Low forehead; sharp ridges for eyebrows; deeply hollowed eye sockets; right eye is raised oval; high cheekbones; large nose widening at nostrils; slit for mouth; prominently jutting chin; sharp jawline; thick neck flaring to lower edge. Bottom surface of neck is smooth and slightly concave, perhaps finished joining surface. Interior is solid. Hand-modeled with much hand-tooling.

Slight trace of red in groove between hairline on right side of forehead and left outside corner of mouth.

Very brittle, highly saline, micaceous clay fired pinkish brown. Munsell: 7.5YR 7/4 (pink)-8/6 (reddish yellow).

Central Anatolian-manufactured.

The battered condition of the head makes any conclusions about the chronology of the figurine tentative. The stratum in which it was found is not well dated, though the level immediately above had Roman material in it. The severity of the head's form and bust-like appearance would be compatible with an Early Roman date, although the coiffure could, equally, be derivative of a Hellenistic style (e.g., D. B. Thompson 1963a: 41).

85 Female Head
   T 12   Trench SET, Central area, Layer 5
   P.H. 0.035; W. 0.0285; Th. 0.029; Th. walls 0.005-0.007 m.
   Pl. 26

Single fragment of head broken at neckline. Features are very worn.

Female head in frontal position wearing veiled stephane. Small oval face. Hair framing forehead is indicated by wavy ridge. Facial features are very indistinct. Back of head forms continuous smooth surface. Interior is partially hollowed. Moldmade.

Entire exterior surface is covered with white groundcoat. Only preserved trace of paint is red dot on upper lip.

Yellow-orange clay with small dark inclusions. No micaceous particles. Munsell: 5YR 6/8 (reddish yellow).

Greek-manufactured.

This female figurine type ranges in date from the late 6th to mid-5th centuries B.C. Comparanda for the type include Töpperwein 1976: 13, nos. 8, 9, pl. 2 (early 5th century, from Pergamon); Higgins 1954: 65, nos. 122, 123, pl. 22 (early 5th century B.C., from Rhodes); Belin de Ballu 1972: pl. 61{4} ("archaic," from Olbia); and Breitenstein 1941: no. 178, pl. 20 ("archaic," from Attica). The context in which the Gordion example was found contains purely 6th- and 5th-century material.

It is likely that this is an East Greek type, possibly mid-5th-century B.C., and that its appearance at Gordion along with the many plastic vessels of East Greek manufacture points to—as would be expected—strong contacts with western Asia Minor and the East Greek islands in this period.

86 Female Head
   T 66   Trench MN-W, Pit 1 through Layer 3 above House 3
   P.H. 0.054; W. 0.047; Th. 0.033 m.
   Pl. 26

Single fragment preserving head and neck. Most of nose missing. Chip around lower break at front and sides, at inside of right eye, eyebrow. Most of fillet missing except left end. Stain on face, especially on right cheek.

Female head with hair above forehead treated with individual wavy strands pulled sideways. Parting divides hair above center of forehead. Behind roll of hair is appliqué fillet, largely lost. Earrings composed of round pellets with raised rim and central knob are set low to left and right at hairline. Round face with low forehead; widely spaced, large, open eyes; large nose; thick, well-shaped lips; full projecting chin; long thick neck flaring slightly toward bottom. Bottom of neck has irregular, concave surface. Top and back of head are smoothed, irregularly rounded surfaces. Interior is solid. Moldmade front with application of handmade fillet and earrings. Back of head and neck are modeled by hand.

Faint traces of white in cracks at hairline and on hair. Reddish brown traces, either stains or paint, on hair, top of head, right side of neck, back of head at lower break.

Slightly micaceous yellow-orange clay with small light and dark inclusions. Munsell: surface 5YR 6/6 (reddish yellow); core: 2.5YR 6/6 (light red).

Greek-manufactured, probably Attic.

Although the context from which the head comes dates after the mid-3d century B.C., the facial features and hair style allow a stylistic date of the 4th century B.C.

87 Female Head
   T 39   Trench NCT-A1/3, ashy layer at floor level inside house
   P.H. 0.026; W. 0.017; Th. 0.015; Th. neck 0.008 m.
   Pl. 26

Single fragment preserving head broken off at neck. Left side of head and back surface are chipped. Front is worn and facial features are blurred.

Female head in frontal position with garland protruding above head and framing face. Hair is arranged in melon coiffure with vertical divisions radiating from forehead. Hair to right and left of face blurred. Pinched narrow face with high forehead, closely set eyes, small mouth and rounded chin. Ball earrings worn on both ears. Back of head is flattish, slightly irregular. Interior solid. Moldmade.

Surface of exterior covered with white groundcoat. Face and neck painted pink; hair dark red. Trace of blue visible at right side of neck at break.

Slightly micaceous, yellow-brown, fine, compact clay. Munsell: 7.5YR 8/4 (pink)-8/6 (reddish yellow).

Greek-manufactured.

The context of this figurine indicates a date after 316 B.C. (from a coin [C 425]) found on the floor. A stylistic analysis of the hair ("melonen frisur" with deep waves) and the facial features, blurred though they are, also suggests a date around the end of the 4th century B.C. (D. B. Thompson 1963a: 31-32, 38).

88 Female Head
T 89   Context unknown
P.H. 0.056; W. 0.03; Th. 0.035 m.
Pl. 26

Single fragment preserving head and neck. Right half of bowknot broken; chips from back of neck, left cheek and jaw and tip of nose. Surface discolored green. Features worn.

Female head with bowknot hairdo. Hair is widely parted in center, drawn to sides in thickened roll with individual hairs defined by shallow grooves and ridges. Hair is bound on top of head into vaguely rendered loose bowknot. Flattish band, perhaps fillet, appears below bowknot. Face is triangular with low, flat forehead, flat cheeks, deeply set inner corners of eyes, slightly bulging eyeballs, straight nose, bowed upper lip set close to nose, slightly parted lips. Earring on right ear. Thick neck flaring toward bottom. Wide band (himation?) applied against right side of neck and ridge on back of neck where band may have continued. Back of head badly shaped, sloping downward from bowknot and ballooning out. Solid interior. Moldmade.

Traces of white groundcoat on hair, face and neck.

Lightly micaceous light reddish brown clay. All surfaces discolored green, making Munsell analysis difficult. Munsell: ca. 2.5YR 6/4 (light reddish brown).

Greek-manufactured.

Stylistic criteria are the sole means of dating this female head. The bowknot hairdo with hair parted in the center and drawn to the sides before being bound on top of the head belongs to a 3d century B.C. type (see D. B. Thompson 1963a: 43, no. 204, p. 130). The frontal head and neck suggest a date prior to the late 3d century B.C., when the trend was toward inclining the head to one side (*ibid*.: 31).

89 Female Head
T 4   Trench SET-W, Cut 8-9, center, Layer 3
P.H. 0.028; W. 0.020; Th. 0.029; D. break at neck 0.012 m.
Pl. 26

Single fragment preserving head broken off at joining surface at neck. Left side of chin and jaw and nose chipped.

Female head turned sharply to right wearing sakkos or kerchief covering hair except curls dangling in front of ears. At back right side of head kerchief holds flattened bun. Facial features are well defined: eyes are finely sculptured ridges; right eyeball is rounded surface; nose widens at nostrils; lips are full and parted with deep incision between them; ears are carefully modeled with deep hollow for interior. Bottom surface of neck is scored with shallow incisions and two small holes for attachment to body. Solid interior. Moldmade.

Slight traces of white groundcoat on face, neck, nose, mouth and kerchief; in ears, corners of eyes.

Very fine red-brown clay with small amount of gold micaceous particles. Munsell: 2.5YR 6/6 (light red).

Greek-manufactured.

A close parallel for this female head is not found among the published examples. The context allows a date in the 3d century B.C., while the strong inclination of the head would suggest a date in the later 3d century B.C. (cf. **93**).

90 Female Head
T 144   Context unknown
P.H. 0.024; W. 0.020 m.
Pl. 27

Single fragment broken at chin with facial features mostly effaced. Back largely intact.

Female head tilted slightly to right. Hair parted in center and pulled back from forehead and sides. From crown of head hair is covered by finely modeled sakkos, folds of which are indicated on sides and at back. Solid interior? Moldmade.

Fine, soft yellow-orange, slightly micaceous clay. Munsell: 7.5YR 6/4 (light brown).

Greek-manufactured.

91 Female Head
T 44   Terracotta Deposit 5 (see pp. 67-69)
P.H. 0.045; W. 0.027; Th. 0.031 m.
Pl. 27

Single fragment preserving head and neck. Surface well preserved except chips from tip of nose, at right side of neck at break, all around neck at break. Back and back right side of head burned. Incrustation on left side of hair.

Female head inclined sharply to right and back. Hair parted in center, brushed back from face to thickened bouffant at back and sides. At back of crown of head are five projecting curls of hair in fan-shaped arrangement. Over top of head behind locks is thin, rolled fillet which terminates abruptly after turning down toward sides. Large button earrings applied at ear level on right and left sides. Face is round and well modeled with low forehead; widely set, almond-shaped eyes with thickened ridges for lids; finely sculptured, upturned nose; mouth set close to nose with bow-shaped upper lip; strong, outturned chin; full neck with one crease of flesh. Back of head is flattish with no modeling except at nape where hairs of bouffant are indicated. Neck flares slightly at lower break at back. At back of head is long, rectangular vent hole. Interior of head and base of neck hollow. Moldmade from relatively sharp mold. Hand-tooling on hair; hand-smoothed back of head and addition of handmade fillet and fine curls at top of head.

White groundcoat preserved on face, especially around nose, left eye and mouth; on hair, especially left side; and on neck. Slight trace of red paint on hair and yellow-orange paint at top of left earring.

Fine, micaceous clay with small amount of small dark inclusions. Fired light red at core. Munsell: 10R 6/8 (light red). Face covered with fine slip fired golden tan. Munsell: 10YR 7/4 (very pale brown).

Greek-manufactured.

For context see discussion of Terracotta Deposit 5 (pp. 67-69).

Stylistic comparisons are compatible with the late 3d-early 2d century B.C. date. The somewhat flamboyant hair style of this female figurine is simply a variation of the "melonen frisur" and lampadion knot (D. B. Thompson 1963a: 41) and is paralleled by that of Thompson's, no. 205 (*ibid.*), a figurine dated to the mid-2d century B.C. The facial features—especially the full, rounded shape (*ibid.*: 29-30), thick-lidded, half-closed eyes (*ibid.*: 29), perky nose and small, well-bowed mouth and the strongly inclined head (*ibid.*: 31) indicate a late 3d- or early 2d-century B.C. date. In general the round facial type is that which develops in the course of the 3d century B.C. (*ibid.*: 32).

92 Female Head
T 51   Terracotta Deposit 5 (see pp. 67-69)
P.H. 0.04; P.W. 0.027; Th. 0.02 m.
Pl. 27

Single fragment preserving front of head and neck. Nose chipped on left side; surface of top of head chipped; small chips missing from right and left sides of neck. Head blackened on exterior and interior.

Female head inclined to left wearing veil over top and wrapped around neck. Hair parted in center and drawn to right and left sides in thick masses with individual hairs indicated by incision. Deep hole on right side of head below hair for ear or earrings. Long triangular face with close-set, wide-open eyes with upper lid emphasized; well-modeled cheeks; long, thin nose with nostril pierced on right side; small mouth with bowed upper lip set off by groove from small, rounded chin. Finished edge along back of fragment. Interior hollow with smoothed surface. Moldmade front in single piece. Back would have been attached in separate section, either hand-modeled or mold-made.

Entire front covered with white slip. Hair painted red.

Red-orange, slightly micaceous, hard-fired clay. Munsell: 5YR 6/6 (reddish yellow).

Greek-manufactured, possibly Black Sea region. See Group II, pp. 79-80.

For the context of the figurine see discussion of Terracotta Deposit 5 (pp. 67-69). Stylistic criteria for a late 3d- or early 2d-century B.C. date are compatible with the *terminus ante quem* of 189 B.C. provided by the contextual evidence. The strong inclination of the head, for example, is a feature typical of terracottas of the late 3d century and is most marked in the early 2nd century B.C. (D. B. Thompson 1963c: 310; 1963a: 31, no. 206; Kleiner 1942: 16, 56, pls. 6a, 9d lower left). The type of the female swaddled in a mantle and the facial features (long, thin face, wide-open eyes with upper lid emphasized, thin nose and small mouth) are typical of later 3d or early 2d century B.C. terracottas (see D. B. Thompson 1963a: 28-32).

The similarities in clay, painted decoration and scale suggest that this head might be assigned to **74**, from the same deposit.

93 Female Head
T 3   Trench SET, W Cut 6-7, Layer 2
P.H. 0.030; W. 0.023; Th. 0.031; D. neck 0.011 m.
Pl. 27

Single fragment broken off at joining surface at neck. Chip at back of skull. Left side of head is burned. Gray enamel paint (modern?) on left side of face and hair. Features are worn.

Female head tipped back and inclined sharply to right. Hair is deeply parted in center and swept in waves to sides in full chignon at back. Facial features are delicately modeled: high triangular forehead; long narrow face; small straight nose; small mouth; eyes are hollows. One "Venus ring" is indicated by shallow groove on neck. Bottom surface of neck is smoothed for joining to body. Interior is solid. Made from worn mold.

White groundcoat is preserved on surface of face, neck and hair. Traces of red-brown paint on hair.

Fine tan-orange clay with no trace of inclusions. No good surface for Munsell test. Munsell: ca. 5Y 7/6 (reddish yellow).

Greek-manufactured.

The hairdo of this figurine can be easily paralleled. See especially D. B. Thompson 1963a: no. 230; F. Winter 1903: 21, no. 2. The very marked inclination of the head probably indicates a date in the late 3d or beginning of the 2d century B.C. (D. B. Thompson 1963c: 310; 1963a: 31). This stylistically derived date may be corroborated by the terracotta's context in a layer with material belonging to the period of Gordion's desertion at the arrival of the Roman army in 189 B.C. The pottery from the layer can be assigned to the latest Late Phrygian/Hellenistic period at Gordion (see F. A. Winter 1984: 319).

94 Female Head
T 91   Trench TBT-E$_2$S$_2$b, Floor 3
P.H. 0.04; W. 0.034; P.Th. 0.029; Th. break of neck 0.015 m.
Pl. 27

Single fragment preserving head and upper neck. Small chips missing from brim of hat. Face much worn.

Female wearing broad stephane at ca. 100° from front of head. Hair is parted in middle and brushed back from face in individual strands rendered by grooves, then gathered at nape in thickened section. Raised circular knobs on right and left ears represent earrings. Irregular lump of clay appears on right side of neck as continuation of hair. Face is triangular with hollows for eyes; short wide nose; rounded cheeks; full chin. Top and back of head form irregular orb. Stephane continues from front as flattened band. Interior is hollow. Face made from worn mold. Stephane handmade. Top and back of head hand-modeled. Grooves of hair gouged out with tool.

White groundcoat preserved in groove between stephane and hair, on lump at right side of neck and on right side of neck. Dark red paint on hair at sides of head and in groove below stephane.

Micaceous yellow-orange clay with lime inclusions. Munsell: 7.5YR 7/6 (reddish yellow).

Greek-manufactured.

For parallels for stephane type see D. B. Thompson 1963a: 49-50, nos. 216-218. The closest of these to this stephane is no. 216, dated to the early 2d century B.C. (*ibid.*: 131).

From same trench and level as **154**, bird.

FEMALES: OTHER FRAGMENTS

95 Female (?) Arm
 T 73   Trench EML-2W, Layer 2, NE of Wall B
 P.L. 0.06; Diameter at attachment surface 0.02; W. 0.01-0.014 m.
 Pl. 27

Single fragment preserved from attachment surface at elbow to end of hand. Hand chipped. Surface roughly worked.

Arm of figurine with thickened circular attachment surface at elbow for fitting and sealing arm into draped arm socket. Arm is thick with little modeling, flattish on inside, rounded on exterior. Hand forms fist and is mitten-like with rounded end and no articulation of fingers. Handmade.

White groundcoat adheres to exterior and interior of arm. No trace of paint preserved.

Hard-fired, micaceous pinkish orange clay. Munsell: 2.5YR 6/6 (light red).

Greek-manufactured.

The only indication that this arm possibly belongs to a female figurine is the white slip, though white is often used as a ground for overpainting and it is likely that the elbow joint would have been masked by drapery.

The context from which this arm comes is certainly Late Phrygian/Hellenistic, though a specific date cannot be assigned to the figurine.

96 Drapery Fragment
 T 120   Terracotta Deposit 5 (see pp. 67-69)
 P.H. 0.077; P.W. 0.059; P.Depth 0.016 m.
 Pl. 27

Composed of one non-joining and five joining fragments (former not shown on Pl. 27). One finished edge. Chips from surface, especially along breaks.

Drapery fragment from left side (?) of large statuette. Long tubular bunch of himation and wide section of flat drapery with diagonal folds. Back unevenly worked, flattish except at top, which curves toward front.

Exterior covered with white groundcoat. Pink preserved on tubular drapery.

Lightly micaceous yellowish red clay laminating at breaks. Few small inclusions. Munsell: 5YR 6/6 (reddish yellow)-2.5YR 5/8 (red).

Greek-manufactured, possibly Black Sea region. See Group II, pp. 79-80.

Males (97-107)

There are, in comparison to female figurines, relatively few male terracotta figurines from Gordion. Typologically, representations of Eros are most numerous among the male deities (see summary of Eros figurines, pp. 42-43), a with possible representation of Attis (**97**) and one of Herakles (**98**). The Dionysiac scene in a mold for a relief medallion (**105**) is a unique reference to Dionysos at Gordion, unless theatrical masks (**110-114**) are linked to Dionysos (see p. 47). The large-scale male head (**106**) may belong to a statuette of a deity but further identification is impossible.

Chronologically, all of the figurines in this category belong to the Late Phrygian/Hellenistic period. With the exception of the possible Attis (**97**) and the medallion with a possible head of Herakles (**98**) the rest of the male representations are Greek imports.

MALES: DEITIES

97 Statuette: Attis (?)
 T 62   Terracotta Deposit 6 (see pp. 69-70)
 P.H. 0.395; P.W. 0.175; Th. 0.012; diameter neck at break 0.039 m.
 Pl. 28

Body joined from many large and small fragments, preserving lower portion of neck, torso, left edge of cloak, upper part of right side of cloak, left leg to above ankle and right knee. Surface chipped and friable, especially badly preserved on lower part. Left arm preserved from near shoulder to hand, lacking half of thumb and all fingers except stump of fourth finger with ring. Ancient plaster adhering to joining surface at shoulder. Also lacking several large fragments and all of lower part of left side of body. Back is preserved except at lower right and bottom left. Some discoloration on upper torso from contact with fire.

Standing figure, possibly Attis, wearing short chiton which falls to above knees. Along left and right sides is cloak falling from back of shoulders. Figure is in frontal position with straight left leg. Right leg is drawn to side. Chiton has broad rounded neckline and is attached at shoulders by buttons. Chiton is belted above waist and deep kolpos hangs to height of hips. Between legs is wall from which legs seem to rise in relief. Left arm is bent at elbow and would have extended forward from shoulder across to middle of body at oblique angle. Palm is open; thumb is held apart from fingers. On outside of arm are shallow diagonal slashes, probably meant to represent sleeves of chiton. At wrist is ridge, meant to represent either sleeve cuff or bracelet. On fourth finger is oval ring with projecting center. Back is roughly worked. Upper back is broad convex surface which ends in finished horizontal edge at mid-back. Rest of back is open with finished edge, 0.01 m. wide, on right and left sides. Lower part of back ends at height of left calf in finished edge, ca. 0.011 m. wide. Interior is hollow. Interior walls on back are smooth, while those on front are rough. Mostly hand-modeled with possible additions of sections of moldmade drapery. Arm modeled separately and attached with plaster. Front of torso is built up of horizontal sections, while back is probably made in single section.

Fine clay slip covers surface of exterior. Traces of white slip adhere at neckline, in grooves of chiton and cloak, and to arm. Yellow paint is preserved on belt; pink paint on chiton, cloak, left kneecap, left arm and palm of hand.

Friable yellowish brown clay fired gray at core. Micaceous with small lime inclusions. Munsell surface: 7.5YR 6/4 (brown)-6/6 (reddish yellow).

Locally manufactured.

There is no doubt that this statuette is a product of a Central Anatolian workshop, probably one at Gordion itself. The style, details of workmanship, clay and size are comparable to those of **52**, the seated statuette of Kybele, which can be shown to have been locally manufactured. The smallest details, e.g., the rings, the manner of depicting the sleeves as slashes, the tooling on the torso, are close enough to indicate that both the Attis (?) and the Kybele are products of the same artist or workshop. Both the Kybele and the Attis (?), as well as other local products (e.g., **36**), bear traces of ancient plaster repairs or attachment).

54, a phiale, is of the right size for this Attis(?)'s left hand; the clay and find-spots are close.

The identification of this figure as Attis is questionable, although there is some evidence pointing in that direction. The costume, a long-sleeved chiton which ends above the knees and a cloak worn over the shoulders, is compatible with representations of Attis and his so-called "Phrygian" attire. Completing the "Phrygian" costume should be long trousers (anaxyrides) and a cap with earflaps. Since the head and most of the legs are missing, it is impossible to be certain about the rest of the costume. The surface preserved on the left kneecap does not indicate any trace of trousers, although the folds of the trousers may have originally been suggested by slashes on the lower legs, in the same manner that the long sleeves are indicated on the left arm. The broad shoulders and robust chest are not decisive evidence for a male or a female figure, and the hermaphroditic character of Attis would allow for some confusion in the representation of sexual attributes (e.g., the finger ring or bracelet). For comparable terracotta representations of Attis see F. Winter 1903: 325, no. 8 (from Tanagra, in British Museum [C286]) and p. 334, no. 2 (from Myrina) = Mollard-Besques 1963: pl. 103b, MYR 215. See also Burr 1934: 56-57, nos. 63-64, pl. 25. Variations in the iconography include a conflation with Eros producing a winged Attis or a "Phrygian" Eros (e.g., Wiegand and Schrader 1904: 339, fig. 383, from Priene), and Attis playing the syrinx (e.g., Perdrizet 1897: 514-528, pls. 5-8, from Amphipolis). A Late Hellenistic bust from the Athenian Agora shows subtle evidence for the sexual duality of Attis (H. A. Thompson 1948b: 181, pl. 61{1}). The alternative identification for this statuette is a male or female, possibly in Oriental costume.

98 Medallion: Head of Herakles?
P 3698   Trench TB8-2, Layer 3
P.H. 0.051; W. 0.042; Depth 0.025 m.
Pl. 28

Intact except chips at lower and upper edges. Surface badly worn and stained green on exterior and back.

Oval medallion with head of bearded male in high relief. Edges of medallion flare to sides with flat rim. Head is frontal and wears lion headdress, with paws tied beneath chin. Face is round with low forehead, deeply sunken eyes, high cheekbones, full mustache and beard. Back is flat with flaring sides and flat edge at bottom. Moldmade.

No painted decoration.

Pinkish gray-brown, lightly micaceous clay fired green-brown at core. Gritty texture. Munsell: 7.5YR 7/4 (pink).

Central Anatolian-manufactured.

See **82** for a medallion of Medusa (?).

The bearded figure wearing a lion's mane may be identified as Herakles. It is likely that this medallion was manufactured as relief decoration for a vessel like P 2562, a black-glazed bowl with relief on the interior; P 1760, a bowl with relief on its exterior rim; or P 851, a closed vessel with a relief set at the base of the handle. All three comparable relief images are of Herakles.

This medallion comes from a Late Phrygian/Hellenistic layer, probably late 4th or 3d century B.C. and the medallion can be dated stylistically to ca. the 4th century B.C.

EROS

After Kybele, the divinity most frequently represented among the terracotta figurines at Gordion is Eros. Eros, as the child of Aphrodite, the goddess of love, enjoys great popularity in the Hellenistic period in Greek and Greek-influenced regions and is very common as a type among Hellenistic terracotta figurines (see, e.g., the large numbers from Myrina alone: Mollard-Besques 1963: 35-63, pls. 39-79).

At Gordion there are five certain representations of Eros, including one on a relief medallion set into the floor of an imported bowl (P 649), not included in this catalogue; one probable one (**103**) and a thymiaterion held by two Erotes (**104**). All are imports to Gordion and all can be firmly dated in the Late Phrygian/Hellenistic period, most in the later 3d and early 2d centuries B.C.

The iconography of Eros is diverse, although the most common Hellenistic image of Eros is winged, standing with a slim youthful body (**100-102**) and a childlike face (**100, 103**). In the case of **99** Eros is reclining in a sensuous pose in a flower; he has a full, almost voluptuous, body and a chubby childlike face. The two Erotes holding the thymiaterion cup both have the heads of children. Unlike the large numbers of Erotes with outstretched wings and feet poised as if in flight or about to take flight, as at Myrina (Mollard-Besques 1963: 35-41, pls. 39-48) or Priene (Töpperwein-Hoffmann 1971: 130), the majority of the Eros representations at Gordion show him in relaxed poses with wings tucked by his side (**100-102**).

99   Eros in Flower
   T 58   Terracotta Deposit 6 (see pp. 69-70)
   P.Diameter 0.138; P.Th. 0.055; L. body 0.100 m.
   Pl. 28
   Sams 1979b: 51, fig. 10.

Intact except broken edges of flower, chips from surface of front. On back, tip of dome is missing. Paint well preserved on front; back is faded and chipping.

Winged Eros reclining in deep petaled flower with head thrown back and eyes closed, right arm resting over head and left arm bent around object. Eros lies on top of mattress (?) with legs and back swathed in himation or blanket.

Flower is composed of eight or ten overlapping petals rising at ca. 45° angle from deep center with small knob. Back of flower is separately applied conical section. At lower edge of flower are two peg-feet. Feet and tip of conical section form tripod arrangement by which object can stand. Two holes are also pierced through back near top for suspension. Back is incised with pattern of single oak-like leaves radiating from center. Molded in two sections, front and back, and joined at outer edges of petals. Front mold has produced very sharp impression.

Interior of flower and body of Eros are covered with white groundcoat. Pink paint is applied over white on flower and body of Eros. Orange-yellow paint also appears on face, body and hair of Eros. Traces of red paint adhere to inside center of flower, on upper molding of object Eros is clutching and in groove of flower petal. Back is white. Traces of pink paint survive around edges of petals.

Dark red-orange clay fired gray at core. Friable and slightly micaceous with small, light sandy inclusions. Munsell: 2.5YR 5/8 (red).

Greek-manufactured, possibly Black Sea region. See Group II, pp. 79-80.

The terracotta type of Eros in a flower is common in the Hellenistic period and the geographic distribution of examples of the type is widespread. The type appears in the Athenian Agora (D. B. Thompson 1962: 254, no. 12, pl. 89, down to second/third quarter of 3d century B.C.; Agora T2733-2735, T2737), at Troy (D. B. Thompson 1963a: 145-146, no. 302a), at Myrina (Mollard-Besques 1963: 55, pl. 67b, MYR 122, 2d century B.C.), at the Heraion on Samos (Vathy Museum T1036), on Delos (Laumonier 1956: 142), at Abdera in Thrace (Lazarides 1960: 27, 62, pl. 3{B54} beginning of second half of 2d century B.C.), and on Crete (Athens National Museum no. 6063). For a catalogue of known examples see Touratsoglou 1968: 58-64; Bielefeld 1950-51: 47 ff. The attributed dates of the examples range from the 4th century B.C. (Touratsoglou 1968: 58, no. 1) to the end of the 2d or beginning of the 1st century B.C. (*ibid.*: 1968: 64, no. 12). None of the dates, except that of the fragment from the Athenian Agora (down to second/third quarter of 3d century B.C.; D. B. Thompson 1962: 254, no. 12; for discussion of dating of the Satyr Cistern see *ibid.*: 244), is derived from stratigraphic evidence.

The Eros in a flower from Gordion, which most closely resembles the Myrina (Mollard-Besques 1963: 55, pl. 67b, MYR 122) and Abdera examples (Touratsoglou 1968: 64, no. 11), can be closely dated to the late 3d or early 2d century B.C., no later than and probably close to 189 B.C. (see discussion of Terracotta Deposit 6). See Group II, p. 79-80, for figurines which can be assigned to the same probable manufacturing source.

100   Eros
   T 63   Trench NCT-S, Persian Cut 4, Layer 4
   H. 0.096; W. 0.054; Th. 0.011-0.013 m.
   Pl. 29

Intact except small chips on top of polos, top and bottom of left wing, tips of feet and hood at back. Paint moderately well preserved.

Standing winged Eros wearing polos on head and chlamys tied around neck and along right and left sides. With right hand he grasps chlamys at side; left arm is bent and hand is resting on hip. Tops of wings arch to height of head and rest along sides in two tiers. Back is smoothed, leaving concave surface. At upper back shallow hood with two suspension holes is formed of clay. Back of head is smoothed and flat. Moldmade front. Head and body probably made from single mold. Back hood applied by hand. Features are not sharp, indicating that mold from which terracotta was made was worn or generation or two old.

Entire front surface and sides of wings are covered with white groundcoat. Face, neck and body are painted pink. Polos is blue with thin red line below upper molding. Wings are blue with red line outlining upper tier of left wing.

Yellow-buff, slightly micaceous clay with some white lime inclusions and small dark inclusions. Munsell: surface 7.5YR 8/6 (reddish yellow).

Greek-manufactured.

Cf. **101** and **102**.

This figurine was recovered from fill with mixed pottery in the area of unidentified building foundations.

101   Eros
   T 31   Trench ET-N, Ext. 4, under floor of room of house
   P.H. 0.081; W. 0.055; Th. 0.013 m.
   Pl. 29

Single fragment lacking head and lower edge. Surface worn. Much white incrustation on interior.

Winged Eros standing in frontal position with chlamys wrapped around back, appearing in front over left shoulder and bent left arm and held at right side in right hand. Wings arch to height of head and frame body to right and left. At upper back is hollowed-out hood with two holes for suspension. Rest of back is carefully smoothed, producing slightly concave surface. Moldmade front with hand-applied back. Figurine made from slightly worn mold.

Traces of white groundcoat adhere to front of wings and body. Over groundcoat is pink paint. Line of dots of red paint appears across both wings at elbow height, to differentiate upper wing-feather section from lower.

Orange-brown, hard-fired micaceous clay with small light inclusions. Munsell: 5YR 6/6 (reddish yellow).
Greek-manufactured.

The pottery found with this figurine suggests a date later than the 4th century, possibly as late as the early 2d century B.C.
Cf. **100** and **102**.

102 Eros
T 45   Trench ET-C3, Level 2 above Floor 2
P.H. 0.066; P.W. 0.04; Th. 0.01 m.
Pl. 29

Single fragment preserving lower body from waist to ankles and most of left foot. Lacking right wing, right side of right leg, right foot and tip of left foot. Chips missing from abdomen and left thigh.

Standing winged Eros in frontal position with chlamys hanging to left side. Left wing is set along side of body, ending in slightly outturned lower tip. Body is long and thin. Back is smoothed, producing concave surface. Moldmade front and hand-applied back. Features are very sharp, indicating that mold was fresh or made from "new" figurine.

Slight traces of white groundcoat preserved in grooves of wings.

Dark red-brown compact clay, slightly micaceous with small amount of tiny inclusions. Munsell: surface 2.5YR 6/6-6/8 (light red).
Greek-manufactured.

Cf. Cat. Nos. **100** and **101**.

This Eros figurine was found in a level with a stamped black-glazed bowl (P 1058) which can be dated to the late 4th or early 3d century B.C. (see F. A. Winter 1984: 122, 127, no. 41).

100-102 are all similar types of standing winged Erotes, but no two are made from the same mold.

D. B. Thompson dates the Erotes with the slim boyish body types to the late 3d century B.C. (1963b: 279). Evidence from the contexts of the three Gordion examples (**100-102**) corroborates this dating and possibly extends the duration of the type at least to the early 2d century B.C.

The closest parallels for the Gordion variety with chlamys over left shoulder come from Callatis in Rumania (Canarache 1969: nos. 41-46).

103 Eros?
T 67   Trench MN-W, Layer 4, fill in House 3
P.H. 0.025; W. 0.018; Th. 0.021 m.
Pl. 29

Single fragment preserving head and neck. Chip from left side of head. Surface is uneven and cracked. Small depression in top of head.

Head of child or Eros. Head is round and cheeks are full. Mouth is smiling; features are dull. On neck are two ridges. Back of head is rounded and roughly finished. Back of neck is smooth. Interior is solid. Moldmade; mold probably worn.

White groundcoat adheres to crack beneath chin and to cracks on head. No paint survives.

Slightly micaceous tan-brown clay with tiny dark, gritty inclusions, fired gray at core. Munsell: 7.5YR 6/4 (light brown).
Greek-manufactured.

If this figurine represents Eros, it is possible that the ridges on the neck are the buckle or tie of the chlamys which Eros wears in other examples (**100-102**).

The context can be dated after the mid-3d century B.C. (coin: C 651, Seleukos II [246-226], Antioch, in fill below house). Also found in the same trench and sequence are **13**, goat rhyton, from Layer 3 fill; **86**, female head, from pit through Layer 3; **65**, standing female, in fill beneath House 3.

104 Thymiaterion: Erotes with Vessel
T 106   Trench TB8-S1, Floor 4
P.H. 0.052; P.W. 0.071; Max.D. 0.051; Th. walls 0.005-0.008 m.
Pl. 30

Single fragment preserving upper part of miniature vessel with upper halves of two Erotes. Only head of right figure survives while head and chest of left one are preserved. Chips are missing from edge of basin, face of right Eros. Head of left Eros cracked. Surface worn. Traces of burning on right Eros. Interior of basin slightly grayer than rest but not burned.

Thymiaterion figurine of two Erotes hoisting footed bowl on shoulders. Basin of bowl has steep flaring sides with floral design in relief on front. Stem of bowl shown between two Erotes is composed of round molding with fluted cone below. Heads of Erotes are turned three-quarters toward center. Projecting from left shoulder of left Eros is small rounded wing. Back of thymiaterion is smooth, slightly convex surface. Upper edge of vent hole preserved in back. Interior below basin is hollow. Moldmade front with basin and back applied by hand. Mold worn. Right side of head of right Eros is flattened from flaw in mold or in removal from mold.

White groundcoat adheres to cracks on front. No surviving traces of paint.

Yellow-orange micaceous clay, fired pink-brown on surface. Many gritty inclusions, both light and dark. Cracked surfaces due perhaps to overfiring. Munsell: surface 5YR 6/4 (light reddish brown)-6/6-6/8 (reddish yellow).
Greek-manufactured.

The closest parallel for this type of vessel-figurine comes from a pithos burial on Samothrace dated to the second quarter of the 3d century B.C. (inv. 57.841; H. 0.108 m.; Lehmann 1975: 31). The size and the clay are also comparable. Many unpublished examples of the type from Amisos (Samsun) are housed in the Archaeological Museum in Istanbul (cf. Mendel 1908: 594, no. 3523). A similar example from the Athenian Agora belongs to the late 3d century B.C. (D. B. Thompson 1963b: 284-285, no. 19, pl. 75). Another example of a similar type of two Erotes holding the base of a vase from Myrina is dated by Mollard-Besques to the end of the 2d century B.C. (1963: 57, Bo30, pl. 70f. For a later derivation of the type from Troy see D. B. Thompson 1963a: 74, no. 7). The type almost certainly originates in Asia Minor.

The context of the Gordion example can be dated close to the abandonment of Gordion in 189 B.C. (see F. A. Winter 1984: 314-315, no. 30 for analysis of pottery). Since the type continues into the later 3d or early 2d century B.C., as demonstrated by the example from the Agora, the Gordion example might date anywhere in this period. The close resemblance to the figurine from Samothrace could, however, indicate a date for the Gordion figurine perhaps as early as the second quarter of the 3d century B.C.

105 Mold: Relief Medallion with Dionysiac Scene
ST 169   Trench X, Building A, Layer 2
Diameter 0.095; Th. 0.015 m.
Pl. 30

Single fragment preserving just over half of complete circumference of mold. One large hole pierced deeply into back. Burned gray to black on front surface; gray circular discoloration at back center.

Baked mold for relief medallion or plaque. Mold is slightly concave on front with straight, uneven sides and no rim, and slightly convex on back surface. Composition is designed for round field of youthful naked Dionysos; female, probably Ariadne; and satyr in rocky landscape. At right side of mold, filling entire right field, is Dionysos, semi-reclining on rocky seat covered by his chlamys. Torso is in three-quarter frontal and thyrsos is at his left side. Dionysos looks back over right shoulder and puts right arm around female, probably Ariadne, who reclines at broken edge. Leaning on her left hand, she turns toward Dionysos. Her long locks fall over left shoulder and body is enveloped in drapery. At bottom, positioned in rocky landscape below Dionysos and Ariadne, is pudgy ithyphallic Silenos seated in three-quarter position. Derivative mold taken from first-generation terracotta. Little evidence of surface tooling.

Hard-fired to stone-like consistency. Micaceous yellow-brown clay with some small inclusions, fired gray all over. Munsell: unburned back surface 10YR 7/1 (light gray).

Greek-manufactured.

The context pottery confirms the indications from stylistic criteria that this mold probably dates to the Early Hellenistic period (late 4th/early 3d century B.C.).

The specific use of the finished product, a round terracotta plaque, is not immediately apparent, although a medallion for the interior of a large ceramic bowl or drinking cup is a possibility. Most of the vessels of this type are South Italian in origin (e.g., Calenian bowls: Pagenstecher 1909), although examples are known from other centers (e.g., Corinth: CP 3053, CP 2626). Black-glazed relief wares are also found at Pergamon in the 2d century B.C. (Schafer 1968: 64 ff.), but the round form of this mold would lend itself better to the decoration of an open vessel's interior than to that of the exterior wall on the Pergamene vessels.

Comparable scenes of Dionysos, Ariadne and a satyr occur in bronze as appliqués for mirror cases (e.g., Züchner 1942: 32-35; KS37 [Abb. 15]; KS38 [Taf. 19]; KS39, KS40; [Scheurleer 1922: 223, Abb. 17]). The figures on this mold do not seem to be cut with the precision necessary for the production of a metal appliqué or metal medallion for a ritual vessel. This mold may have been made to produce copies in terracotta of a mirror scene (see von Rohden 1884: 30 ff.; Berger 1982: 105-107, no. 154).

MALES: OTHER

106 Male Head
T 14   Trench SET-S, pit through Floor 4, Layer 3
P.H. 0.081; P.W. 0.063; P.Th. 0.035; Th. walls 0.010 m.
Pl. 30

Two joining fragments preserving entire face, portion of upper neck and front half of top of head. Broken at point of juncture between front and back sections. Nose is broken off at tip and right side of hair and chin are chipped. Right side of face is scarred.

Large-scale male head turning off axis to left. Hair is rendered by ca. ten high ridges, radiating from forehead in symmetrical arrangement on right side and sweeping at diagonal on left side. Hairline forms peak at center of forehead. Face is long and triangular with flat cheeks. Eyes are large and set deep beneath heavy ridges for eyebrows. Mouth is short and lips full. Interior is hollow and interior walls are smoothed with fingers. Probably moldmade with much hand-modeling of front. Very thick walls. Traces of final tooling exist on cheeks. Front and back sections were joined at point of break just in front of ears.

Face preserves traces of white groundcoat. Hairline is marked by reddish brown paint. Hair is covered with same color to crown of head where ca. 0.007-m.-wide band of red paint survives across top. On face are traces of reddish pink near breaks on right and left sides, on cheeks, above and between lips and on neck. Eyebrows are painted dark brown. Eyes are outlined in elongated oval with brown-black paint and pupils are defined by brown-black circles.

Very hard-fired tan-brown clay, fired grayish brown at core. Clay contains small silver and large gold micaceous particles in large amounts and tiny sandy and lime inclusions in small amounts. Munsell: surface chip 10YR 7/3 (very pale brown); interior 7.5YR 5/4 (brown).

Greek-manufactured.

This head is a unique specimen at Gordion and in the terracotta repertoire of Asia Minor. The large size and the plastic, portrait-like qualities of the face suggest affinities with large-scale stone sculpture. An especially close parallel is a marble head from Rhodes in the Metropolitan Museum, New York (11.91.1; Richter 1954: 72, no. 118, pl. 91; Frel 1971: 121-124, pls. 42, 43{2}).

Stylistic comparison (especially of the facial features) with stone sculpture indicates similarities to works of the late 4th century in the "Lysippan style." The slightly turned head, the large, deep-set eyes and the leonine hair recall the portrait type of Alexander sometimes identified as that of Lysippos.

The head was found in a pit together with a considerable amount of Late Phrygian/Hellenistic pottery, the latest belonging to the late 4th or 3d century B.C.

107   Male (?) Figure
T 139   Context unknown
P.H. 0.050; P.W. 0.044; Th. 0.004-0.007 m.
Pl. 31

Single fragment preserving lower legs from knees to ankles. Uncleaned.

Bare human legs, probably male, in high relief against irregular background. Right leg is bent at knee; left leg is straight. Moldmade.

White groundcoat (Munsell: 5YR 8/1 [white]) covers front. Traces of red paint (Munsell: 10R 5/6 [red]) over groundcoat.

Light orange clay. Munsell: core 2.5YR 6/8 (light red); surface 10YR 7/2 (light gray).

Greek-manufactured.

The unrecorded context makes assessing the chronology of this figurine difficult, but on the basis of scale and painted details, it is likely that this figurine belongs to the Late Phrygian/Hellenistic period.

Unidentifiable Humans (108-109)

The two human terracotta representations in this category bear no indications of sex, one because it was never intended as a finished product (**108**), the other because it probably simply served as a scary or apotropaic charm (**109**). Both representations are Central Anatolian products, the former surely locally produced.

108   Archetype Fragment?: Neck with Torque
T 72   Terracotta Deposit 5 (see pp. 67-69)
P.H. 0.04; P.W. 0.064; P.Th. 0.014; Th. walls 0.002-0.005 m.
Pl. 31
F. A. Winter 1977: fig. 1; 1988: 64, 70, n. 31 (Romano catalogue number incorrectly cited as **103**).

Single fragment preserving front of lower neck and turn to upper chest. Broken on all sides.

Poorly modeled, thick, angular neck and upper torso fragment; probably unfinished kiln discard. On neck rests torque composed of single narrow rolled band with two balls meeting at center of neck. Roughly worked surface of back of neck preserved on lower area. Handmade.

No painted decoration.

Pinkish orange, lightly micaceous clay, hard-fired with tiny light and dark inclusions. Munsell: 5YR 6/6 (reddish yellow).

Locally manufactured.

By virtue of the identification of the torque around the neck, this poorly preserved and poorly modeled unfinished fragment may represent one of the few bits of archaeological evidence for the Galatians at Gordion. See F. A. Winter 1977: 60ff., fig. 1: and Conclusions, p. 75. Its find-spot in the Pottery Establishment and unfinished state suggest that this neck may be an archetype or secondary archetype fragment.

109   Pendant: Grotesque Head
T 49   Trench ET-012, Level 4
P.H. 0.043; P.W. 0.04; Th. 0.031 m.
Pl. 31

Intact except chips at bottom and back right edge. Surface burned.

Circular pendant with grotesque head on front, pierced at top for suspension. Eyes are incised circles with added clay pellets for pupils. Nose is large with deep indentation defining underside and nostrils. Mouth is deep fold of clay with upper lip rolled beneath nose. Back of pendant carries intaglio impression of shell. Handmade.

No painted decoration.

Lightly micaceous gray-brown clay with small dark and light inclusions. Munsell: 10YR 5/3 (brown).

Central Anatolian-manufactured.

Context pottery and coins suggest a date for the level at least as late as the second half of the 4th century B.C.

This pendant was surely worn as a necklace.

Masks (110-114)

All of the comic masks from Gordion are New Comedy types, a theatrical form which replaced Middle Comedy ca. 330 B.C. The references in the Catalogue to Pollux correspond to his listing of New Comedy masks in *Onomasticon* IV, 143-154.

Specific dates for each of the Gordion masks are difficult to establish but **110** and **111** are probably the earliest of the group (late 4th-early 3d century B.C.), with **112** dating to the first half of the 3d century B.C. **113** and **114** could be as late as the early 2d century B.C.

All of the comic masks from Gordion are certainly Greek imports, but from which specific manufacturing sites is unclear. None of the clays appear to be Attic. Workshops in Asia Minor are the probable source of the Gordion examples. Pergamon may be the manufacturing site of **113**, to judge from the appearance of its clay and a comparative examination of the clays of the Hellenistic terracotta figurines from Pergamon and the Pergamene shrine of Mamurtkale.

FUNCTION

It is not clear what function these comic masks had at Gordion. None were found in contexts which might be useful in this regard; four were recovered from trenches where houses and shrines of the Late Phrygian/Hellenistic period were excavated, but the masks did not come from any specific architectural units. The only specific clues to their function come from the holes pierced through the top or back of two of the masks (**111**, **112**) which indicate they were meant to be suspended.

The general function of small-scale terracotta masks is debatable. Obviously, these terracotta masks are miniature versions of the large masks worn by actors in dramatic productions. The miniatures are meant to evoke the theatrical originals and the dramatic world in general. Connections between terracotta masks or figurines of actors and Dionysos are cited to prove the votive nature of these objects (Webster 1950: 23; 1969: ix); the link between masks and Dionysiac cult is clearer at Sarkiné in ancient Colchis (Georgia), where Hellenistic busts of Dionysos and Ariadne were found with theatrical masks (Lordkipanidze 1974). Associations with Demeter are also suggested (Peredolskaja 1964: 10 ff; Webster 1969: ix). Terracotta masks are found in houses, e.g., at Priene the walls of a Hellenistic house were decorated with New Comedy masks (Wiegand & Schrader 1904: 360-361, figs. 446-450); in graves, e.g., many in Lipari (see Webster [1965: 319 ff.], who implies that their primary function was as souvenirs of certain plays or theatrical performances); and in sanctuaries, e.g., that of Demeter and Kore at Corinth (Stroud 1965: pl. 2E). It is likely that, originally, small-scale terracotta theatrical masks were produced with religious associations in mind, e.g., as votives to Dionysos as the god of the theater. These masks later probably became popular for their comical or decorative effects and became widespread as decorations, souvenirs or collectors' pieces. The unique appearance of each of the character types would appeal to the collectors' instincts.

There is only limited evidence of worship of Dionysos at Gordion. The only representation of Dionysos at Gordion, in this case together with Ariadne and a satyr, is on the mold for a relief medallion (**105**). There is also a satyr bust-thymiaterion (**35**). The site has yielded no traces of an ancient theater or theatrical area and no reason to suppose that these five comic masks bear any immediate relation to a cult of Dionysos as the god of the theater. Private worship of Dionysos may well have been conducted at Gordion, and if these masks have any connection to that deity, they may have been used in domestic shrines. It is preferable, however, to think of these masks as popular tourist souvenirs or collectors' items which made their way to Gordion through dealers in terracotta figurines or through individuals.

110 Comic Mask
   T 20   Trench ET-N, brown fill with stones over Level 4 between two faces of wall
   P.H. 0.046; P.W. 0.032; P.Th. 0.022; Th. walls 0.005-0.007 m.
   Pl. 32

Single fragment preserving face, lacking right side from outside of eye, lower part of mouth and chin. Chips from all edges except part of left cheek.
Comic mask of slave with hair rising around face in *speira* (Pollux no. 22); low sloping forehead and high arching eyebrows formed by one thick ridge; protruding eyeballs; small nose with bulbous end; gaping cavity for mouth. Back of mask is smoothed and forms concave surface. Interior hollow. Made from worn mold.
No trace of painted decoration.
Reddish orange clay, well fired and fine with many tiny silver micaceous particles and small number of gritty inclusions. Munsell: 5YR 6/6 (reddish yellow).
Greek-manufactured.

This type of mask is described by Pollux (no. 22) as a leading slave with a *speira* of red hair, raised brows and a frown. See Webster and Green 1978: 15, B Slave, for examples and description of general type of slave. The type was created in Attica during the course of the 4th century, and was popular by the beginning of New Comedy at the end of the 4th century B.C. (*ibid*.: 15). This is one of the comic slave mask types that became popular as supports on Hellenistic molded relief bowls (e.g., Edwards 1975: 171, Corinthian example dated close to 146 B.C.).
A date in the late 4th or early 3d century B.C. is probable for this mask based on stylistic comparisons:

• Athens, Agora T942 (Webster 1960: 276, 282, no. C2, pl. 68): end of 4th century B.C.;
• Munich SL 201 (Sieveking 1916: 17);
• Madrid 3373 (Laumonier 1921: no. 859, pl. 101{8}): provincial version;
• Nicosia (Webster 1969: 75, KT4): local version;
• Lipari (Webster 1965: pl. 185{4}, C6): local version.

The context in which the mask was found cannot further narrow the stylistically derived date.

111 Comic Mask
   T 102   Trench WS 4-5, S2, Layer 6
   P.H. 0.085; P.W. 0.035; P.Th. 0.04; Th. walls 0.003-0.005 m.
   Pl. 32 and Color Pl. I

Single fragment preserving two-thirds of front of mask, broken across left side of face and hair. Back of head is missing from crown. Finished edge exists along right jaw. Surface and paint very well preserved. Traces of carbon adhere to interior at lower edge and right break, but fragment is not burned.
Comic mask of slave with high *speira*, wrinkled brow, recurved eyebrows, pop-eyes, pug nose, open mouth and hairy beard and mustache (Pollux no. 22). On crown of head is small suspension hole. Interior is hollow with rough walls and finger impressions. Made from fresh mold. Possibly some reworking of details by hand.
Entire exterior surface is covered with white groundcoat and pink slip or paint. Over white and pink is coat of orange or tan paint for skin color, hairline on left side of forehead and right eyelid. Ring of red is painted around inside edge of mouth. Very thin line of black is painted above right eyeball. On left side,

eyebrow is marked by thin arching brown line. Interior is neither slipped nor painted.

Very slightly micaceous, hard-fired fine orange-pink clay, few dark inclusions. Munsell: 5YR 7/4 (pink)-7/6 (reddish yellow).

Greek-manufactured.

This mask is the same type as **110**, i.e., Pollux no. 22. A date no earlier than the late 4th/early 3d century B.C. is likely based on context. An Ephesian coin of ca. 387-295 B.C. (C 1232) provides a broad date for the layer.

112   Comic Mask
T 90   Trench TBT 7a, Layer 2, NW quarter
H. 0.048; W. 0.064; P.Th. 0.04; Th. walls 0.005-0.01 m.
Pl. 32

Single fragment preserving entire section of hair from top to finished edge at bottom, lacking most of face except right edge at hairline. Chipped surfaces on left side of face and hair. Interior discolored green with black splotches. Some paint preserved.

Comic mask wearing thick rolled fillet around top of head (probably Pollux no. 16). Hair is swept back from face on right in horizontal mass defined by closely packed grooves and ridges. On left side hair is modeled in varying convex and concave surfaces with ridges for individual locks. Through top of head is small oval hole (0.019 x 0.004 m.) for suspension or attachment of object. Individual strands of hair radiate from center of back of head. In back of head to right and left of center are two holes, not pierced through to interior; their purpose is unclear. Interior is hollow, walls smooth. Moldmade front with addition of fillet and some hand-tooling of hair. Back of head is modeled by hand and hand-tooled.

Traces of white groundcoat on exterior surface. Hair was painted but color is now blackened. Traces of pink paint on topknot, at left hairline and beneath fillet. Fillet is red.

Red-orange, very slightly micaceous, hard-fired clay with tiny dark particles. Munsell: 5YR 5/6 (yellowish red).

Greek-manufactured.

This comic mask is probably the type described by Pollux (no. 16) as a young man with a fillet coming home from a banquet (Webster and Green 1978: 19, O Young Man). The mask is similar to one from Centuripe (de Morant 1956: 32, pl. 55B), though not of the same type. It can be compared to a fragment of a "female mask" from Pergamon (Töpperwein 1976: no. 506, pl. 74).

The latest datable pottery dates the context not much later than the first half of the 3d century B.C.

113   Comic Mask
T 22   Trench SET-N, Cut N-6-D, Layer 1
H. 0.0615; W. 0.0425; Th. 0.032 m.
Pl. 32

Intact. Lacking only tiny fragments, e.g., tip of nose, tip of right side of topknot and edge of face on right side.

Comic mask of pseudokore type (Pollux no. 34). Hair is parted in middle and pulled back above ears. At top of head is large rectangular bowknot bound at base by ribbon. Face is oval; eyelids defined by upper and lower ridges with empty slit for pupil; nose exceptionally long with pointed tip; mouth forms open rectangle; inside of mouth is concave with tongue projecting over thin lower lip. Back of mask is open with back edge forming 135° angle. Back of bowknot is flat surface. Interior is hollow. Moldmade.

Surface of face is covered with white groundcoat. Traces of white slip on hair, especially on bowknot. Bowknot is painted red, while rest of hair is black. On face are traces of blue-green paint.

Fine yellow-orange clay with few micaceous particles and no visible inclusions. Munsell: 7.5YR 7/6 (reddish yellow).

Greek-manufactured.

This New Comedy mask is the first pseudokore or hetaira described by Pollux (no. 34). See Webster and Green 1978: 23, W Hetaira, for general type. The Gordion example is probably derivative of an Attic mask of the late 4th century B.C. See Töpperwein 1976: 236, no. 518 (from Pergamon) for close stylistic comparison for type.

Although the pottery from this layer contained 5th-, 4th-, and 3d-century B.C. material, the latest sherds in the fill can be dated to the end of the 3d or early 2d century B.C. The mask could be as late as the latest pottery or be among the 3d century B.C. objects.

The clay of this mask closely matches that of terracotta figurines from Pergamon and the Pergamene Kybele shrine at Mamurtkale.

114   Comic Mask
T 118   Trench SE-NW, Stratum 1c
P.H. 0.025; P.W. 0.033; P.Th. 0.031; Th. walls 0.002-0.005 m.
Pl. 32

Single fragment preserving lower left half of mouth, chin and face. Finished surface below left jaw. Paint well preserved.

Comic mask with gaping mouth and broad lower jaw and chin (probably Pollux no. 16). Interior is hollow and interior walls are smooth. Moldmade.

Exterior surface is covered with white groundcoat. On top of white is pinkish orange paint for skin color. Inside of mouth on lower lip is painted red.

Light red, very fine, slightly micaceous clay. Munsell: 2.5YR 6/6 (light red).

Greek-manufactured.

This fragment probably belongs to a comic mask of a young male type, perhaps like **112**, Pollux no. 16

This fragment was found with a Rhodian stamped amphora handle, an imitation Megarian bowl (P436), a locally made black burnished imitation of West Slope ware and a stamped red-glazed sherd. The stratum could be as late as the last half of the 3d or early 2d century B.C. but this fragment, on stylistic grounds, might well be one of the earliest pieces in the stratum.

Animals: Central Anatolian and Non-Central Anatolian (115-155)

CHRONOLOGY

Animal figurines are the most numerous of all categories of terracottas from Gordion. Chronologically, animal terracottas span the history of the site from the Early Bronze Age to the Byzantine period, with Early Phrygian, Roman and Byzantine examples barely represented or non-existent. (See Tables 1 and 2, pp. 50 and 73. for general chronological groupings.) This chronological pattern is consistent with the overall picture of the terracotta figurines from Gordion. Zoomorphic vessels, animal attachments for vessels, or animal spouts, not included in this catalogue (see Gunter 1991: nos. 254, 508-514), are common in the Hittite period. The local production of terracottas in the Early and Middle Phrygian periods seems to have been limited to handmade animal figurines, animal vessels (see **1-11, 17**) and a few other non-figural objects—boots (see **162-168**), a model cart (**156**), and miniature wheels (**159-161**, with only one of the latter (**159**), dating surely to the Early Phrygian period. Only three animal figurines can possibly be placed within the Early Phrygian (or Middle Phrygian) period (**122, 137, 138**). Animal figurines as plastic attachments for pottery are also rare in the Early Phrygian period (see Sams, *Gordion* IV, p. 122). The majority (at least 18 examples) of the handmade animal figurines belong to the Middle Phrygian period. Unlike other categories of figurines at Gordion, the Late Phrygian/Hellenistic period is not well represented by handmade animals, with only two definite examples, **146** and **148**. No Roman-period animals and one medieval period quadruped are represented at Gordion.

Non-Phrygian or non-Central Anatolian figurines are limited in this category to three examples (**153-155**).

TECHNIQUE AND DECORATION

The animal figurines represented in this catalogue are handmade with the exception of one Greek example (**153**). Although the surviving animal figurines which are Anatolian-manufactured display handmade techniques, some of the figurines probably once had hollow cylindrical bodies, now missing, turned on the wheel and then reshaped by hand (e.g., **126, 127, 131**). See also **1-5**: animal vessels with wheel-turned bodies.

The majority of the Central Anatolian animal figurines are simple representations, although for the most part executed with great care. Almost without exception the animals are decorated or finished by polishing. They may be slipped and/or polished dark gray, brown or black in a typically Phrygian technique (**122, 126, 127, 130, 137, 140, 149**); slipped and polished to a dark red-maroon or orange with added painted details (**123-125**); slipped and/or polished to orange or red (**129, 131, 136, 144, 152**); covered with white groundcoat and painted in red (**132, 151**); painted orange (**134**) or black (**135, 142, 150**); or covered with a buff slip (**128, 133**).

SCALE

While the majority of the Central Anatolian-manufactured animal representations are on a small scale, with average estimated restored lengths of 0.05-0.12 m. or heights of 0.05-0.10 m., a few are truly miniatures: **116** (Early Bronze Age) and **139** (Middle Phrygian period), two quadrupeds of estimated restored lengths of ca. 0.04 m.; **133**, a yoked (?) animal only 0.02 m. in preserved height. A number of the animal representations are of a very substantial size. All the animals in the category of Large Quadrupeds and Large Quadrupeds Attached to Plinths would, if restored to complete representations, be larger than the average figurines. The three comparable horses' heads, slipped, polished and fired red (**123-125**), could be restored to the size of statuettes of perhaps 0.35-0.40 m. in height. And a group of ungulates' legs (**126-132**) are of a size that would suggest, for complete animal bodies, statuettes of ca. 0.15-0.30 m. in height. Since there are no complete or even near-complete examples of these larger animals, it is impossible to be certain that an entire animal form was ever rendered.

ANIMAL TYPOLOGY

The majority of the animal types represented by the Central Anatolian-manufactured terracotta figurines from Gordion are quadrupeds, with a small class of birds. Ten of the quadrupeds are not specifically identifiable; there are eight representations of otherwise unidentifiable ungulates and eleven probable representations of horses including two stallions and two harnessed horses. In addition, represented by a single or a handful of examples each are a ram, two bulls, a possible stag and a lion. Among the Anatolian bird figurines, none are specifically identifiable, although among the imports one may be identified as a cock (?) and one a dove.

One miniature animal (**133**) is unidentifiable, although a strap appears across its back as if to suggest a yoke or harness. In addition, five quadrupeds wear bridles, yokes or some other form of harness: e.g., two of the horses from the Hittite period (**117, 118**) wear bridles or halters; **135** wears a harness strap across its rump; **123** and **125** wear painted bridles or halters; and on **134** and **135** harnesses are represented by strips of clay. The small yoked or harnessed figurines may be part of group compositions followed by vehicles such as carts or chariots (see Miscellaneous category for carts and wheels, **156-161**). One may have had a rider (**134**).

TABLE 1. CHRONOLOGICAL CHART
Central Anatolian Manufactured Animal Figurines

Early Bronze Age 3000-2000 B.C.		115	(probably) Animal Head
		116	(probably) Quadruped
Middle and Late Bronze Ages (Hittite Old Kingdom or Empire) 1650-1200 B.C.		117	Horse's Head
		118	Horse's Head
		119	Horse's Head
		120	Ram's Head
		121	Bull's Head
Early Phrygian Period ca. 1000 to early 7th century B.C.		122	Quadruped: Ungulate's Leg
Early or Middle Phrygian Period ca. 1000 to 323 B.C.		137	Quadruped
		138	Quadruped
Middle Phrygian Period early 7th century to 323 B.C.		123	Large Quadruped: Horse's Head?
		124	Large Quadruped: Horse's Head?
		125	Large Quadruped: Horse's Head?
		126	Large Quadruped: Ungulate's Leg
		127	Large Quadruped: Ungulate's Foot
		128	Large Quadruped: Ungulate's Leg
		129	Large Quadruped: Ungulate's Leg
		130	Large Quadruped: Bull Horn?
		131	Large Quadruped on Plinth: Ungulate's Leg
		132	Large Quadruped on Plinth: Ungulate's Leg
		133	Yoked Quadruped
		136	Wheeled Quadruped: Horse Pull-Toy
		139	Quadruped
		140	Quadruped: Stag?
		141	Quadruped
		142	Quadruped
		145	Quadruped: Ungulate's Legs
		149	Bird
Middle or Late Phrygian/Hellenistic Period early 7th century to 189 B.C.		134	Harnessed (?) Quadruped: Horse?
		135	Harnessed Quadruped: Horse?
		143	Quadruped: Stallion
		144	Quadruped: Stallion
		150	Bird
		151	Bird
		152	Bird
Late Phrygian/Hellenistic Period 333-189 B.C.		146	Quadruped's Legs
		148	Lion's Paw
Roman Period 1st century B.C. to 6th century A.D.		no examples	
Medieval Period 7th-14th centuries A.D.		147	Quadruped

Non-Phrygian or Non-Central Anatolian Animal Figurines

Bronze Age 3rd to 1st millennia B.C.		no examples	
Early Phrygian Period ca. 1000 to early 7th century B.C.		no examples	
Middle Phrygian Period early 7th century to 323 B.C.		153	Plaque: Bull
		154	Bird: Cock?
		155	Bird: Dove
Late Phrygian/Hellenistic Period 333-189 B.C.		no examples	
Roman Period 1st century B.C. to 6th century A.D.		no examples	
Medieval Period 7th-14th centuries A.D.		no examples	

FUNCTION

Animal representations were, of course, popular as rhyta or other vessels and as attachments for vessels (see **1-18**). Of the animals in the figurine category, it is possible to assign a specific function to only a small proportion. One stylized horse representation is by its form identifiable as a pull-toy (**136**) and was recovered from the fill between floor levels in Building C, a Middle Phrygian megaron. A total of only two animals have definite funereal associations: **128**, an ungulate's leg and **140**: a stag (?) (from the cremation burials beneath Tumulus D). **126**, an ungulate's leg, was found in the mantle of Tumulus F and was not, therefore, intended as a burial gift. Information about other types of burial gifts in the Phrygian tumuli indicates that most were not made specifically for use in burials.

Some of the animal figurines or statuettes have associations with identifiable architectural units: e.g., **127**, an ungulate's foot, from either the houses beneath Tumulus E or the fill brought in to level the area on which Tumulus E was built; **133**, an unidentifiable quadruped wearing a yoke or strap, from a floor level inside Building D, a Middle Phrygian megaron whose function is unknown; **137**, a quadruped, from the Phrygian houses beneath Tumulus H; **144**, a stallion, found in the ashy fill in a coil-built clay oven; **153**, an imported bull plaque, found in the clearing of a 4th-century or Late Phrygian/Hellenistic house wall.

Four figurines come from pits:

116: Quadruped, of probably Early Bronze Age date
131: Large Ungulate's Leg on Plinth
147: Medieval-Period Quadruped
149: Bird

Most of the remaining figurines or statuettes come from functionally undefinable earth fills.

Anthropological models might be tested here in attempting to classify the Gordion animal figurines by function. M. M. Voigt's study (1983: 186-195) of the terracotta figurines from the Iranian site of Hajji Firuz Tepe is useful in this regard. Voigt (p. 190) suggests criteria based on the figurine's size and form on its method and place of disposal, and on its degree of wear or breakage patterns to indicate possible functions. Ethnohistoric and ethnographic sources form the basis for Voigt's categories.

Since our knowledge of Phrygian daily life, practices and belief systems is based on the archaeological finds, including some inscriptions which are very limited in content and in a largely undeciphered language (see Brixhe and Lejeune 1984), and on a small number of Assyrian, Greek and Latin literary sources which mention Phrygia or the Phrygians, it is difficult to back up a classification system for the Gordion figurines with historical sources. An ethnography of Yassıhöyük, the modern village around which the ancient site of Gordion lies, has been published (METU 1965), but little written information is available on the general accouterments of Anatolian daily life or rituals.

Voigt's basic functional categories for animal and human figurines (1983: 188) are as follows: (1) vehicles of magic—in the case of animals, used in rituals associated with fertility, success in agriculture or the hunt; (2) didactic figures; (3) toys (this probably applies to the small-scale terracotta figurines from Gordion). To judge from the number of depictions of domesticated animals, including yoked or harnessed quadrupeds, the first functional class probably encompasses most of the animal figurines from Gordion. The interest in the careful representation of the genitalia of two of the horses, making them identifiable as stallions (**143**, **144**), may suggest the function of these as vehicles for magic associated with fertility or as didactic models for instruction in animal husbandry. That some of these terracotta animal figurines were used as toys is likely but difficult to prove. The large number of animal vessels (see **1-5**), the wooden animals (TumP 106-114, 148-149) and a miniature bronze quadriga (TumP 40) in Tumulus P, a child's burial, suggest that animals were pleasing gifts for the deceased child and possibly playthings for the child in his or her lifetime. While it is possible to add a fourth category for terracotta figurines of the Late Phrygian/Hellenistic period, that of household bric-a-brac or decoration, it is unlikely that any of these animals served in this capacity.

ANIMALS: CENTRAL ANATOLIAN-MANUFACTURED

BRONZE AGE ANIMALS

115 Animal's Head
T 125   Trench PN-3, fallen earth to NW of Meg. 12
P.H. 0.043; P.Th. neck 0.018 m.
Pl. 33
Gunter 1991: 23, no. 81.

Single fragment of head and neck, broken across neck leaving irregular surfaces. Surface cracked and pitted with small irregular notches. Evidence of secondary burning on snout and neck.

Head and neck of animal with long neck and snout. Ears are two small bumps separated by flattened area. Interior solid. Handmade.

No slip.

Reddish brown, somewhat coarse clay with some inclusions. Surface smoothed with reddish yellow slip on exterior. Munsell: slip 5YR 7/6 (reddish yellow)-2.5YR N4/ (dark gray); core 2.5YR N3/ (very dark gray).

Central Anatolian-manufactured.

Early Bronze Age? (3000-2000 B.C.). This figurine comes from the edge of one of the trenches which reached Early Bronze Age levels.

Cf. Fischer 1963: 159, no. 1325, pl. 137, Boğazköy, from an unstratified context.

116 Quadruped
T 98   Trench M7A, pit in Floor 4
P.H. 0.033; P.L. 0.057; P.W. 0.033 m.
Pl. 33
Gunter 1991: 26, no. 101.

Single fragment preserving body, stumps of four legs and tail. Surface badly chipped and cracked. Body burned to dark gray-black.

Quadruped with thick-set, squarish body, four legs set apart and erect. Tail is thick, arching slightly and extended horizontally at break. Interior solid. Handmade.

No painted decoration. Surface is smooth as if polished, although burning has altered surface appearance.

Sandy dark brown clay fired dark gray-black (or burned?). Munsell: surface 2.5Y N3/ (very dark gray).

Central Anatolian-manufactured.

Context pottery is mixed with material as late as 4th-3d century B.C., but this animal has been assigned to the Early Bronze Age (3000-2000 B.C.) on the basis of its appearance (cf. Gunter 1991: 26, no. 101).

117 Horse's Head
P 4388   Trench CC3A, clay layer
P.H. 0.061; P.Depth 0.035 m.
Pl. 33
Gunter 1991: 84, no. 524.

Single fragment preserving head and neck, broken at lower neck. Missing tops of ears, chips from underside of muzzle, front of neck, right side at break, much of mane.

Horse's head with bridle. Head is short and small with ears applied to either side, thick section of mane between ears and down back of head. Bridle loops over muzzle in flattened band and crosses cheeks to behind head to meet at upper neck. Interior solid. Bottom surface concave for attachment to body of vessel or to hollow wheelmade body of statuette. Handmade.

Yellow-buff slip on exterior.

Slightly micaceous, gritty clay fired yellowish pink. Munsell: core 7.5YR 8/6 (reddish yellow).

Central Anatolian-manufactured.

Hittite, Old Kingdom or Empire period (1650-1200 B.C.), but found in Middle Phrygian clay deposit.

118 Horse's Head
T 43   Phrygian Gate, N Court, Cut B, top layer of clay
P.H. 0.06; P.W. 0.051; Th. 0.0325 m.
Pl. 33
Gunter 1991: 84, no. 523.

Single fragment preserving head and upper neck, lacking tips of ears, end of muzzle, chip off bridle at muzzle and across neck. Mane mostly missing.

Horse's head wearing bridle. Erect triangular ears are set low and close to head. Head is thick and short with bump on upper forehead. Bridle crosses muzzle as thick roll and cuts across cheeks. Above forehead bridle is rendered as two thin ridges looping from base of ears to between ears, meeting in low knob. Interior solid. Handmade.

Entire surface, except strip where mane is missing from neck, has thin buff slip.

Hard-fired, slightly micaceous gritty clay with tiny white and dark inclusions, fired light reddish brown. Munsell: 2.5YR 6/4 (light reddish brown).

Central Anatolian-manufactured.

Hittite, Old Kingdom or Empire period (1650-1200 B.C.), but found in Middle Phrygian fill.

119 Horse's Head
T 50   Trench Deep Cut 4, clay layer over Early Phrygian "Polychrome House"
P.H. 0.043; W. 0.02; Max.Depth 0.033 m.
Pl. 33
Gunter 1991: 84, no. 525.

Single fragment preserving head and neck of animal. Missing right ear, most of mane down back of head, part of muzzle strap. Surface chipped.

Horse's head with bridle. Head is short and muzzle is long and pointed. Triangular left ear stands up on head. Two punched holes on either side of central bridle strap mark eyes. Another smaller and deeper hole pierced through below left eye. Tiny hole is pierced through left nostril. Mane stands up as high ridge on lower neck. Bridle is applied over muzzle as flattened band and down front of face. Bottom of neck has concave finished surface. Interior solid. Handmade.

Surface slipped pink-buff.

Orange-red clay, lightly micaceous, hard-fired and filled with tiny sandy and gritty inclusions. Munsell: 2.5YR 6/8 (light red).

Central Anatolian-manufactured.

Hittite, Old Kingdom or Empire period (1650-1200 B.C.), but from Middle Phrygian context.

120 Ram's Head
T 111   Trench TB8-S3, in clay layer for Middle Phrygian rebuilding
P.H. 0.034; W. 0.032; P.Th. 0.021 m.
Pl. 33
Gunter 1991: 84, no. 522.

Single fragment preserving head broken off unevenly at neck. Surface chipped on right back side. Muzzle, underside of neck and right side of head slightly gray from burning.

Ram's head with long muzzle, flat on top and tapering to rounded tip. Horns are set on top of head, tightly curled into two raised coils with flat tops. Neck is flat on back side. Interior solid. Handmade.

No slip.

Gritty, lightly micaceous reddish orange clay with buff slip on exterior, fired buff on exterior. Munsell: core 2.5YR 6/8 (light red).

Central Anatolian-manufactured.

Hittite, Old Kingdom or Empire period (1650-1200 B.C.), but from Middle Phrygian fill.

This piece is probably a plastic attachment for a vessel. Another ram's head from this same period which is more certainly a plastic attachment is P 3329 (Gunter 1991: 62, no. 254).

Cf. Fischer 1963: 158, no. 1304, pl. 137, from fill in front of Hittite citadel gate on Büyükkale.

121 Bull's Head
   T 141   Küçük Hüyük, Tower 3, robbers' fill
   P.L. 0.028; W. 0.033; P.H. 0.020 m.
   Pl. 33

Single fragment preserving head including snout, one horn and one eye. Broken at top of neck.

Triangular head with short stubby cylindrical horns and added clay pellet eyes. Flattened nose has nostrils roughly indicated. Front of face and back of head are flat. Handmodeled.

range-buff slip over exterior.

Pale yellow-buff medium-coarse clay. Munsell: slip 10YR 7/3 (very pale brown); core 10YR 7/2 (light gray).

Central Anatolian-manufactured.

This animal comes from a context disturbed by ancient robbers, but the period of use of the Küçük Hüyük, ending ca. 550 B.C., provides the lower limits for the figurine. The style of the animal form, the color of the clay and the slip would be compatible with Hittite figurines of the Old Kingdom or Empire period (1650-1200 B.C.).

ANIMALS: LARGE QUADRUPEDS

122 Quadruped: Ungulate's Leg
   P 2611   Terrace Building 1
   P.H. 0.031; D. 0.019 m.
   Pl. 33
   Sams 1994: **1033**.

Single fragment broken above hoof.

Bottom of hoof broad and flattened with deep groove forming cleft. Thick leg flaring above to attachment. Handmade.

Vertical lines and ladders on leg in dark paint. Surface polished in vertical strokes.

Coarse clay, fired gray throughout.

Central Anatolian-manufactured.

Context allows date in Early Phrygian period (Early Phrygian Destruction level).

123 Large Quadruped: Horse's Head?
   T 30   Trench NCT-S, Section A, Cut 4b, Level 1c-2
   P.H. 0.06; P.L. 0.109; P.W. 0.047 m.
   Pl. 33

Single fragment preserving left side of head, broken at muzzle and top of neck. Surface of eyeball, harness, cheek and ears broken. Many surface chips.

Animal head, probably of horse, wearing harness. Horse has broad muzzle, large eye protruding from head, surrounded by groove and broad ridge. Harness is rendered in relief as wide rolled band over muzzle, forehead and cheek with knob at midpoint of cheek. Solid interior. Handmade, but probably attached to hollow wheelmade body.

Surface is slipped, polished and fired to dark red-maroon. Munsell: 10R 4/4 (weak red). Eye has ring of white and ring of black added over red.

Tan clay (Munsell: 7.5YR 7/4 [pink]) fired completely gray at core. Many dark and some lime inclusions. Some mica.

Central Anatolian-manufactured.

This animal head, like the comparable animals from Gordion (**124** and **125**), comes from a 4th-century or Late Phrygian/Hellenistic context. The red-maroon fired color of the polished slip combined with white and black additions is similar to the decoration of Middle Phrygian bichrome pottery, but not characteristic of the Late Phrygian/Hellenistic period. It is, therefore, possible that these bridled horses are remnants of the Middle Phrygian period from later contexts. For a Hittite animal of similar style see Fischer 1963: no. 1262, pl. 134.

124 Large Quadruped: Horse's Head?
   T 18   Trench SET-N, Cut 2F, Layer 2
   P.H. 0.041; P.W. 0.04; Th. walls at neck 0.005-0.007 m.
   Pl. 33

Single fragment preserving head and upper neck, missing muzzle, ears, entire surface of top of head. Surface chips and flakes missing.

Head of animal, probably horse, with thick neck and modeled jaws. Eyes are rendered as ovals with single incision producing slight ridge around convex eyeball. Interior solid. Handmade, probably for attachment to hollow, wheelmade body.

Surface is slipped, burnished unevenly and fired golden orange to red-brown. Munsell: 5YR 5/6 (yellowish red).

Pinkish brown clay with small amount of silver micaceous particles and gritty inclusions, fired silver-gray at core. Munsell: 7.5YR 6/4 (light brown).

Central Anatolian-manufacturd.

Comparable animal figurines are **123** and **125**. The pottery in this layer indicates that the context is no earlier than the late 4th or 3d century B.C.

125 Large Quadruped: Horse's Head?
   T 23   Trench SET-N, Cut N-4-D, Layer 4
   P.H. 0.042; P.L. 0.056; W. 0.022 m.
   Pl. 33

Single fragment preserving head and upper neck. Surface chipped on right and left sides of neck, along ridge of neck's underside and tip of muzzle.

Head of animal, probably horse, wearing harness. Muzzle describes long arching line from forehead with sharp ridge along line. Muzzle narrows considerably at mouth. Eyes are large ovals raised above plane of rest of head and set off by deep groove around perimeter. Small, triangular ears are laid back on head; forelock is swept back between ears; mane forms sharp ridge down back of neck. Harness is incised in front of ears, behind head and along sides of head to mouth. Interior solid. Handmade, probably originally attached to hollow, wheelmade body.

Surface is slipped, burnished and fired reddish brown.

Highly micaceous pink clay fired gray at core with many white lime inclusions. Munsell: 5YR 6/4 (light reddish brown).

Central Anatolian-manufactured.

See comparable animals: **123** and **124**.

The pottery in the stratum with the animal head indicates a date for the context no earlier than the 4th century B.C.

126 Large Quadruped: Ungulate's Leg
T 128   Tumulus F, Trench SW-NE, mantle fill
P.H. 0.035; W. hoof 0.026 m.
Pl. 33
Kohler, forthcoming: Tumulus F.

Single fragment of animal foot broken above hock.
Modeled leg splaying into split hoof with hock defined by two lumps. Solid interior. Handmade.
Hard gray ware, slipped and burnished. Munsell: core: 10YR 6/2 (light brownish gray); surface 10YR 4/1 (dark gray)-10 YR 3/1 (very dark gray).
Central Anatolian-manufactured.

This animal leg comes from the earth cover of Tumulus F, a cremation burial, which can be dated tentatively to ca. 630-615 B.C.

127 Large Quadruped: Ungulate's Foot
T 131   Below Tumulus E, Deep Cut V, E., level of bronze deposit and below
P.H. 0.06; P.W. 0.045 m.
Pl. 33

Single fragment of foot.
Animal foot with slightly concave sides and flat bottom. Short vertical groove spreading at floor indicates split hoof. Hock is defined behind. Handmade.
Burnished in vertical strokes.
Coarse clay fired gray to black on surface and gray at core with some fine white mica. Munsell: core 10YR 5/1 (gray); surface: 10YR 5/2 (grayish brown) to 3/1 (very dark gray).
Central Anatolian-manufactured.

This figurine comes either from the lowest fill over the houses over which the tumulus was constructed *or* from the upper fill of these houses. Tumulus E can be tentatively dated to the last quarter of the 6th century B.C. and, thus, the animal probably dates to this time or before (see Kohler, forthcoming: II, 2 for description of Tumulus E and analysis of its date).

128 Large Quadruped: Ungulate's Leg
T 127   Beneath Tumulus D, in Pit Z
P.H. 0.069; W. hoof 0.0235 m.
Pl. 33

Broken at attachment to body.
Round leg with slight incurve at front. Hoof split. Interior solid. Handmade.
Slipped and burnished.
Hard-fired yellow-buff ware. Munsell: core 7.5YR 6/4 (light brown); surface 10YR 7/3 (very pale brown).
Central Anatolian-manufactured.

Dates in or prior to period 550-450 B.C. (for context see **140**).

129 Large Quadruped: Ungulate's Leg
T 113   Trench SET-N, Layer 2
P.H. 0.044; W. 0.019; Th. 0.021 m.
Pl. 33

Single fragment preserving lower leg and portion of hoof. Surface chipped.

Animal leg, rectangular in section at top with flattish sides and ridge down front. Begins to flare out toward hoof with bulge at back to form hock. Interior solid. Handmade.
Exterior is slipped and polished unevenly, producing high sheen in orange-red over much of leg.
Clay is lightly micaceous with small black inclusions. Core is fired to charcoal gray with outer ring of buff-brown. Munsell: outer ring 7.5YR 6/4 (light brown).
Central Anatolian-manufactured.

Comparable animal legs: **131** and **132**.
Context pottery is mixed, Middle Phrygian to latest Late Phrygian/Hellenistic period at Gordion (189 B.C.).

130 Large Quadruped?: Bull's Horn?
T 142   Küçük Hüyük, Level 1
P.L. 0.075; D. base 0.020 m.
Pl. 33

Single fragment, broken at attachment to head.
Horn (?), perhaps of bull. Conical, slightly curved and circular in section. Interior solid. Hand-modeled, probably rolled in hand.
Matte black slip.
Coarse, dark gray clay with large inclusions including small chunks of flint. Munsell: slip 10YR 4/1 (dark gray); core 10YR 6/1 (gray).
Central Anatolian-manufactured.

Comes from mixed upper level with pottery ranging from 6th century B.C. to Roman period. Size of horn (?) indicates animal figurine of substantial size.

ANIMALS: LARGE QUADRUPEDS ATTACHED TO PLINTHS

131 Large Quadruped on Plinth: Ungulate's Leg
T 81   Trench WML-4M, Room A, Pit N, under Floor 6
P.H. 0.065; P.W. 0.022; Th. 0.032 m.
Pl. 34

Single fragment preserving lower leg and hoof to bottom. Surface of left front of hoof chipped off. Broken edge at left side of hoof as if base continues. Surface well preserved with few nicks.
Right foreleg of ungulate. Round in section, with two knobs projecting for hocks and concavity beneath. Hoof flares to side with front of hoof coming to point with applied pellet at right front. Deep vertical incision down front of hoof divides foot in half. Bottom of hoof is attached to flat base. Interior is solid. Handmade.
Surface of leg and hoof is slipped and burnished to high gloss, red-brown after firing.
Buff-pink, very lightly micaceous clay with lime inclusions. Munsell: 7.5YR 6/4 (light brown).
Central Anatolian-manufactured.

For comparable animal legs see **129** and **132**; the latter also rests on a plinth.
Datable pottery is no later than the second half of 6th century, possibly soon after 546 B.C.

132   Large Quadruped on Plinth: Ungulate's Leg
T 75   Trench WML-2E, Layer 4, SW quarter
P.H. 0.088; P.W. base 0.034; P.Depth 0.032 m.
Pl. 34

Single fragment preserving leg from upper thigh to bottom, right side front and small portion of bottom of base at right front corner. Chips around leg at top; surface missing halfway down back of leg and from bottom. Paint well preserved.

Right foreleg of animal, possibly bovine, attached to low rectangular plinth. Leg is modeled with wide thigh, narrowing with flat sides, convex curve for knee. Hoof projects forward in lump to front of base, merging with top and sides of low (H. 0.012 m.) rectangular base. Interior solid. Handmade.

Leg and hoof are covered with thick white groundcoat, polished to smooth surface. Hoof is covered with matte red paint. Top and sides of base are painted with same matte red as hoof. Streak or thin line of red down outside of leg. Inside back of leg mostly unslipped. Bottom of base unpainted.

Fine, light red clay; slightly micaceous with tiny light inclusions. Munsell: 2.5YR 6/8 (light red). Surface slipped with fine orange-red clay.

Central Anatolian-manufactured.

Similar ungulates' legs on animals: **129** and **131**.

In the same layer with the animal leg was a bronze coin of Alexander III (330-315 B.C.).

ANIMALS: YOKED OR HARNESSED QUADRUPEDS

133   Yoked (?) Quadruped
T 82   Trench D2b, Building D, in cleaning Floor 4
P.H. 0.02, W. 0.015; Th. 0.016 m.
Pl. 34

Single fragment preserving upper body and head of animal, lacking tips of front legs, chip from back of strap and back half of body.

Animal with applied strap on back, perhaps harness or yoke. Head is pointed at top and at muzzle with small projections at right and left sides for ears or horns. Neck is thick, widening toward body. Two legs are applied at sides and curve out from body. Handmade.

No painted decoration or polish over well-smoothed surface.

Fine pink-orange clay, light gray at core, covered with buff slip. Munsell: 5YR 7/6 (reddish yellow).

Central Anatolian-manufactured.

This animal figurine comes from a 6th-century B.C. context and may belong to a plowing cart or chariot group.

134   Harnessed (?) Quadruped: Horse?
T 11   Trench SWT, Section C, Cut 17, Level 1
P.H. 0.040; P.L. 0.051; W. body 0.025 m.
Pl. 34

Single fragment preserving neck and back of head, stumps of four legs and three-quarters of body.

Four-legged animal, probably horse, with upright neck, small head and body which balloons toward rear. Interior solid except for large hole (D. 0.009 m.) through animal's rear forming hollow inside back half of body. Handmade with extra layer of clay applied very unevenly to left flank and other areas.

Traces of bright orange paint on entire body, especially well preserved on underside.

Very hard-fired, lightly micaceous brown clay, fired gray at core. No clean breaks to allow Munsell test.

Central Anatolian-manufactured.

Although this quadruped comes from a Roman-period context, it is likely to be Middle or Late Phrygian/Hellenistic in date. The hole into the interior of the body and the layer of clay applied unevenly to the exterior might suggest that a rider or a harness was attached, perhaps as part of a chariot group.

135   Harnessed Quadruped: Horse?
T 92   Trench TBT-CC1, fill between Floors 1 and 1B
P.H. 0.055; P.L. 0.06; P.W. 0.036 m.
Pl. 34

Single fragment preserving body, left foreleg, upper right foreleg, stumps of hind legs and tail. Missing neck and head. Paint flaking off.

Quadruped, probably horse, with applied strap, perhaps harness, across rump; long front legs; thick body, rectangular in section; wide rump and tail. Legs are thick and erect, set wide apart in front and back. Left leg turns out into flattened surface at hoof. Handmade.

Brown-black paint over entire animal. On back behind neck is brown dot.

Very fine, lightly micaceous, light red clay with brown ring around exterior. Munsell: 2.5YR 6/6 (light red).

Central Anatolian-manufactured.

Pottery indicates a date no earlier than the 4th century B.C. for the stratum.

The horse (?) may have been attached to a plinth, as suggested by the treatment of the left hoof, and thus may have been part of a chariot group.

ANIMALS: WHEELED QUADRUPED

136   Wheeled Quadruped: Horse Pull-Toy
T 129   Trench ETV-1 and -2, Building C between Floors 2 and 3
H. 0.059; L. 0.061; Max.W. 0.029 m.
Pl. 34

Single fragment preserving hindquarters of horse, broken at mid-body, tail and right rear leg.

Pull-toy in form of stylized horse with hind legs pierced for attachment of wheels. Back has sharp ridge; tail is round in section; rear legs are plank-like and squared at bottom. Handmade with evidence of tooling with knife.

Traces of red slip or paint (Munsell: 10R 6/6 [light red]-5/6 [red]) on hindquarters and tail, although not on lower legs. Lightly polished.

Light orange to red clay with small inclusions, mostly black. Munsell: core 5YR 6/6 (reddish yellow); surface 5YR 7/6 (reddish yellow).

Central Anatolian-manufactured.

The second period of Building C from which this pull-toy comes dates to the latter part of the 6th century B.C. and the building lasts possibly to the late 5th century B.C. (see description of Building C in R. S. Young 1955: 6-8, esp. 8).

ANIMALS: OTHER QUADRUPEDS

137 Quadruped
    T 21   Beneath Tumulus H, Pit 2, below House I, Level A
    P.L. 0.048; P.W. 0.0265; D. body at break 0.017 m.
    Pl. 34
    Anderson 1980: 14, 348, no. 161.

Single fragment preserving head, neck and upper portion of forelegs. Missing tips of ears, chip of muzzle and surface chips.

Animal, probably bull with erect head, long flat muzzle, widely spaced ears and long thick neck. Solid interior. Handmade.

Surface is black polished to medium sheen in Phrygian technique.

Pinkish brown clay, lightly micaceous with small white gritty inclusions, fired to dark gray-black surface. Munsell: core 7.5YR 6/2 (pinkish gray).

Central Anatolian-manufactured.

The burial in Tumulus H is dated by an East Greek bird bowl to ca. 650 B.C. or later (Kohler 1995, 48-49). House I beneath the tumulus probably spans the Early and Middle Phrygian periods and lies, as do all the houses in this area, on top of a Hittite-period cemetery. The black polished surface of this animal makes it unlikely to date to the Bronze Age and, therefore, the figurine can probably be dated to the Early or Middle Phrygian period.

138 Quadruped
    T 79   Clay deposit under Building C
    P.L. 0.048; P.H. 0.022; P.W. 0.015 m.
    Pl. 34

Single fragment preserving body, beginning of neck, stumps of tail and four legs. Nicks on surface.

Long-bodied quadruped with neck extended forward and downward-curving tail. Handmade.

No painted decoration. Partially polished?

Hard-fired pinkish brown, very slightly micaceous clay with tiny dark inclusions. Munsell: 5YR 6/4 (light reddish brown).

Central Anatolian-manufactured.

The context suggests a date for this animal no later than the mid-6th century B.C. A much earlier date than the 6th century is, however, possible.

139 Quadruped
    T 41   E-W Trench, Gate Building W, beside Building B, in clay fill
    P.L. 0.037; P.H. 0.024; W. 0.017 m.
    Pl. 34

Single fragment preserving body and head, lacking lower parts of legs, tip of tail, back of head, all of left ear and part of right ear. Surface burned black with cracking on head.

Quadruped with round body, sagging belly, raised ridge on back, downward-arching tail, thick neck, short rounded muzzle and ears or horns set at sides of head. Handmade.

Slight traces of burnishing on outside of left foreleg.

Tannish or yellowish orange clay with small dark inclusions. No Munsell reading possible.

Central Anatolian-manufactured.

The clay fill from which this animal comes was probably laid down in the first half of the 6th century B.C. to raise the level of the gateway for the construction of a new fortification gateway. The clay fill also contained earlier material, dug up from other places on the mound.

140 Quadruped: Stag?
    T 17   Beneath Tumulus D, in Pit Z
    P.H. 0.042; P.L. 0.082; W. body 0.015 m.
    Pl. 34

For description of Tumulus D and contents: Kohler, forthcoming; initial report of excavation of Tumulus D: R. S. Young 1952: 20; 1953: 30.

Single fragment preserving head and body; lacking upper portions of ears or antlers, end of muzzle, four legs, end of tail. Surface chips on body. Partially burned, especially heavily on left side of body.

Four-legged animal, possibly stag, with flat-sided, erect ears or antlers; separately applied pierced circles for eyes; long muzzle with two holes pierced for nostrils; long, thick neck; round body with arching tail. Interior solid. Handmade.

Slipped and burnished to high gloss over uneven surface.

Pink-brown clay, lightly micaceous and fired to dark-brown surface. No clear surface to test Munsell color.

Central Anatolian-manufactured.

140 comes from the same pit as **128**, although they do not belong to the same figurine. The context for these two animals, in the cremation burials over which Tumulus D was built, allows a *terminus ante quem* for both figurines of 550-450 B.C. Comparable treatment of the eyes is seen on a plastic attachment from Gordion (P 3491) which can be dated prior to the 4th century B.C. from context.

141 Quadruped
    T 114   Trench SET-N, Building A, Layer 5, W of Wall E
    P.H. 0.046; P.L. 0.060; P.W. 0.043 m.
    Pl. 34

Single fragment preserving back half of body, upper portion of hind legs and stump of tail.

Quadruped with round body, arching buttocks and tail. Interior solid. Handmade.

No slip, burnish or painted decoration.

Lightly micaceous brown clay with small grit inclusions, fired charcoal gray on surface, darker on lower flanks and stumps of legs.

Central Anatolian-manufactured.

The animal comes from a layer which was probably laid down in the first half of the 6th century B.C.

142 Quadruped
T 94   Trench T-E1, Layer 6
P.H. 0.031; P.L. 0.072; P.W. 0.029 m.
Pl. 34

Single fragment of body, missing neck, four legs, tail and lower legs. Paint well preserved.

Quadruped with long thick body and tail appended to top of rump, held horizontally at break. Four legs set squarely. Interior solid. Handmade.

Upper body and tail are painted with narrow hatched lines in orange and polished.

Hard-fired, pinkish orange, lightly micaceous fine clay. Munsell: 5YR 7/4 (pink)-7/6 (reddish yellow).

Central Anatolian-manufactured.

Closely comparable in clay and painted decoration is **50**. From Erythrai is a probably East Greek horse figurine with crosshatched painted decoration (Bayburtluoğlu 1977: no. 64, pl. 36). This animal figurine (**142**) was found in a layer with a 5th-century black glazed lamp and black-polished wares.

143 Quadruped: Stallion
T 112   Trench M12-E, Layer 10
P.H. 0.032; P.L. 0.055; W. 0.024 m.
Pl. 34

Single fragment lacking neck and head, right foreleg, surface of rear right flank, left foreleg, other small chips, especially tips of hind legs.

Stallion standing with legs spread apart. Tail arches away from buttocks. Appended to belly toward back legs is small round pellet to represent penis. Interior solid. Handmade.

No slip, painted decoration or polishing.

Lightly micaceous, gritty brownish clay fired light gray all over. No Munsell reading.

Central Anatolian-manufactured.

The latest datable pottery in this layer is no earlier than the mid-4th century B.C.

144 Quadruped: Stallion
T 107   Trench TB8-S2, Layer 1, ashy fill in oven
P.H. 0.036; P.L. 0.059; P.W. 0.023 m.
Pl. 34

Single fragment lacking forelegs, left hind leg and tip of right hind leg, tail, left ear, tip of forelock, most of genitals and small chips.

Horse standing with four legs spread. Head narrow and pointed, tapering to snout with no definition of eyes or mouth. Ears are small, pointed projections, mane is sharp ridge from top of head down back of neck. Back is flattish with body narrowing sharply in middle before widening and arching at rump. Genitals are partially preserved on underside of belly toward rear. Handmade.

Exterior slipped matte red-orange (Munsell: 2.5YR 5/8 [red]). Surface texture of paint is rough.

Fine, lightly micaceous yellow-orange clay (Munsell: 7.5YR 7/8 [reddish yellow]) fired browner below surface (Munsell: 7.5YR 7/4 [pink]).

Central Anatolian-manufactured.

Context can be dated to Late Phrygian/Hellenistic period.

145 Quadruped: Ungulate's Legs
T 124   Trenches NCT-A3 and ET-O5, over NW corner of Building C
P.H. 0.047; W. 0.030 m.
Pl. 35

Single fragment preserving lower portion of legs broken at knees. Bottom of one leg and hoof broken; chips in vertical support on back; bottom surface irregular.

Lower legs, hocks and hooves of bull or goat. Well-modeled musculature. At back at juncture of legs is upright cylindrical member (support?). Interior solid. Handmade.

Traces of white groundcoat on back of both legs and support.

Highly micaceous buff-brown clay fired gray at core. Munsell: core 7.5YR 6/4 (light brown)-10YR 5/1 (gray)-5YR 6/6 (reddish yellow); surface 7.5YR 6/4 (light brown).

Central Anatolian-manufactured.

Context can be dated after late 5th century B.C., probably 4th century B.C.

146 Quadruped's Legs
T 57   Terracotta Deposit 5 (see pp. 67-69)
P.H. 0.069; W. legs 0.047; P.W. top break 0.03 m.
Pl. 35

Single fragment preserving two hind legs broken off at top of rump and juncture with body.

Hind legs of quadruped. Outsides of legs are flat with legs tapering to blunt-ended, narrow hooves. Handmade.

Traces of white groundcoat or incrustation (?) on legs. Two tiny traces of red paint on outside of right leg.

Lightly micaceous yellow-buff clay with few inclusions. Munsell: 10YR 7/3 (very pale brown).

Central Anatolian-manufactured.

147 Quadruped
T 97   Trench M5B, big pit in Level 1 and below
P.H. 0.035; P.L. 0.101; W. 0.031 m.
Pl. 35

Single fragment preserving body, missing neck and head, four legs and tail. Surface chipped and glaze flaked.

Quadruped with long body, round in section. Neck rises at right angle to body. Four legs are set in standing position. Interior solid. Handmade.

Slashes cut across back in short, shallow strokes. Over white groundcoat thick vitreous glaze is applied. Over back, neck and legs is light green with diagonal stripes of black-brown along sides of body. Brown blobs on front of chest. Underside of body and inside of hind leg are glazed blue-green over lighter green.

Hard-fired, pinkish orange, lightly micaceous clay with few light inclusions. Munsell: 2.5YR 6/6-6/8 (light red).

Anatolian-manufactured?

A medieval date (probably 9th-14th centuries A.D.) is indicated for this animal by the type of glaze. Other green-glazed Byzantine pottery fragments were found in the same pit.

148 Lion's Paw
T 29   Trench SET-NW, Cut 1c, Layer 3
P.L. 0.085; P.W. 0.077; Th. 0.04-0.047 m.
Pl. 35

Single fragment broken at both ends. Surface chipped. Green discoloration.

Large, rounded fragment of lion's paw and foreleg, possibly primary archetype for mold producing lion's-foot attachments. Oval in section, fragment widens at one end with two raised areas resembling claws. Solid interior. Handmade.

Surface is partially slipped with pink-buff clay and polished.

Hard-fired, orange-red clay turned gray at core with many lime and small grit inclusions. Munsell 10YR 6/8 (light red).

Central Anatolian-manufactured.

This fragment comes from a stratum with the latest datable pottery belonging to the early 3d century B.C.

ANIMALS: BIRDS

149 Bird
T 93   Trench M4-C, small pit in Floor 4
P.H. 0.04; P.L. 0.047; P.W. 0.05 m.
Pl. 35

Single fragment preserving back, beginning of neck and legs. Missing tip of tail, top of neck and head, tip of right wing. Surface well preserved.

Stylized bird with flat, triangular body with incised pattern on top. Neck begins to rise from back at oblique angle. Legs are wide and flat on sides with ends widening toward front and back. Two legs are separated from each other by arching hollow area. Handmade.

On top surface is incised pattern composed of large diamond in center within which is smaller diamond divided into four squares. To right and left of diamond are two triangles. No painted decoration. Body and neck burnished to high sheen.

Fine clay fired light gray with few visible inclusions. No Munsell reading.

Central Anatolian-manufactured.

Late Phrygian/Hellenistic pottery on Floor 4 suggests a probably late 4th- to early 2d-century B.C. date for the context, but the gray polishing of the bird may indicate an earlier date for the figurine.

150 Bird
P 4247   Trench PPB-SE5, under Floor 3
P.H. 0.042; W. 0.021; P.Th. 0.023 m.
Pl. 35

Single fragment preserving lower body of bird; lacking head and upper neck, tail and tip of left leg.

Bird sitting in upright position with tail support. Body is circular in section, with irregular convex sides. Tail fans out in back and turns up at break. In front are two peg-legs with hollow between. Bottom of body and tail is flat. Interior is solid. Handmade.

Body is painted in orange with irregular crosshatched lines. Large stripe is painted down back at center and horizontal stripes are painted down right and left sides of body. In front on breast is confusing mass of painted lines.

Fine, hard-fired lightly micaceous light pink-orange clay. Munsell: 5YR 7/4 (pink)-7/6 (reddish yellow).

Central Anatolian-manufactured.

142 is comparable in clay and crosshatched painted decoration. **156** has same clay and similar design, though paint is black on white groundcoat.

Context pottery on the floor above includes rouletted black-glazed wares and can be dated to the 4th century B.C. This figurine may belong to the 4th century or earlier.

151 Bird
T 133   Trench ET-O5, Balk
P.H. 0.047; P.W. 0.020 m.
Pl. 35

Single fragment of head, broken at beak and base of neck.

Bird, possibly goose or dove, with cylindrical neck curving and tapering to beak. Eyes incised. Handmade.

White groundcoat all over with vertical red stripes on back of neck, vertical red band on front of neck, incised eyes with red paint.

Fine light brown clay with micaceous particles. Munsell: core 7.5YR 6/4 (light brown)-10YR 6/4 (light yellowish brown); surface 10YR 6/2 (light brownish gray); paint 2.5Y 8/2 (white) and 2.5YR 5/8 (red)-5/4 (reddish brown).

Central Anatolian-manufactured.

The balk contained a range of material of the 4th century B.C., but the figurine may be earlier.

152 Bird
T 132   Trench ET, Layer 2, Sections 4, 4b, 4c
P.H. 0.041; P.L. 0.033; P.W. 0.025 m.
Pl. 35

Single fragment preserving body of bird broken at neck and legs. Surface worn.

Bird with rounded body and flattish sides, tapering to neck. Body bulges toward legs. Probably handmade.

Polished red.

Fine reddish orange clay, fired gray at core with few fine white inclusions. Munsell: core 7.5YR 6/4 (light brown); surface 2.5YR 5/6 (red).

Central Anatolian-manufactured.

Pottery indicates a date for the context no earlier than the second half of the 4th century B.C.

ANIMALS: IMPORTS

153 Plaque: Bull
T 110   Trench PBX-E, Level 4b, clearing N wall of house
P.H. 0.104; W. 0.095; L. 0.07; Th. walls 0.007-0.013 m.
Pl. 35

Single fragment of plaque preserving left side of head, neck and beginning of body. Left horn, left ear, tip of muzzle and surface fragment at lower break missing. Slip almost completely missing.

Relief plaque of bull with head and body in left profile. Head is small and well modeled. Horn set at right angle to head; ear laid back on neck behind horn; left eye is puncture in convex surface, nostril is deep hole. Cheek and neck have rippled surface; large fatty mass hangs below chin. On interior, edges are raised flat surfaces and surface is concave. Moldmade.

Traces of white groundcoat survive on exterior and edge of interior.

Reddish pink slip over surface of exterior. Slightly micaceous, very gritty clay fired unevenly pink and gray at core. Munsell: near surface 2.5YR 6/6 (light red)-10YR 5/8 (red).

Greek-manufactured.

The pottery in this level is consistently 4th-century B.C. to Late Phrygian/Hellenistic.

154 Cock?
T 126   Trench TB-E2-S2b Floor 3
H. 0.032; L. 0.064; W. 0.014 m.
Pl. 35

Single fragment preserving some of head, much of neck, body and tail of bird with much of surface missing. Bottom totally broken away.

Bird, perhaps cock, with small, plump body, long neck, small head and broad arching tail. Interior solid. Handmade.

Fugitive red paint on head, back and tail (in bands?); yellow on neck.

Light buff clay with black core. Munsell: core 10YR 5/1 (gray) -7.5YR 6/4 (light brown); surface 10YR 7/3 (very pale brown); paint 10R 5/6 (red) and 10YR 7/8 (yellow).

Probably Greek-manufactured.

The cock is from the same context as **94**, a Hellenistic female head, but possibly earlier in date to judge from technique and style.

155 Dove?
T 85   Trench PN, Layer 2
P.H. 0.065; P.L. 0.072; W. 0.037; D. base 0.025 m.
Pl. 35

Single fragment preserving body of bird on base; missing end of tail, head and fragments from right side of base. Surface well preserved.

Bird, possibly dove, on conical base. Bird stands with neck erect and wings folded. Long tail is held in horizontal position. On back and wings are incised lines for feathers. Instead of legs bird has conical base with small hollow shaft beneath. Interior is solid. Probably handmade.

No painted decoration.

Fine, lightly micaceous yellow-red clay, fired gray at core. Munsell: 5YR 7/8 (reddish yellow). Surface covered with fine slip, fired brownish orange.

Greek-manufactured.

Similar dove in Delos Museum from deposit in Heraion (no inv. no.).

Also found with the bird were a figurine of Kybele (**62**) and a coin of Alexander the Great. The pottery in this layer belongs to the Late Phrygian/Hellenistic period (ca. 3d century B.C.), but this dove belongs stylistically to the 5th or 4th century B.C.

Miscellaneous (156-171)

MISCELLANEOUS: VEHICLES AND WHEELS

The precise function of these model chariots (or carts) and wheels is not known. Their uses may be linked to those of the animal figurines, to which some of the vehicles may have been attached (see p. 49 above). Functions as votives or funerary gifts are also possibilities. In Greek practice a wagon was used to transport the corpse in the ekphora to the tomb or place of cremation (see Kurtz and Boardman 1971).

Four-wheeled wooden wagons were found in two of the 6th-century Phrygian tumuli with cremation burials at Gordion (Tumuli A and E; see Kohler, forthcoming). These are presumably the vehicles by which the burial gifts and funeral participants were brought to the site of the cremation pyre. The horses were unhitched and removed from the site and the wagon was buried under the tumulus along with the gifts and burned body. The significance of the wagons in the tombs was probably limited to their use as objects of everyday life which might, therefore, be needed in the afterlife. Also, a miniature quadriga group in bronze was recovered from Tumulus P at Gordion (R. S. Young 1981: 21-26, TumP 40).

Miniature chariots with charioteers are found in great numbers at the Cypriote Sanctuary of Apollo Hylates at Kourion (J. H. and S. H. Young 1955: esp. 29-30), where their use as votives is clear. That these charioteers and also riders on horseback symbolized persons of prestige who were bringing themselves before the god is speculated by the Youngs. If votives, these wheeled vehicles from Gordion may suggest images of agricultural plenty (if carts or wagons) or success in warfare (if chariots) and may have been presented to a deity at a private shrine.

Whatever their meaning, the animal figurines and the vehicle fragments when examined as a corpus mirror the types of Greek votive material, including terracottas from Early Iron Age contexts (see Nicholls 1970). It is unclear whether this correspondence (of, e.g., the quadrupeds on plinths and the animals attached to vehicles) directly evolves from Early Greek contacts with the Central Anatolians. None of the animals and only one of the wheels (**159**) can be placed in the Early Phrygian period. The majority in both categories can be assigned Middle Phrygian dates.

156 Model Chariot
T 80   Trench TBT-2, clearing E-W wall overlying House N
H. 0.062, L. 0.105; W. 0.099; Th. walls 0.003-0.013 m.
Pl. 36

Joined from eight fragments preserving 90% of vehicle. Missing back left corner, front left edge, upper right side and numerous chips from front, back and inside. On inside at front is broken stump. Surface and paint well preserved.

Square model chariot with three straight sides, open back and rectangular "post," possibly lower part of rider or seat, set off center to right inside back edge. At front, applied to bottom of vehicle is pierced tang for attachment of chariot pole (?). On each side is applied curving piece of clay pierced for attachment of wheel's axle. Floor of chariot on inside is unevenly smoothed by hand. Bottom is flat. Handmade.

White groundcoat covers exterior of sides and back of rider or seat inside chariot. Over white is applied streaky black-brown matte paint. On front side is lattice pattern composed of seven horizontal lines crossed by ten verticals, forming irregular squares. On right and left sides is similar pattern, less carefully executed. Post inside vehicle on back is painted over white with four thin horizontal bands. Interior of sides, floor and underside are all unpainted. Paint and white groundcoat have worn off in circle around axle hole from turning of wheel.

Pink-orange, very light micaceous fine clay with few inclusions, fired slightly gray at core. Munsell: 2.5YR 5/6 (red).

Central Anatolian-manufactured.

The clay and the lattice design are close to **142** and **150**.

Pottery suggests a 4th-century or Late Phrygian/Hellenistic date for the context, but the chariot is most likely earlier in date.

157 Miniature Cart or Chariot
   MC 151   Trench EML-2E, Layer 2
   P.H. 0.055; W. 0.117 m.
   Pl. 36

Single fragment preserving corner and part of base and sides.

Miniature cart or chariot with concave interior surface, slightly flaring sides with scalloped rim. Handmade.

Flat upper surface of rim is reserved with spiral-like decoration in purplish red. Red paint inside and on undersurface.

Micaceous buff clay. Munsell: core 10YR 6/3 (pale brown); surface 10YR 7/3 (very pale brown); paint 10R 6/6 (light red) and 7.5R 4/4 (weak red).

Central Anatolian-manufactured.

Cf. **156**, a model chariot.

The layer from which the object comes can be dated to the Late Phrygian/Hellenistic period, but the cart or chariot is likely to be earlier.

158 Painted Panel
   T 37   Trench ET-O3, mixed fill and clay, below Floor 2
   P.L. 0.071; P.W. 0.051; P.Th. 0.021; Th. walls 0.008-0.011 m.
   Pl. 36

Single rectangular fragment preserving front painted surface, one corner and small portion of one side. Paint well preserved.

Slightly convex rectangular panel for chariot (?) with raised flat border along two edges and rounded molding at break on one edge and turning corner to side. Oval hole is pierced through at top middle of fragment. Interior is hollow, carefully smoothed. Handmade.

Entire exterior surface is covered with white groundcoat. Large wide matte red-orange X decorates center of panel. Exterior is polished lightly. Borders of central panel are black on light wash. Along one raised border are small brown Xs. Molding is painted brown. Side is slipped white with uneven line of black along edge of molding.

Very hard-fired, lightly micaceous clay with small light inclusions fired buff-gray at core. Munsell: 2.5YR 7/2 (light gray) but no clean broken surface to test.

Central Anatolian-manufactured.

While the polishing technique and painting style are clearly Phrygian characteristics, the use of this panel is not certain (possibly a fragment of a chariot).

A date after the early 4th century B.C. is suggested for material in the fill.

159 Miniature Wheel?
   MC 264   Trench Z1, Phrygian clay overlying Early Phrygian Building V and area to N/NE
   D. 0.058; D. hole 0.009; Th. 0.009 m.
   Pl. 36

Complete. Worn on outer edge and inside of hole.

Flat disk pierced through slightly off center. Probably cut from sherd. Hand-tooled.

Orange slip or wash over exterior.

Coarse gritty clay with sandy temper. Hand-finished and fired gray-white at core. No Munsell reading.

Central Anatolian-manufactured.

The slightly off-center hole indicates its probable use was not that of a spindle whorl. The signs of wear on the edges and inside the hole would be compatible with its function as a miniature wheel for a wagon, cart, chariot or wheeled animal.

The clay fill from which this wheel comes can be dated prior to the early 7th century B.C. (pre-Kimmerian Phrygian).

160 Miniature Wheel
   MC 212   Trench M5E, S Cellar
   D. 0.075; Th. through axle holes 0.038 m.
   Pl. 36
   R. S. Young 1966: 268-269.

Complete except chips from edges and surface.

Lentoid wheel for wagon, cart, chariot or wheeled animal with uneven thin edges. Raised collars in center of each side are pierced for axle. Wheelmade?

Polished to gray-black on surface.

Fine brownish gray clay. No Munsell reading.

Central Anatolian-manufactured.

The South Cellar building from which this wheel comes goes out of use in the 5th or 4th century B.C. but has material ranging in date from the 8th century down to ca. 400 B.C. (Sams 1971: 184; but see also R. S. Young 1966: 268-269).

161 Miniature Wheel
   T 108   Trenches M7-F and WS-10, Layer 6b
   D. 0.09; H. 0.043; Th. wheel 0.004-0.008; D. axle holes 0.008 m.
   Pl. 36

Single fragment preserving both hubs and ca. one-quarter of wheel. Chips missing from edge.

Miniature wheel for model wagon, cart or chariot, pierced through for axle. Handmade.

Exterior is covered with purplish red paint and polished to smooth finish.

Tannish brown clay with gold micaceous particles, grit and other dark and light inclusions, fired gray at core. Munsell: near surface 7.5YR 6/4 (light brown).

Central Anatolian-manufactured.

Pottery dates this layer no earlier than the 5th century B.C. The polished red-painted surface is most common on Phrygian pottery of the Middle Phrygian period, but also occurs in the Early Phrygian period. Gold micaceous clay is characteristic of both Phrygian and West Anatolian pottery.

MISCELLANEOUS: BOOTS OR SHOES

The specific meaning and use of the boots or shoes from Gordion is unclear. Boot-shaped vessels or shoes of statuettes are known from Central Anatolia in the Bronze Age (e.g., Metropolitan Museum of Art, New York, 67.182.2, ca. 1900-1600 B.C.; from Boğazköy, Fischer 1963: 79-80, pl. 131{1238-1243}; from Alişar Hüyük, von der Osten and Schmidt 1932: 37, Abb. 28{1106, 1533}; von der Osten 1937: 174, Abb. 216{C730, D1119, D2756}; see also Bittel et al. 1967: 111 ff. [Hittite examples]; Mellink 1956: 12, 40 ff., 23a-d [shoe-shaped amulet from Hittite cemetery at Gordion]), in the Iron Age (at Kululu near Kültepe, Özgüç 1971: 101, pl. 34{1a-b}) and from Kamir-Blur in Urartia in the 8th century B.C. (Piotrovsky 1969: pls. 47-48). The Anatolian examples are all from settlement sites with the exception of the amulet from the Hittite cemetery at Gordion.

In Greece vessels in the form of shoes or boots appear in tomb contexts: e.g., in Geometric graves in Eleusis (Skia 1898: Taf. 4{4}; 1912: 36, Abb. 16) and in the Athenian Agora (H. A. Thompson 1948a: pl. 54B; R. S. Young 1949: pls. 70-71). At Lefkandi in Euboea, a vessel of uncertain origin with a strutted handle terminating in a boot was excavated in a tomb with Late Protogeometric vases (Catling 1981-82: 16, fig. 30). Model or real shoes in funerary practice probably served in the last journey of the deceased (Kurtz and Boardman 1971: 211). Three 9th-century B.C. examples of probably Corinthian origin from the sanctuary of Poseidon at Isthmia are, however, unrelated to funerary ritual (Mitten 1978).

Unguentaria in the form of shoes are manufactured on Rhodes and other East Greek sites in the 6th century B.C. (Higgins 1959: nos. 1650, 1651, 1655-1658) and in Sicily in imitation of East Greek types (*ibid*.: 47, no. 1680, pl. 33). From the East Greek site of Pitane (Çandarlı) comes an aryballos in the shape of a boot with an elaborate handle which probably dates to the 6th century B.C. (on exhibit in Izmir Archaeological Museum). A Chian boot comes from the harbor sanctuary site at Emborio (Boardman 1967: 198, no. 83, pl. 77), is probably of local Chian manufacture and belongs to the late 7th/early 6th century B.C. In this case it is clear that the small boot, decorated with white slip and brown-black glaze for laces, is not a vessel but the booted foot of a large figure.

Of the Gordion examples, only two, because of their open form and hollow interiors, could possibly be identified as vessels (**167** and **168**) but that identification is highly dubious. The roughly finished interior walls would suggest that the use of these boots or shoes was not that of vessels. All of the other boots or shoes are solid with holes or irregular openings in the upper surfaces (except the earliest and smallest of them, **162**) as if for attachment to something. That the Phrygian boots or shoes belong to large-scale terracotta figures (e.g., the Lydian exhibitionist from Sardis [Greenewalt 1971: 29 ff.]) is also unlikely. No fragments of large-scale human figures from the Early or Middle Phrygian period have been recovered from Gordion, none of these shoes form a pair, and the irregular bottom surfaces of most of the shoes or boots would not provide a sturdy resting surface for a freestanding human figure. The only other possible identification for some of these boots (the ones with solid interiors) is as attachments, perhaps as the feet of terracotta tripod stands or other exceptional vessels. An 8th-century Iranian example, probably from Hasanlu, of such a vessel is in the collection of The University Museum, Philadelphia (83-2-1).

To judge from context, polished or painted decoration and form, the shoes or boots from Gordion represent a range in dates. The smallest of the boots can be dated prior to the Kimmerian destruction of Gordion (**162**); its brown surface, polishing technique and upturned toe suggest a Bronze Age date and an identification as Hittite. One boot comes from a pit with 6th- and 5th-century pottery (**163**), another comes from a context which can be dated no earlier than the second half of the 5th century B.C. (**167**). The other four boots were recovered from 5th-century to Late Phrygian/Hellenistic contexts, two from pits (**164** and **168**). To judge from the technique and decoration, the majority of these boots, even those from late contexts, are probably survivals from previous centuries and can be dated in the Middle Phrygian period.

162 Boot
P 4157   Trench TBT-8, S3, terrace fill over Meg. 8
L. 0.037; W. 0.018; P.H. 0.021 m.
Pl. 37

Single fragment broken across at ankle height. Traces of burning (?) on one side.

Plain boot or shoe with upturned toe. Contour of sole is plain oval. Ridge from toe to ankle in front. Interior solid with no hole in upper surface. Handmade.

Slipped and polished and fired to brown.
Clay fired light gray-brown throughout.
Central Anatolian-manufactured.

The context clearly indicates a date for this boot before the Kimmerian destruction of Gordion in the early 7th century. The brown polished decoration and the upturned toe of the boot are similar to examples of boots from Boğazköy which date to the Hittite Old Kingdom or Empire period (1650-1200 B.C.) (Fischer 1963: 79-80, pl. 131{1238-1243, esp. no. 1239}).

163 Boot
    T 38   Trench ET-V2, Pit 5
    P.H. 0.079; L. 0.126; Max.W. ankle 0.041 m.
    Pl. 37 and Color Pl. II

Single fragment preserving entire foot and lower ankle, broken above ankle. Paint well preserved.

Right boot with upturned pointed toe with bump on tip. Contour of foot is long and narrow with high arching instep and narrow heel. Through top broken surface is large irregular hole (L. 0.023; W. 0.016; D. 0.043 m.). Boot swells to sharply convex bump at midpoint between toe and ankle. Surface of sole is slightly convex and does not provide stable resting surface. Through bottom of sole is long slit (L. 0.03 m.) which runs lengthwise and is cut through to hollow section in toe of boot and which in turn connects with large hole in ankle by narrow passage. Handmade.

Sole is painted with white groundcoat defined around contour of boot by thin matte black line. On tip of toe protuberance is painted white and bordered in black. On top of boot from central convexity to break at ankle, "laces" or fasteners in shape of pendent triangles are painted on white groundcoat in black (for outlining and interior lines) and red (for interior dots). On both sides vertical ladder-like design is painted from central ridge to sole in black with red dots as filler ornament. Remaining areas of boot are slipped golden brown and polished to smooth finish.

Micaceous yellow-brown clay, fired gray at core, with many small light and dark inclusions. Munsell: 7.5YR 6/6 (reddish yellow).

Central Anatolian-manufactured.

This boot was found in a pit with a black burnished animal rhyton (P 892), three lydia (P 906: end 6th century), a gray burnished dish (P 987), tile fragments with spiral design and some black-glazed fragments. The context can be dated no earlier than the 5th century B.C.

164 Boot
    T 27   Trench SET-NW, pit in Floor 7, E edge
    P.H. 0.048; P.L. 0.09; Max.W. 0.0345 m.
    Pl. 37 and Color Pl. II

Single fragment preserving front half of boot broken off irregularly at instep. Surface chipped on right side, top and lower left. Sole slightly worn.

Well-shaped narrow boot with pointed toe and strongly curving contour. Probably for right foot. Upper surface slopes sharply from toe to break below ankle. Flat sole with slight concavity at midpoint. Interior is solid with one small round hole (D. 0.004 m.) running horizontally toward toe in broken upper surface to depth of 0.01 m. Handmade.

Boot is slipped light tan-brown and painted matte red on front and sides. White paint covers arch of foot in roughly oval area and vertical band on outside of foot. Over white are painted "laces" or fasteners in alternating lines of black and red. On inside of boot is broad white vertical band near back break. All painted surfaces are polished. Sole of boot is unpainted except near tip, which has thin red slip. Sole is polished.

Lightly micaceous clay with small light inclusions and grit, fired gray below surface. Munsell: polished, unpainted sole 5YR 6/4 (light reddish brown)-6/6 (reddish yellow).

Central Anatolian-manufactured.

The boot was found in a pit with material dating to the early 4th century B.C. or later. The polishing technique and bichrome painting style are common to Middle Phrygian bichrome pottery and indicate a local origin for the boot.

165 Boot
    T 101   Trench M7B, cleaning cellar wall
    P.H. 0.079; L. 0.098; W. ankle 0.039 m.
    Pl. 37 and Color Pl. II

Single fragment broken at top above ankle. Chips on surface around break. Bottom of heel worn. Tip of boot chipped. Trace of burning on instep.

Ankle-high, long and narrow right boot or shoe with pointed toe, high arch and very narrow heel. Front of boot rises steeply with convexity at midpoint. Sides of boot curve in markedly above instep and flare slightly at upper break. Top surface is irregular with round hole (D. 0.006; Depth 0.03 m.) drilled through. Sole does not provide stable surface for standing boot upright. Handmade.

Exterior surface except sole at ball of foot is slipped red-orange and polished to smooth sheen. Down front of boot are painted black "laces" or fasteners, consisting of pendent triangles to right and left of central ridge. Dark paint appears gray and is only faintly visible under the polish.

Lightly micaceous red-brown clay fired gray at inner core and red around hole in top surface. Much grit. Munsell: 2.5YR 5/6 (red).

Central Anatolian-manufactured.

The arching top of the foot and painted "laces" are close in design to those of **163**. The black-on-red painting style and the polishing technique are known on both Phrygian and West Anatolian pottery. The pottery from this layer is mixed, but the context probably does not indicate a date any earlier than the 5th century B.C.

166 Boot
    T 77   Trench WML-4N, Layer 3
    P.H. 0.045; L. 0.074; Max.W. 0.034 m.
    Pl. 38

Single fragment preserving full length of foot and ankle, lacking upper surface of ankle, surface of left back of foot, chips from upper right side, and bottom edge at right and sole, especially toward heel. Sole slightly worn.

Short, thick, open-toed left (?) boot or shoe. Boot is pointed at front with triangular opening cut out at toe; ridge inside opening to indicate toe of foot. Ankle rises in thick, solid, vertical mass. Back and bottom of boot are flat. Interior solid. Handmade.

No painted decoration. Boot is slipped and polished to smooth surface. On upper surface polish is especially heavy, producing uneven, dark tan-brown.

Lightly micaceous, yellowish brown clay fired gray at core. Compact clay with few small lime inclusions. Munsell: at break 7.5YR 6/4 (light brown); on burnished surface 7.5YR 5/4 (brown).

Central Anatolian-manufactured.

This boot was found in the same layer and trench as **64**, a Hellenistic female with tympanum, but the layer is not otherwise datable.

167 Boot
T 88   Trench TBT-5, Floor 4, NW part
P.L. 0.069; P.W. 0.081; P.H. 0.051 m.
Pl. 38 and Color Pl. II

Single fragment preserving lower back and right side, bottom and portion of plinth. Left back side broken off. Front half has nicks on bottom. Paint well preserved.

Boot or shoe on flat plinth with rounded heel and straight outer walls. Plinth continues beyond left edge of boot as if plinth was meant to serve as base for another foot. Bottom of plinth is flat and smooth. Interior is hollow with rough walls. Handmade.

Over right side of boot, over matte ivory groundcoat, in lustrous paint (black-brown and red) are abstract designs in vertical panels defined by brown-black lines. From back to front patterns within vertical units are triangles, wavy lines and rectangles alternating solid and dot-filled. Edge of boot's sole is red.

Pinkish orange slightly micaceous clay, fired pinkish brown on interior surface and grayish at core, with large dark inclusions and few small white inclusions. Munsell: below surface 10R 6/8 (light red).

Central Anatolian-manufactured.

The motifs in red and black lustrous paint over matte ivory groundcoat are typical of Middle Phrygian bichrome pottery, especially of the 6th century B.C. The other material found in the same level with this boot, including late lydia, a black-glazed fish-plate rim and a red-figure sherd, indicates a date for the level no earlier than the second half of the 5th century B.C.

168 Boot
P 2174   Trench WML-4N, Layer 2, Pit A
P.H. 0.066; P.L. 0.125 m.
Pl. 38 and Color Pl. II

Single fragment preserving front right side of boot, broken in front of heel, down central "seam" and along bottom right of sole.

Boot has squared-off toe and peak down central "seam" ending in raised side "seam," and slightly convex sides. Sole is slightly convex. Hollow interior with rough walls as if formed over fingers. Handmade.

Exterior covered with matte white groundcoat. "Seams" are indicated by red-wash zone outlined in black for "tie" area. Raised moccasin-like sides are defined by red line between single black lines. Over toe are black triangles with red and black oblique lines in front. Sole is solid red with black line defining upper edge. Painted areas are burnished. Red is glossy.

Thick buff fabric.

Central Anatolian-manufactured.

The context in which this boot was found can be roughly dated to the 4th century or Late Phrygian/Hellenistic period.

MISCELLANEOUS: OTHER

169 Mold: Wing
T 48   Trench Deep Cut 3, in clay deposit at Phrygian gate
P.L. 0.063; P.W. 0.049; Th. 0.011-0.013 m.
Pl. 38

Single fragment broken all around, preserving upper surface of mold. Highly friable; surface blackened from fire, chipped and flaking.

Baked clay mold of wing. Three tiers of overlapping feathers curving up. First two rows will appear in relief on finished product while outermost row will appear incised and on lower plane. At lower right edge is part of head or body of creature. Back of mold is smoothed. Molded from metal or terracotta object.

Very gritty, reddish orange clay burned charcoal gray on upper surface. No Munsell test possible.

Central Anatolian-manufactured.

The very crisply defined lines of the mold might suggest that it was taken from a metal prototype (see Richter 1958: 369 ff.; D. B. Thompson 1949: 365 ff.). The friable surface of the mold would not lend itself to the casting of metal wings. It is likely that the final products were meant to be in terracotta.

The clay fill from which this mold comes probably dates to the first half of the 6th century B.C., but contains earlier material.

170 Unfinished Fragment
T 69   Terracotta Deposit 5 (see pp. 67-69)
P.H. 0.075; P.W. 0.036; P.Th. 0.067; Th. walls 0.005-0.009 m.
Pl. 38

Single fragment preserving one side and front surface, broken off on all other edges.

Unidentifiable, unfinished triangular fragment with convex front surface marked by four vertical flutes and raised leafy pattern. Possibly drapery fragment. Interior is hollow with roughly worked walls. Back roughly smoothed. Possibly moldmade front.

No painted decoration.

Pinkish orange clay, lightly micaceous, very hard-fired with lime inclusions. Munsell: 5YR 7/6 (reddish yellow).

Locally manufactured.

This fragment may be a test-piece or discard reused as a kiln prop or possibly an archetype or secondary fragment.

171 Votive Cake?
MC 311   Trench SE, Layer 5, Bag 21
D. 0.043; H. 0.025 m.
Pl. 38

Single fragment preserving upper surface except two small chips and most of undersurface.

Votive cake(?) in form of small cylinder with flat upper surface with small knob of clay added at center; incised lines divide upper surface into slices. Handmade.

Undecorated.
Coarse pink-buff clay. Munsell: core 2.5YR 5/6 (red); surface 5YR 8/3-7/3 (pink).
Central Anatolian-manufactured?

Pottery indicates a late 4th-3d century date for Layer 5.

Model cakes are sometimes interpreted as votive offerings to Dionysos (Goldman 1950: 344-345), but they can equally be interpreted as substitutes for real cakes which are common gifts to other deities (Rouse 1975 [1902]: 200, 290).

II

Terracotta Deposits

Six deposits or context groups of figurines can be isolated from among the corpus of terracotta figurines from Gordion. A deposit is defined here as a group of terracotta figurines or hand-modeled or molded vessels which were found together in a confined area, in a single level, a pit, or within an identifiable architectural unit, and which can therefore be associated with one another. In addition to these deposits, individual terracotta figurines may have come from deposits of pottery and other finds. This information is included in the discussion of context following each catalogue entry.

TERRACOTTA DEPOSIT 1

Tumulus P, S side of Tomb
NB 43, pp. 120 ff., esp. pp. 153-159: October-April 1955
R. S. Young 1957: 325 ff.; 1981: 1-77
See Fig. 5 for reconstructed floorplan of the chamber of Tumulus P.

TERRACOTTA VESSELS

1 TumP 49 Animal Vessel: Goose (S side of tomb)
2 TumP 50 Animal Vessel: Goose (S side of tomb)
3 TumP 58 Animal Vessel: Ram Jug (SW corner of tomb)
4 TumP 62 Animal Vessel: Goat Jug (S side of tomb)
5 TumP 63 Animal Vessel: Deer or Bull Jug (S side of tomb)

DESCRIPTION OF CONTEXT AND CONTENTS

These five Central Anatolian-manufactured animal vessels were all found near the south wall inside the wooden tomb chamber of Tumulus P. It is supposed that most of the group, along with other fine pottery, had been placed on a wooden table which collapsed and disintegrated. The tomb has been identified as that of a child on the basis of the identification of the teeth as those of a four- or five-year-old. The grave goods of wooden toy animals (TumP 106-114) and animal attachments (TumP 148-149), a tiny bronze quadriga (TumP 40) and these terracotta animal vessels seem appropriate for a child of perhaps royal status.

DISCUSSION OF VESSELS

These five vessels from Tumulus P are the only terracotta animal vessels datable to the Early Phrygian period. The manufacturing technique is similar for all of them, i.e., wheel-turned bodies with modeled heads and other parts added, though the decorative schemes vary: brown-on-buff painted, black-on-red painted and black polished. The matching pair of goose vessels (**1** and **2**) were attempted with lifelike details, while the other three vessels in the deposit are more stylized animal forms. There is no stylistic closeness between the locally made wooden animal figures (TumP 106-114, 148-149) in Tumulus P and these terracotta animal vessels.

DATE

The size of the tomb deposit and the wealth of archaeological data allow a secure date for the burial just prior to the Kimmerian invasion of Gordion, ca. 700 B.C.

TERRACOTTA DEPOSIT 2

Trench NE-1, W section, Level 2B
NB 52, p. 118: June 4, 1955; NB 96, p. 40: April 1961
DeVries 1988: 51

TERRACOTTA VESSELS

19 Plastic Vessel: Anatolian (?) Couchant Animal
20 Plastic Vessel: East Greek (?) Hedgehog
25 Plastic Vessel: East Greek Pomegranate (Trench NE-1, robbed foundation trench of Middle Phrygian citadel enclosure wall).

26   Plastic Vessel: East Greek Pomegranate
28   Plastic Vessel: East Greek or Lydian Kore Bust

DESCRIPTION OF CONTEXT AND CONTENTS

Four plastic vessels (**19**, **20**, **26**, **28**) were found together with a banded lydion (P 1158), a gray burnished plate (P 1159), an alabaster hawk (S 32), and other small finds and sherds at the edge of a trench, partially embedded in the scarp, in what seems to have been a pit of some kind. The soil is described as dark gray, ashy and gritty with flakes of a white lime-like substance. The architectural features in the area, several stone walls and paving stones, were never completely excavated or interpreted. The East Greek pomegranate vessel **25**, found near the rest of the group in the same trench but interpreted by the excavator as coming from a different level, is likely to be part of the same group.

DISCUSSION OF VESSELS

Of the eleven molded vessels of Greek type from Gordion, five are from this deposit. Most are probably from East Greek centers, with the possible exception of **28**, which may be Lydian, and **19**, which is likely to be an Anatolian imitation of an East Greek type. An interpretation of the use of these plastic vessels is hampered by the archaeological data's lack of clarity. It is possible that this group of plastic vessels represents a collection made by an individual or the wares of a dealer.

DATE

The catalogued objects from the deposit represent a range in dates from the first half to the late 6th century B.C., with the hedgehog and pomegranate probably among the earliest datable objects and the banded lydion (530/10-500 B.C.) among the latest. The group was deposited in the second half of the 6th century, possibly as late as the end of the century. The Anatolian (?) polished couchant quadruped (**19**) is the latest of the plastic vessels in the group.

TERRACOTTA DEPOSIT 3

Trench SET, "Level 2 House," "Room South of Pithos Room"
NB 2, pp. 145, 159, 161: June 6, 9, 10, 1950
F. A. Winter 1984: 312-313; 1988: 64-65, fig. 4; R. S. Young 1951b: 7, figs. 1 and 2, pl. 2
See Fig. 6 for plan of "Level 2 House."

TERRACOTTA FIGURINES

57   Kybele Riding Lion
59   Enthroned Kybele
66   Standing Female with Wreath
67   Standing Female
68   Standing Female
93   Female Head (from Layer 2 of house outside of court at west)

DESCRIPTION OF CONTEXT AND CONTENTS

The "Level 2 House" was at the southeastern edge of the City Mound and was oriented in a northeast/southwest direction. Composed of a large courtyard and a series of square rooms to the east and two rectangular rooms to the southwest, the complete plan of this sprawling building was never recovered, especially at the southwest edge. The two rooms to the southwest of the court, the "Pithos Room" and the "Room South of Pithos Room" contained most of the pottery and other finds from this house. In the "Pithos Room" were four large pithoi, suggesting that the room was used for storage. The "Room South of Pithos Room" was entered from the "Pithos Room" and measured 4.5 by at least 5.5 m. (the southwest end of that room was never excavated). In addition to the five terracotta figurines, large quantities of coarse and fine pottery were inventoried from the room (see F. A. Winter 1984: 313 for listing of catalogued black-glazed ceramics). F. A. Winter's analyses of the pottery from this house, including thirteen Rhodian stamped amphora handles, fusiform unguentaria, black-glazed fish plates, West Slope plates, fruit dishes and black-glazed plates with stamping, indicate that it is chronologically consistent and can be identified as material in use just prior to and left behind at the abandonment of Gordion in 189 B.C. (see *ibid*.: 313).

The "Room South of Pithos Room" may also have served as a storage facility and the figurines mixed with the pottery were probably part of the household supplies, perhaps components of a domestic shrine (to Kybele?).

DISCUSSION OF TERRACOTTA FIGURINES

The figurines in this deposit represent some of the best-preserved and highest-quality imported terracottas from Late Phrygian/Hellenistic Gordion. All are imports to Gordion, all are female, two are of Kybele and two are made from the same mold (**67** and **68**). All except **93** are close in style, painted decoration and clay and can be assigned to the same manufacturing site, perhaps even the same workshop. Close parallels can be found for the Kybele riding a lion among Pergamene terracottas (see **57** and p. 79) and the clay of **57** and **59** is comparable to that of figurines from the acropoles of Pergamon and Mamurtkale. Pergamon is a likely manufacturing source for the entire group of figurines (see Group I, pp. 78-79). It is not without interest that among the pithos fragments from the "Level 2 House" are five inscribed with Ionic numbers used to record Pergamene units of measurement (Roller 1987a: 63-64, 67, 68; 3B-34, 3B-38). Since the majority of Pergamene terracotta figurines and all of the sherds with the Pergamene notation system were recovered from this house, one can speculate that this "Level 2 House" belonged to a Greek, perhaps one from Pergamon or at least with Pergamene ties.

DATE

All of the figurines can be dated to the late 3d and early 2d centuries B.C. and the dating of the pottery confirms the conclusion that the material in the "Room South of Pithos Room," as from the rest of the house, was left behind when the City Mound was abandoned at the impending arrival of the Roman army in 189 B.C.

TERRACOTTA DEPOSIT 4

Trench SET-NW, Level 1 Room
NB 21, pp. 55, 57, 66, 72: Oct. 16-17, 19-20, 1951
F. A. Winter 1984: 314; R. S. Young 1953: 6-9

TERRACOTTA FIGURINES

- 15 Animal Vessel: Goat
- 33 Vessel Handle Attachment?: Nike Protome
- 35 Bust-Flower Thymiaterion: Satyr (from small hole in Floor 1)
- 38 Bust-Flower Thymiaterion: Female
- 52 Large Kybele Statuette
- 60 Enthroned Kybele

DESCRIPTION OF CONTEXT AND CONTENTS

The SET-NW, Level 1 Room is located in the southeastern part of the mound near the earlier monumental entranceway to the site. The entire plan of this area was never established. The contents of this deposit were found on a hard-packed floor level within a room enclosed by stone walls. Over the floor was a thick stratum, ca. 0.10-0.20 m. deep, of burned debris.

The terracotta figurines were found clustered toward the northeast side of the room, while **35** was found in a small hole nearby in quantities of ash and with an alabaster loom weight (ST 158). The majority of the pottery was found in a group north of the room's south wall (see F. A. Winter 1984: 314 for list of catalogued black-glazed ceramics from room). The quantities of pottery from this room include West Slope ware; black-glazed bowls; black burnished, red burnished and gray ware; unglazed table ware; unguentaria; cooking vessels; coarse ware and four stamped amphora handles, including two Rhodian. Other finds include a lamp stand, faience bowl fragments, a glass fragment, iron blades and clamps, a bronze knucklebone, stone whorls and a pestle. The pottery can be dated to the final Late Phrygian/Hellenistic phase of Gordion just before its abandonment in 189 B.C.

DISCUSSION OF TERRACOTTA FIGURINES

The terracottas of this Late Phrygian/Hellenistic structure are remarkable for their size and quality and for the probably local origin of many of them. The two bust-flower thymiateria, the satyr (**35**) and the large female head (**38**), are local products. The Nike protome handle (?) (**33**) from this deposit and the animal rhyton (**15**) are Central Anatolian products, to judge from the Nike's intentionally gray-fired fabric, typical of Phrygian pottery from Gordion, and the black polishing of the goat rhyton, another typically Phrygian pottery technique. The clay of the large Kybele (**52**) is close to other suspected local products (e.g., **38**) and the style of the head is comparable to locally made bust-flower thymiateria. The Kybele was probably made at Gordion. This large Kybele is on a scale and of a quality appropriate for a cult image in a household shrine, and it might be equally fitting to find bust-flower thymiateria of the local type in a domestic shrine. Since the entire plan was never recovered, it is impossible to establish a definitive use for this building. The contents of the room, however, suggest a domestic establishment, one which might have had a substantial shrine to Kybele within it.

DATE

The figurines and pottery can be assigned to the late 3d and early 2d centuries B.C. The deposit may have been formed as a result of the burning and destruction of the building close to, at the time of, or just after the abandonment of Gordion in 189 B.C.

TERRACOTTA DEPOSIT 5: POTTERY ESTABLISHMENT AND ADJOINING STRUCTURES

Trenches NCT-W, NCT-W1, NCT-W3, NCT-S, MN, MN-Ext. 3
NB 19, pp. 93-94, 144: June 1951; NB 43, pp. 113, 114: Oct. 1955; NB 66, pp. 52, 57: Apr. 1957; NB 72, pp. 17-18, 68, 134: June-Aug. 1958, May 1961
Edwards 1959a: 267 ff., pls. 67, 68; 1959b: 13, pls. 4-5; F. A. Winter 1984: 308-309
See Fig. 7 for plan of area.

TERRACOTTA FIGURINES

KILN AREA (ROOM 3):

- 39 Bust-Flower Thymiaterion: Female (Trench NCT-W3/4, Layer 4 below Floor 3 in Room 3)

44 Mold: Thymiaterion Flower (Trench NCT-W1, S section, E half, in firing chamber of later, small kiln)
50 Mold: Female Bust (Trench NCT-W1, S section, E half, in firing chamber of later, small kiln)
108 Neck with Torque (Trench NCT-W1, S section, E half, Layer 1 below floor, possibly chamber of kiln)
170 Unfinished Fragment (Trench NCT-W1, S section, E half, Layer 1, below floor, possibly chamber of kiln)

ROOMS 1 AND 2:

45 Thymiaterion Fragment (Trench NCT-W3, Room 1, destruction filling)
46 Thymiaterion Fragment (Trench NCT-W3, Room 1)
47 Thymiaterion Fragment (probably Trench NCT-W3 Pottery Establishment)
48 Thymiaterion Fragment (Trench NCT-W3, Room 1, destruction filling)

ROOMS 5 AND 6:

40 Bust-Flower Thymiaterion Fragment (probably Trench NCT-S, Level 1a = probably Pottery Establishment Room 5 or 6)
42 Bust-Flower Thymiaterion: Artemis? (Trenches NCT-S, Level 1a and NCT-W, "House A," Room 2 = Pottery Establishment Room 5)
56 Tympanum? (possibly Trench NCT-W, "House A," Room 1 or NCT-S, Level 1a = Pottery Establishment Room 6)
61 Enthroned Kybele (Trench NCT-W, "House A", Room 1 and NCT-S, Level 1a = Pottery Establishment Room 6)
63 Kybele (?) Fragment (Trench NCT-S, Section A, Cut 3, Level 1b = Pottery Establishment Room 5 or 6)
70 Standing Female (Trench NCT-W, "House A," Room 1, filling = Pottery Establishment Room 6)
74 Standing Female (Trench NCT-S, Level 1a = probably Pottery Establishment Room 5 or 6)
91 Female Head (Trench NCT-S, fallen from scarp between walls in S part of "House A" = Pottery Establishment Room 6)
92 Female Head (Trench NCT-W, "House A," Room 2, in upper fill = Pottery Establishment Room 5)
96 Drapery Fragment (Trench NCT-W, "House A," Room 1 = Pottery Establishment Room 6)

ROOM 7:

34 Vessel: Tyche? (Trench MN-Ext. 3, Layer 4 in fill = "Pottery Establishment" Room 7)
69 Standing Female (Trench MN, Layer 5 fill = "Pottery Establishment" Room 7)
146 Quadruped's Legs (Trench MN-Ext. 3, Layer 5, fill behind house = "Pottery Establishment" behind Room 7)

DESCRIPTION OF CONTEXT AND CONTENTS

The Late Phrygian/Hellenistic Pottery Establishment at Gordion is a rambling multi-unit complex which was excavated in several different sections, several years apart, in at least three trenches. There are many peripheral areas of the complex which were not completely excavated and the total plan is not yet understood. A plan and description of the establishment was published by Edwards (1959a: 267-268, pls. 67, 68). There is a large open court (labeled "3" on the plan) with at least two kilns: an earlier, larger kiln with an oval firing chamber and a semicircular mouth; and a later, smaller kiln with a lower ovoid firing-chamber, a stacking floor and a dome-shaped upper chamber. (It was in the latter kiln that terracotta molds were found.) The large numbers of fired and unfired sherds in the kilns indicate that the Pottery Establishment was employed in the manufacture of both ceramic vessels and terracotta figurines.

The court is bordered on the northwest by a partly open-air kitchen (1) with a fire-pit, brazier and pithos and an adjoining pantry (2). East of the court is a wall through which is an informal entrance to the court (4). To the southeast of the court is a megaron-like structure (7) whose entrance was probably from the southwest side away from the court. Inside this building is a longitudinal partition wall with a hearth against its east side. It is not clear from the excavation of this area if this structure is directly linked in function to the Pottery Establishment. This building (7) is contemporary, at least in its final phase, with the rest of the Pottery Establishment.

To the east of the structure are two rooms, 5 and 6 (originally identified as Trench NCT-W, "House A," Rooms 2 [to north] and 1 [to south]). In the north wall of the southern room, as a modification to the building after its original construction, a niche was built (H. 0.60; W. 0.17; Depth 0.28 m.). The original use of this structure is not known but in its later phase, Rooms 5 and 6 served as cellars. Again, it is not certain that this structure is a part of the Pottery Establishment. It is significant in terms of the function of this southeastern area that from the fill of Rooms 5, 6 and 7—along with fine pottery, amphora fragments, a piece of gold foil and a glass bowl—came seven stone sculpture fragments on a small scale (S 37-S 40, S 42, S 49, S 50), including a shield, a male leg wearing a sandal, a child's arm and drapery fragments and three stone bases for statuettes (S 41, I 162, I 184), two of which are locally made and inscribed possibly with the same name (EXEβIOΣ) (Roller 1987b: 112-113, nos. 7, 8).

With the exception of two thymiaterion fragments (**40** and **42**), the figurines from Rooms 5, 6 and 7 represent different types than those from the kiln area and Room 1 of the Pottery Establishment. In this southeastern area are female figurines and goddesses (Tyche?, Artemis?, Kybele). If Rooms 5, 6 and 7 are linked to the Pottery Establishment, it is likely that this is the domestic quarter. It is, however, justifiable to think of Structure 7 and perhaps Room 6 in its earlier phase as shrines with the niche in the south wall of Room 6 as one possible cult spot.

Some of the terracotta figurines from Rooms 1 (**45** and **48**), 5 (**92**), and 6 (**61, 70, 91**) show definite signs of burning or contact with carbonized material. Over the floor of Room 6 was a layer of ash and burnt debris including charred wooden beams and seeds, and there is also ample evidence of severe burning in Room 1. It is therefore very probable that the Pottery Establishment and adjoining structures were destroyed by fire. F. A. Winter, concludes that the pottery in the destruction debris over the floors of the complex and in the later kiln is so similar to pottery from abandonment (189 B.C.) levels of Gordion that the destruction of this complex most likely occurred close to 189 B.C. (1984: 309). This pottery includes red-banded bowls, dark and buff echinus bowls with angular profiles, a gray polished situla and fusiform unguentaria.

DISCUSSION OF TERRACOTTA FIGURINES

The molds and unfinished terracotta figurines from the kilns and Room 1 of the Pottery Establishment are of inestimable importance for our knowledge of the local production of terracottas in the Late Phrygian/Hellenistic period at Gordion. The partially fired or lightly baked mold of a flower-container (**44**) used for the bust-flower thymiateria, the rim fragments of the flowers (**45-48**) and the female heads for busts (**39**) provide firm evidence of the local manufacture of this thymiaterion type. In addition, the mold for a female bust (**50**) may have been used for the production of the front halves of busts of the bust-flower type of thymiaterion.

108 and **170**, both unfinished but fired terracotta fragments, may have been test-pieces used as props or for temperature-control trials in the kiln, or archetype or secondary archetype fragments. **108** is one of the only archaeological traces of the Celtic occupation at Gordion. The torque around the neck of the figure is a typically Celtic type of ornament and provides the clue that Celtic ways of life and dress may have had some influence, no matter how slight, on the coroplastic industry at Gordion.

The terracotta figurines from the structures (Rooms 5, 6 and 7) on the southeast side of the courtyard are all female types with one representation of Tyche (?) (**34**), one of Artemis (?) in the form of a bust-flower thymiaterion (**42**) and two of Kybele (**61** and **63**?). **61, 70, 74, 92**

and **96**, all from Rooms 5 and 6, are imported figurines similar to one another in style, clay and painted decoration, suggesting the same source of manufacture (see discussion of Group II, pp. 79-80).

DATE

A late 3d-early 2d century B.C. date for all the figurines in this group is supported by stylistic criteria and the chronology of the ceramics in the Pottery Establishment. Both the Pottery Establishment proper (Rooms 1, 2, 3 and Entranceway 4) and the structures to the southeast (Rooms 5, 6 and 7) were probably destroyed by fire just prior to or at the time of the abandonment of the City Mound in 189 B.C.

TERRACOTTA DEPOSIT 6

Trench Q_2E_2, cindery fill over Floor 2
NB 60, p. 159: Apr. 13, 1957.

TERRACOTTA FIGURINES

36	Bust-Flower Thymiaterion: Female
37	Bust-Flower Thymiaterion: Female
58	Enthroned Kybele
73	Standing Female
97	Statuette: Attis?
99	Eros in Flower

DESCRIPTION OF CONTEXT AND CONTENTS

This group of figurines comes from the cindery fill over the floor of what may be the cellar of a Late Phrygian/Hellenistic house. The plan of the structure was never recovered. The figurine types suggest that the area may have contained a shrine to Kybele.

The pottery over the floor was identified as Late Phrygian/Hellenistic by the excavator but only one fragment was inventoried: a large thin gray-ware fusiform unguentarium (P 1666) dating to the last quarter of the 4th or early 3d century B.C.

DISCUSSION OF TERRACOTTAS

The types of terracottas in this group compare closely with those of other household deposits, e.g., Terracotta Deposits 2 and 3. In this deposit all of the figurines with the exception of two are female; one statuette of Kybele (**58**) is represented as are two of the locally made bust-flower thymiateria (**36** and **37**). One of the more unusual of the Gordion terracottas is found in this deposit: a very large statuette possibly of Attis (**97**). Its style, clay and size compare closely with those of the large statuette of Kybele from Terracotta Deposit 3 (**52**) and both are probably products of the same workshop, perhaps located at Gordion. It is worth noting that the three probably local products in this group, **36**, **37** and **97**, all exhibit traces of ancient plaster for repairs or adhesion.

The Eros in a flower (**99**) is a well-executed and well-preserved example of its type and an obvious import to Gordion. The two probably imported products (**73** and **99**) seem to have been made from the same clay (see Group II, pp. 79-80), and are remarkable for their painted decoration's heavy use of pink and good state of preservation.

DATE

Despite the late 4th/early 3d century B.C. date for the fusiform unguentarium, most of the figurines from this deposit can be placed in the later 3d or early 2d century B.C. The fact that a figurine of Kybele (**59**), made from the same mold as **58**, was found in an "abandonment level" (see, e.g., Terracotta Deposit 3) and that large heads of the bust-flower thymiaterion type are also found in the latest Late Phrygian/Hellenistic levels suggests that this group dates to the final Phrygian phase of the citadel of Gordion. Stylistic criteria, especially of the Eros in a flower, a type well documented at various Hellenistic sites, also support a date around the turn of the 3d to 2d centuries B.C. for this group.

III

Conclusions

OVERALL CHRONOLOGY

Terracotta figurines are represented in every period at Gordion, beginning with the Early Bronze Age, but with the majority dating to the Late Phrygian/Hellenistic period (Table 2). To some extent, conclusions about the interest in using or manufacturing terracotta figurines are skewed by the excavation history of the site. For example, Early Bronze Age levels were reached primarily in only one area on the City Mound (in two soundings: see Gunter 1991: 1-3) and the few probably Early Bronze Age figurines from Gordion (**115** and **116**) are most likely not representative of the site as a whole. Because the sample of excavated Old Hittite-period burials at Gordion is adequate, it is safe to say that terracotta figurines were not as a rule given as gifts in burials in the Old Hittite period at Gordion (see Mellink 1956). Our knowledge of Hittite-period habitation at Gordion, however, is limited to scattered finds and two deep soundings on the City Mound (see Gunter 1991: 1-3). Of the four or five Hittite-period animal figurines, all are scattered finds, mixed in upper fills. It is therefore through comparisons with Hittite figurines at other sites, especially Boğazköy (Fischer 1963: 154-160), that these figurines can be identified as Hittite (Old Kingdom or Empire period, 1650-1200 B.C.). In addition to these four or five Hittite-period figurines included in the Catalogue, Hittite-period animals produced in the Middle and Late Bronze Age were used as handles, spouts or plastic attachments (e.g., P 2400, P 1080, P 1358, P 3329). These are not included as a part of this corpus but see Gunter 1991: nos. 514, 508, 509, 254.

Similarly, our archaeological knowledge of pre-8th-century Central Anatolian coroplastic production is very limited: only a wagon wheel (**159**), one animal (**122**) and five animal vessels (**1-5** are catalogued here as definite examples of the period, and possibly **6**). A significant jump in the statistics for the occurrence of terracotta figurines and figural vessels takes place in the period after the Kimmerian destruction of Gordion, down to the arrival of Alexander the Great (Middle Phrygian period). This is also, not coincidentally, the period about which the most complete archaeological data are available. The majority of these Middle Phrygian objects are animal vessels or animal figurines, in addition to other Central Anatolian-produced objects like boots or shoes (**162-168**) and model chariots or carts (**156** and **157**). There are also a substantial number of imported Greek plastic vessels from this period.

It is in the Late Phrygian/Hellenistic period that we see a proliferation of imported Greek terracottas, with representations of Kybele, standing draped females, Eros, and theatrical masks being the most common imported types. The number of imported figurines in this Late Phrygian/Hellenistic period equals that of the Central Anatolian and local products, and the majority of these imports can be assigned to the period just before the abandonment of Gordion in 189 B.C. Enhancing the local coroplastic repertoire in this period are a type of bust-flower thymiaterion and large statuettes of Kybele and Attis (?) (**52** and **97**).

After the abandonment of the City Mound in 189 B.C., Gordion never seems to have regained its importance as a fortress/town in Anatolia. The period of sparse Roman rehabilitation of the site is represented among the figurines by only two possible examples, both female heads (**83** and **84**). Again, since little excavation has taken place in the zone where it has been recognized that Roman resettlement occurred, the picture of the coroplastic industry in this period may be skewed. We know nothing historically about Gordion in the Medieval period, except that sporadic finds, like the green- and brown-glazed animal (**147**), occur on the City Mound.

LOCAL AND CENTRAL ANATOLIAN COROPLASTIC PRODUCTION

We know that terracotta figurines were manufactured at Gordion in the Late Phrygian/Hellenistic period by the presence of molds (e.g., **31**, **44**, **50**, **51**, **169**), fragments from kilns (**170**) or unfinished figurines (**108**), and a large pottery establishment of this period, in the kilns of which were found molds and figurine fragments (see Terracotta Deposit 5, pp. 67-69). All of the evidence of this type for coroplastic production at Gordion itself is restricted to the Late Phrygian/Hellenistic period. No kilns or workshops for pottery or terracotta figurine production dating to the Bronze Age or Early or Middle Phrygian period have been located at Gordion.

CHRONOLOGY

BRONZE AGE, EARLY AND MIDDLE PHRYGIAN PERIODS

Handmade animal figurines and wheel-turned and hand-modeled animal vessels are the most numerous of the Phrygian and Central Anatolian-manufactured terracottas found at Gordion, and there seems to be a persistent interest in terracotta representations of animals, both free-standing figurines and vessels, as well as decoration for pottery (spouts, handles or decorative attachments). Vases in animal form seem generally to have fascinated the Phrygians. Imported East Greek plastic vases are documented at Gordion (**20-23**) as well as Central Anatolian-manufactured vessels from the Early Phrygian period (e.g., **1-5**). It is mainly on the basis of their polished, slipped or painted decoration that these animals can be identified as Phrygian or Central Anatolian. See full discussion of animals on pp. 49-51, especially regarding technique on p. 49, and of animal vessels on pp. 5-6.

Among the handmade Phrygian/Central Anatolian products from Gordion are boots or shoes (**162-168**), which are also produced in Hittite times (see **162** for a Hittite period-example). These can also be identified as the work of Central Anatolian coroplasts on the basis of comparable decoration on Phrygian/Central Anatolian ceramics or by form and clay in the case of the Hittite-period example. Two lack painted decoration but are slipped and polished, one with an uneven dark tan-brown surface (**166**), like local Iron Age pottery. The painted examples are all decorated in a bichrome technique (**163, 164, 167, 168**) with the exception of **165**, which is slipped, given decoration in black and polished to a red-orange. This "black-on-red" painting style is typical of both Phrygian and West Anatolian Iron Age pottery.

A group of miscellaneous models can be assigned, again by virtue of their painted decoration, to this group of local Phrygian/Central Anatolian products. **156**, for example, a model chariot decorated with brown matte paint over a white groundcoat, comes from a 4th-century or Late Phrygian/Hellenistic context, but is likely to be earlier in date. Miniature wheels for carts, chariots or wagons from the Middle or Early Phrygian period (**161**: 5th century; **160**: pre-5th or 4th century; **159**: pre-Kimmerian) can also be assigned to Central Anatolian workshops. **157** and **158** are other examples of carts or parts of other objects which are manufactured in the region.

The only evidence for the use of molds in the manufacture of terracottas prior to the Late Phrygian/Hellenistic period is a fragmentary mold for a wing (**169**). We are uncertain of the type of terracotta object this shallow mold might have produced.

LATE PHRYGIAN/HELLENISTIC PERIOD

In the Late Phrygian/Hellenistic period the production of figurines at Gordion itself and in the region becomes more diverse and ambitious. In addition to a small number of animal figurines and animal vessels, simple hand-modeled terracottas in human form (e.g., **108**: neck with torque; **109**: grotesque head pendant) are still in evidence but are augmented by molded products. Among the less pretentious of these molded terracotta figurines are a female head (**83**) on which there is ample evidence for hand-tooling of details and handmade additions, and a standing female (**65**) with a handmade back and sloppily executed tooling for the chiton folds. The latter is an adaptation of a Greek "Tanagra-type" standing female but can be assigned an origin in the region of Gordion on the basis of its workmanship and clay composition. The clays of **53, 65, 83** and **108** are all very closely comparable and the inferior workmanship and style indicate that all four were probably made in a single Central Anatolian workshop.

A moldmade rhyton handle (?) in the form of Nike wearing a painted torque around her neck (**33**) adds another dimension to the coroplastic industry at Gordion. The fabric is comparable to Late Phrygian/Hellenistic bucchero wares fired in a kiln in a reducing atmosphere. The finished product is a unique creation combining a Greek deity wearing a typically Celtic ornament with a Phrygian firing technique.

The largest of the terracottas from Gordion are two locally manufactured moldmade statuettes, one of Kybele (**52**) and one probably representing Attis (**97**). The two are so close in clay composition, style, workmanship, scale and details that it is likely that they were manufactured in the same workshop, probably at Gordion itself. The clue to their local origin comes in the stylistic affinities to the unquestionably Gordion-manufactured bust-flower thymiateria (see below, pp. 74-75).

The Kybele statuette (**52**) almost certainly served as a cult image for a small shrine. There is evidence of thick ancient plaster which was painted over, masking breaks on the throne and drapery. Although the Attis (?) (**97**) does not exhibit any evidence of ancient repairs, plaster was used to attach the separately modeled arms (only left arm preserved) to the torso.[2]

The group of bust-flower thymiateria form the largest single category of locally manufactured moldmade terracottas from Gordion. It is the presence of molds and fragments of these thymiateria in the kiln area of the Late

TABLE 2. TYPES OF GORDION FIGURINES AND THEIR CHRONOLOGY

	Early Bronze	Middle/Late Bronze	Early Phrygian	Early/Middle Phrygian	Middle Phrygian	Middle/Late Phrygian	Late Phrygian	Roman	Medieval	Total
Animal Vessels: Central Anatolian Manufactured			5		7	3	3			18
Plastic Vessels: Greek or Greek-inspired					13	1	2			16
Bust-flower Thymiateria							17			17
Kybele and Related Types							13			13
Females					2	1	27	2		32
Males						1	10			11
Unidentified Humans						1	1			2
Masks							5			5
Animal Figurines	2	5	1	2	21	7	2		1	41
Vehicles and Wheels				1	2	1	2			6
Boots or Shoes		1			4	2				7
Other Miscellaneous					1		2			3
Total	2	6	7	4	49	18	82	2	1	171

Phrygian/Hellenistic Pottery Establishment (see Terracotta Deposit 4), and a fragmentary head fired in a bucchero technique (39), which provides the clue that coroplasts at Gordion were producing these terracotta figurine containers. An examination of the fabric of these bust thymiateria, and of the large statuettes (52 and 97) and phiale (54), indicates that all were probably made in the same local workshop. In addition, the use of plaster to secure the flower container to the hole in the top of the head (easily seen on 36, and traces on 37 and 38) is comparable to the use of plaster on both of the large statuettes.

The busts are all female types with the exception of one, the satyr (35). Artemis can possibly be identified in one of the busts (42), on the basis of an object she wears strapped over her back, apparently a quiver case. The ingenuity and humor of representations such as the satyr and the careful workmanship and ambitious compositions of these and of the large Kybele and Attis (?) indicate a highly sophisticated coroplastic industry which depended on Greek sources of inspiration for much of its moldmade production. To judge from the relatively small number of these local molded terracottas, and the lack of any specific matches of figurines made from the same mold series among the published figurines from other sites in Greece and Asia Minor, it is unlikely that Gordion was an exporter of terracotta figurines in the Late Phrygian/Hellenistic period.

Two molds dating to the Late Phrygian/Hellenistic period (31 and 105) add yet another dimension to the coroplastic assemblage at Gordion. The mold for a relief medallion (**105**) is an anomaly at Gordion. Terracotta molds did travel in trade situations. This mold appears to be a secondary one, taken from a first-generation terracotta. This first-generation terracotta, with a Greek theme and in a purely Greek style, can be recognized as very high-quality work. This style is unlike any of the known local products at Gordion and it can probably be assumed that the mold was taken from an imported Greek terracotta plaque for use in producing other plaques for local distribution. The lion mold (**31**) was probably produced in the region of Central Anatolia and was possibly manufactured for an animal-head vase. In addition, a lion's paw (**148**) may be a primary archetype for a mold for producing lion's foot attachments.

Lastly, a group of molded medallions in high relief decoration (**80-82** and **98**), all of which can probably be assigned functions as plastic decoration for ceramic vessels, exhibit uniformly poor clay, sloppy firing technique and inferior styles. These medallions and plastic decorations can be related to a larger group of Central Anatolian vessels with molded decoration (P 1760, P 1607, P 3972, P 379, P 2562, P 102, P 709, P 3535) which are not included in this corpus (see F. A. Winter, forthcoming). Included among the relief images of the latter group of vessels are representations of bearded males, female heads and Medusa. Some of these males and females may be identified as Celts, and some as Hellenistic rulers wearing the lion's skin associated with Herakles, adopted by Alexander and later by the rulers of the Hellenistic kingdoms.

ROMAN PERIOD

Two female heads which probably belong to the Roman period, **83** and **84**, may be Phrygian/Central Anatolian products, modeled and tooled by hand. The style of the former can be related to a general Central Anatolian style exhibited in limestone sculpture.

LOCAL COROPLASTS

Although graffiti, dipinti and potters' or owners' marks are found on ceramics from Gordion (see Roller 1987a, 1987b) there are no marks of these kinds on the figurines from Gordion, either local or imported. It was not common practice elsewhere for coroplasts to sign their works until the second half of the 2d century B.C. (see below, p. 78), so this absence is not unusual.

There is mounting evidence from the epigraphy (Roller 1987b) that Greeks settled at Gordion alongside the Phrygian and Celtic population of the 3d and 2d century B.C. (see also F. A. Winter 1988). Greek inscriptions, including a potter's signature incised before firing on a locally manufactured ceramic fragment (Roller 1987b: no. 9), indicate that there were Greeks living at Gordion. The very Greekness of the local products of the Late Phrygian/Hellenistic period, the deities depicted and the forms and decorative techniques indicate a close familiarity with Greek products and would allow the possibility that some of the coroplasts, especially of the most ambitious works, were Greek. Two of these very ambitious locally manufactured terracottas, statuettes of Kybele (**52**) and Attis (?) (**97**), are both obviously deities which are Greek in type and iconography. Although Kybele is in essence an Anatolian goddess, it is in the form and with the iconography established by the Greeks that she appears in the Late Phrygian/Hellenistic terracottas at Gordion, even in the examples manufactured in the region or at Gordion itself (**52** and **53**). Holloway proposes, probably correctly, that the large Kybele statuette from Gordion (**52**) was modeled after a large-scale sculptural image, probably a Pergamene one (1957: 32 ff.). If correct, this raises interesting questions regarding the means of transmission of the Pergamene model, the historical relationship between Pergamon and Gordion and the identity of the coroplasts at Gordion (see below, pp. 77-80 for imported figurines).

Late Phrygian/Hellenistic pottery shows an interest in Hellenized shapes and decoration yet a lack of skill which is almost never apparent in true Greek ceramics of the period, and suggests that Phrygians may have had a hand in this production (see F. A. Winter, forthcoming). For the figurines, the adoption by the Phrygians at Gordion of Greek deities such as Nike and Artemis and creations such as the bust-flower type of thymiaterion, which seems ultimately borrowed from a Magna Graecian source, can be explained by pointing not only to the remarkably widespread diffusion and popularity of Hellenism throughout the East in the 4th, 3d and 2d centuries B.C., but also to the presence of Greek craftsmen at Gordion. The Phrygians of the period from the end of the 4th century were, it seems, a Hellenized people, using a Greek alphabet and adopting some of the cults and ways of the Greeks. The presence of Greek personal names, Greek deities and Greek cults suggests a Greek community at Gordion, though how large is unknown (Roller 1987b).

It is virtually certain that Phrygians were also involved in the coroplastic industry as the manufacturers of the handmade animals and wheelmade and hand-modeled animal vessels from the Early and Middle Phrygian periods and that they continued to manufacture a portion of the terracottas to the end of the Late Phrygian/Hellenistic settlement in 189 B.C. This is suggested by, for example, the gray fabric of the Nike vessel handle (?) (**33**) and the female bust thymiaterion (**39**), a fabric typical of Phrygian pottery and other handmade products.

Two human representations of the Late Phrygian/

Hellenistic period, one unfinished and found in the Pottery Establishment (**108**) and one vessel handle (?) in the form of Nike, produced in a typically Phrygian fabric (**33**), wear around their necks what appear to be torques, a distinctly Celtic form of adornment (Powell 1960: 71-73). This may be interpreted as a sign that it was from the Celtic population of the region that some of the coroplasts came, but more probably, simply that close contact with these Celts created an interest in one of the most attractive aspects of their material culture, the torque.

It seems likely, then, from the combined evidence that in coroplastic production in the late 3d and early 2d centuries B.C. at least Greeks and Phrygians participated. It may have been the Greeks at Gordion who produced (or commissioned) most of the Greek-like products—the bust thymiaterion, the Kybele (**52**) and the Attis (?) (**97**). Of the Celts' role in the coroplastic workshops we are able to say virtually nothing. The few products bearing Celtic ornament (**33** and **108**) may have, in fact, been produced by non-Celts. It was probably Phrygian coroplasts who continued to produce the mostly handmade, traditional figurines and had an influence on or made some of the very special products in gray-ware fabrics (e.g., **33** and **39**). We also cannot discount the possible influence of Persian animal vessels on Central Anatolian products (e.g., **14** and **15**); this lingering Persian influence may have been due to Anatolized Persians living in the region (see Cook 1983: 176-182; F. A. Winter 1988: 71, n. 45).

CENTRAL ANATOLIAN FABRICS

It has not been possible to conduct any technical analyses of the composition of the clays used for the terracotta figurines from Gordion. F. A. Winter has been able to analyze by the PIXE method samples from Late Classical and Hellenistic pottery from Gordion (forthcoming; E. T. Williams et al. 1987: 430-432). For a very thorough study of the clays used for local pottery of the 8th to 6th centuries B.C. see Johnston 1970.

EARLY BRONZE AGE

The two probably Early Bronze Age figurines (**115** and **116**) are made of somewhat coarse reddish brown or dark brown clay (Munsell: 2.5YR N3/ [very dark gray]).

MIDDLE AND LATE BRONZE AGE

The clays used for the figurines of the Hittite period are gritty and slightly micaceous, fired to a yellowish pink, orange-red or light reddish brown (Munsell: 7.5YR 8/6 [reddish yellow]; 2.5YR 6/4 [light reddish brown]-6/8 [light red]-N3/ [very dark gray]). Some light and dark inclusions are found in most examples, and most are slipped with a yellow-buff or buff-pink, although at least one (**162**) is burnished to a slightly reddish brown. The similarities of the clays used for both the pottery of this period and the figurines indicate Central Anatolian manufacture.

EARLY PHRYGIAN PERIOD

The group of five Central Anatolian-manufactured animal vessels from Tumulus P exhibit a variety of clays from fine buff (**1** and **2**) to medium-fine light brown (**5**) to fine red clay (**3**). The one Early Phrygian-period animal figurine was manufactured of coarse clay (**122**) as was the miniature wheel (**159**). For a description of the clays used in Early Phrygian ceramics see Sams, 1994.

MIDDLE PHRYGIAN PERIOD

A great variety of fabrics are used in the Central Anatolian production of figurines in the Middle Phrygian period. The colors of the clays range from gray to buff-yellow to pinkish yellow or brown to red. Small or moderate amounts of micaceous particles are common and gritty inclusions, dark and light, are visible in most. The clays range from moderately fine to somewhat coarse. Most figures of the period are covered with polished slip. Surface colors after firing often range from pinkish brown to light brown to gray.

LATE PHRYGIAN/HELLENISTIC PERIOD

The handmade animal figurines of this period are made from clays which range in color from light reddish brown (Munsell: 5YR 6/4 [light reddish brown]) to reddish yellow (Munsell: 7.5YR 7/4 [pink]-7/8 [reddish yellow]) or light red (Munsell: 2.5YR 6/6 [light red] or 10YR 6/8 [light red]), sometimes fired light gray all over or often gray at the core. The clays range from fine with few inclusions to gritty clay with many dark and some lime inclusions. Almost all have some micaceous particles. One Late Phrygian/Hellenistic animal vessel which is likely to be Central Anatolian-manufactured (**12**: stag's head) has light red clay (Munsell: 2.5YR 6/6 [light red]) with small amounts of mica and dark inclusions.

Among the Greek-inspired molded figurines probably made at Gordion itself in the Late Phrygian/Hellenistic period, several distinct groups can be isolated on the basis of clay, technique, design and style. For example, **52**, **54** and **97** belong together as a group from a single workshop and the clays of all are close: hard or friable, micaceous yellowish brown or yellowish red clay fired gray at the core with small lime inclusions (Munsell: 7.5YR 6/6 [reddish yellow]-6/4 [brown]). Although the bust-flower thymiateria can be linked to these statuettes by style and details of the technique, the clays vary slightly. The satyr's bust (**35**) is made from a highly micaceous light reddish brown clay (Munsell: 2.5YR 6/8 [light red]) fired gray at the core. Large and small dark inclusions are visible. The rest of the bust-flower thymiateria are made from a reddish yellow clay (Munsell: 7.5YR 7/6-7/8 [reddish yellow]) which is lightly micaceous with small light inclusions. As in the statuettes (**52** and **97**) a gray core is common in the bust-flower thymiateria. Often the products of this bust-thymiaterion workshop are poorly fired, producing a friable surface.

Another Central Anatolian- or locally made group of molded Late Phrygian/Hellenistic figurines can be isolated: **53**, **65**, **83**, and **108**. The clays of these are consistently micaceous, pinkish brown or light reddish yellow (Munsell: 5YR 6/4 [light reddish brown]-6/6 [reddish yellow]), filled with large dark gritty particles and white lime inclusions, fired gray at the core.

TECHNIQUE

In the Early Phrygian period, the Central Anatolian animal vessels (**1-5**) seem all to have been produced by a combination of wheel-turning technique (for the vessel bodies) and hand-modeling. The other Early Phrygian-period products are handmade. For the Middle Phrygian-period products, e.g., the animal figurines and animal vessels, hand-modeling is the rule, although many of the larger animals and animal vessels probably had wheel-turned sections, mostly for the bodies of the animals.

The groups of Late Phrygian/Hellenistic molded figurines allow an insight into the coroplastic techniques employed by Central Anatolian or local craftsmen. The two large statuettes (**52** [Kybele] and **97** [Attis?]) use both molded and hand-modeling techniques. The large seated Kybele is composed of separately molded sections (e.g., head, upper torso, lower torso, feet and stool, sphinxes) joined together. The attributes, a phiale and a tympanum, are probably wheelmade and the back is applied and tooled by hand. Other details are incised or hand-modeled. A round firing hole is cut through the back of the head. The interior walls are roughly finished. The surface is covered with a fine clay slip over which painted details are rendered. Thick white plaster is used to repair breaks.

The techniques used in the manufacture of the Attis (?) are similar, though the less complete state of preservation inhibits a thorough comparison. The torso of the figure seems to have been largely built up in horizontal sections by hand, with sections of the drapery made in a mold. The arm is modeled separately by hand and attached with thick white plaster. The upper back is hand-modeled in a single section, while the lower torso is left open. The interior walls are smooth on the back and left rough in front. As in the case of the Kybele, the exterior surface is covered with a fine clay slip over which are a white groundcoat and painted details. Hand-tooling is evident for details (on drapery and arm). On both the Kybele and the Attis (?) there are no vent holes on the backs of the torsos because the backs are largely left open. A hole would probably have been cut into the back of Attis's (?) head.

The fronts of the busts of the bust-flower thymiateria are made from molds. The satyr's head (**35**), for example, is made from a single mold for the front of the torso and the head, while the "fillet" is handmade and separately added. **36** was also made with a separate front (head and torso) mold which was joined to the handmade back and the joins masked by the braids at the shoulders and "fillet" on top of the head. On **41** the join of the front and back of the torso is cleverly masked by braids of hair. The technique of attaching the sections is seen on **40**, where gouges or scoring marks are visible along a finished edge of the back section or the head. The backs of the heads and torsos were mostly worked by hand. The back of the satyr's head and **38** may have been molded. **42** appears to have both a molded front and back with the addition of a hand-modeled or molded quiver. That the fronts of the head and torso were sometimes made in a single mold is shown by **50**. If **51** can be assigned to this group of bust-flower thymiateria, fronts of heads were also sometimes molded separately from the torso. The flower containers of these thymiateria, as is evident by **44**, are made from a single mold and set into the holes cut into the tops of the busts' heads. The conical shape of the mold with a narrow interior diameter at the base would make molding a difficult task, and the sloppily executed fragments of the finished products (e.g., **45** *etc.*) demonstrate how unwieldy use of this mold might have been.

The exterior surfaces of the busts' heads and torsos, as well as of many of the flower fragments, were given a slip of fine buff-pink clay. Vent holes vary in size and shape. The satyr's head (**35**) and **36**, for example, each have a large triangular opening cut through the backs of their torsos, while **41** has a circular vent hole in the center of the back. The openings in the head for the flower containers would have been either cut into the leather-hard clay before firing or molded as such (as is possibly shown by **51**). The interior walls of the heads and torsos are well smoothed on some examples (**37**, **40-42**) and left rough on others (e.g., **35**, **39**).

The group of **53**, **65** and **83** are distinguished by their sloppily rendered hand-tooling to augment the molded figurine. In all three cases a tool is heavily used in the rendering of drapery or hair and all three exhibit a lack of facility with the molding technique. Although a much more finely executed figurine, **33** also shows an extensive use of incised details on the hair and drapery. This is one of the few molded figurines of this Late Phrygian/Hellenistic period which have been fired in the Phrygian bucchero technique (see also **39**).

DECORATION

Most of the Central Anatolian-manufactured figurines and vessels are decorated by painting or polishing or a combination of both. The Early Phrygian-period animal vessels show two different decorative schemes, with polishing and painting: monochromatic black on red ground (**3**) and bichromatic brown and yellow on buff ground. Among the handmade animal figurines, few are completely unpolished or undecorated (e.g., the Bronze Age animals, some of which are slipped, and **133** [probably 6th century], **141**, [mid-6th-4th century] and **143**, [mid-4th-century context]). See p. 49 for a discussion of the technique and decoration of animal figurines. All of the boots are polished (**162, 166**) or painted in a bichromatic (**163, 164, 167**, and **168**) or a monochromatic (**165**) technique; and most of the non-figural, miscellaneous objects are painted in a bichromatic (**156-158**) or a monochromatic technique and are polished (**161**) or slipped and polished (**160**).

Among the Greek-inspired Central Anatolian products, the decoration is much the same as for the Greek products of comparable type. For example, a white or light groundcoat over which painted decoration is applied is common on many of the Central Anatolian and locally made figurines: some of the bust-flower thymiateria, the large statuettes of Kybele (**52**) and Attis (?) (**97**), the rhyton handle (?) in the form of Nike (**33**). The colors used for the decoration of these figurines include red, light blue, pink, yellow and black, the same palette used by Greek coroplasts in the Hellenistic period.

NON-PHRYGIAN AND NON-CENTRAL ANATOLIAN FIGURINES

TYPOLOGY

Non-Phrygian or non-Central Anatolian, imported figurines can be defined as composing approximately 50% of the total number of figurines and related figural vessels included in this corpus. The extent of Western—i.e., mostly Greek—influence on and trade with Gordion can be measured in the importation of varieties of figurines from the 6th century on. Greek or imitation-Greek molded vessels in the form of animals, pomegranates or korai are typical finds at East Greek sites in the 6th century B.C. and turn up at Gordion, not too surprisingly, to form a group of eleven vessels (**19-29**). These are the earliest of the terracotta types imported to Gordion in this catalogue, but by no means constitute the earliest Greek objects at Gordion (see Sams 1979b: 45-53, esp. 47 for 8th-century Corinthian and Euboean pottery fragments) or the earliest East Greek material. Pottery imports from East Greek centers are fairly steady from Late Geometric times into the 6th century B.C. (*ibid.*: 47-49; DeVries, forthcoming). The molded vessels, unlike the other categories of terracottas in the corpus, were probably imported to Gordion more for their contents than for the containers.

The first purely terracotta figurines to be imported to Gordion belong to the 5th century B.C. (e.g., **77** and **85**). It is in the Late Phrygian/Hellenistic period at Gordion that the number of imported Greek figurines increases and that a pattern emerges in the popularity or presence of certain types. Representations of females, especially standing and draped types, outnumber all other categories. Mostly imports from Greek regions, these females can largely be associated with religious functions, probably as votives at private shrines.

The group which follows the females and bust-flower thymiateria in frequency is that of Kybele. Her popularity in the Hellenistic period in mainland and eastern Greek regions and in Phrygia is well attested by the shrines dedicated to her (e.g., at Mamurtkale near Pergamon [Conze and Schazmann 1911], and at Pessinus in Phrygia, where literary and epigraphical sources confirm the existence of a shrine by the period of the Attalids of Pergamon [Strabo 12, 5, 3, C 567; Welles 1934: nos. 55-61; Virgilio 1981]), and by the small votives at many sites (see discussion of Kybele, above, pp. 22-24).

That Kybele was worshiped at Gordion in the region of her purported birthplace (at Mt. Dindymus near Pessinus) is not surprising. One temple girl or attendant can be connected with the cult of Kybele at Gordion by the tympanum, an attribute of Kybele which the girl holds (**64**), and the possible identification of one locally manufactured statuette as Attis (**97**) adds additional evidence for a thriving local cult devoted to Kybele.

Eros is also a popular divinity represented among the terracottas at Gordion (**99-104**). In view of a general interest in Eros at Greek sites in the Hellenistic period, it is not surprising that these Greek figurines turn up as imports at Gordion. Other Greek deities represented at Gordion include Nike (in a locally manufactured example, **33**); Tyche (**34**); Artemis (in a locally manufactured thymiaterion, **42**); Dionysos with Ariadne and satyr (**105**); possibly Herakles (**98**); and other mythological subjects including a possible Medusa (**82**) and two satyrs (**32** and **35**), one imported and the other locally manufactured.

The identification of imported terracotta figurine types and manufacturing centers which are lacking in the figurine assemblage at Gordion is, perhaps, as instructive as an examination of the types and export centers which can be identified. For example, there are no figurines from any period at Gordion which can be specifically identified as Carian (Higgins 1954: nos. 301-522) or as Cypriote (e.g., J. H. and S. H. Young 1955). Among the Greek imports at Gordion there are no nude female types, which are very popular elsewhere in mainland Greece and Asia Minor in the Hellenistic period and occur more frequently at Troy, for example, than do draped females (D. B. Thompson 1963a: 87-95). Aphrodite is not represented at Gordion, although Eros is popular. There are at Gordion representations of the child-Eros, Eros reclining in a flower and Eros as a young boy standing with wings at his side, in addition to two chubby Erotes supporting a thymiaterion. There are no examples of Eros in flight, very common at Myrina (Mollard-Besques 1963: 35-39, pls. 39-47; Burr 1934: 47-56). A possible rationale for the absence of Aphrodite among the figurines may be the special position Kybele enjoyed in Phrygia as a mother goddess, the goddess who would have usurped the power of Aphrodite in the realm of love and fertility. Eros may have enjoyed his popularity as a result of a kind of conflation with Attis, the handsome shepherd boy born on the banks of the river Gallus near Pessinus and devoted to Kybele with an almost maniacal fidelity (for the legends of Attis and iconography see Vermaseren 1977b: 31, 88-95). There is only one possible terracotta representation of Attis at Gordion (**97**). One of the figurines of Eros was found in a terracotta deposit with an enthroned Kybele figurine and a large statuette which may be Attis (see Terracotta Deposit 6) in what may be a group of votives for a shrine to Kybele. This connection between Eros and Kybele may be purely coincidental, and it may well be that the number of representations of Eros at Gordion reflects less his local appeal than the numbers of terracotta figurines of Eros on the general market in the Hellenistic period, when his popularity was very widespread.

While very popular in Greek regions in the Hellenistic period, at Gordion only one possible representation of a lone dancer is identifiable among the terracotta figurines (**75**): a mantle dancer (see D. B. Thompson 1963a: 102-105). In addition, a group composition may be reconstructed as a trio of dancing women (**76**). At other sites, in Thrace, Asia Minor, Mesopotamia and Egypt, Phrygian dancers (i.e., dancers wearing Oriental costume and a so-called Phrygian cap, which may in fact be Persian) of 3d- or 2d-century B.C. date are found (*ibid.*: 100-102; 1963c: 312, no. 19, first half of 2d century B.C. from Athenian Agora). Because these so-called Phrygian dancers are often associated with the cult of Kybele, as representations of orgiastic devotees of the Anatolian goddess (D. B. Thompson 1963a: 102), it is surprising that none have been found at Gordion, where the cult of Kybele is very well attested in the Late Phrygian/ Hellenistic period. Similarly, mantle dancers are linked to Kybele at Troy (*ibid.*: 104) and at Mamurtkale near Pergamon (Conze and Schazmann 1911: pl. 12{6-8}; Töpperwein-Hoffmann 1978: 84, 89, pl. 37 {MK 27}); and to Demeter elsewhere (see D. B. Thompson 1963a: 59 ff., 104; Töpperwein-Hoffmann 1978: nos. 161, 164). Since the one example from Gordion has no more specific context than its trench designation, we cannot be certain that it was used there in the cult of Kybele.

Absent from Gordion are imported terracotta figurines with signatures of coroplasts. This can, clearly, be explained through an examination of the site's chronology. From her study of the Myrina figurines, Dorothy Burr [Thompson] (1934: 7-16) concluded that the practice of signing figurines is not manifested in Asia Minor until toward the end of the 2d century B.C.; and the earliest signature of a coroplast that can be identified at Pergamon is dated to the third quarter of the 2d century B.C. (Töpperwein 1976: 166-168). The *terminus ante quem* for the settlement at Gordion helps to reinforce a date after 189 B.C. for the introduction of coroplasts' signatures.

ORIGINS

Groups of imported Greek figurines of the Late Phrygian/Hellenistic period can be isolated according to the composition of the clay, the painting technique and style, and assigned to probable manufacturing sites or workshops on the basis of these criteria. Two such groups have been defined and, in the absence of technical analyses, it is only possible to suggest a specific manufacturing site for one of the two groups, and a general region for the second. Together these two groups account for the most ambitious figurines and stylistically and technically the highest in quality of the imports to Gordion in the Late Phrygian/Hellenistic period.

GROUP I

57 Kybele Riding Lion
58 Enthroned Kybele
59 Enthroned Kybele
66 Standing Female with Wreath
67 Standing Female
68 Standing Female

Included in this first group are standing females and Kybele types, all of which, with the exception of **58**, were recovered from a single household deposit (see Terracotta Deposit 3). **58**, an enthroned Kybele, was found in another household deposit (see Terracotta Deposit 6). It is likely that all are votives from small Kybele shrines (see pp. 66-67 and pp. 69-70 for Terracotta Deposits 3 and 6). All date to the late 3d or early 2d century B.C.

The composition of the clay of all the figurines in this group is uniformly fine with a few lime inclusions and no micaceous particles, fired to a tan-orange (Munsell: 7.5YR 7/6 [reddish yellow]) and sometimes gray at the core. Heavy, usually well preserved painted decoration is applied in all cases over a white groundcoat in pink-red or brick-red, blue, black and orange. The miniaturist style of the painted decoration of the Kybele figurines, e.g., **57-59**, link these figurines together as a subgroup, and the standing females (**66-68**) in a solid, full-bodied style can be assigned to another subgroup, perhaps indicating two different coroplasts or workshops working at the same manufacturing site or utilizing the same clay source.

The composition of the clay of the Group I figurines closely matches that of terracotta figurines found on the acropolis of Pergamon and at the Attalid sanctuary of Kybele at Mamurtkale. For descriptions of the clay of the Hellenistic terracottas from Pergamon, see D. B. Thompson 1963a: 15; Töpperwein 1976: 6-7, 10. Although Töpperwein-Hoffmann identifies the clay of the figurines at Mamurtkale as Aeolian, similar to that of 5th- and 4th-century figurines from Larisa (1978: 80-81), the current excavators at Pergamon can, by virtue of sheer numbers of figurines, isolate the local products from the imports (W. Radt, personal communication, 1981; Radt 1973: 267-268, fig. 10; 1978: 419-423, Abb. 11-18, 20) and match these with figurines at Mamurtkale.

The Hellenistic figurines at Pergamon are made of clays which are finely washed and fired to buff golden-yellow with no micaceous particles (D. B. Thompson 1963a: 15), very like the description of the clay of the figurines in Group I from Gordion. Additional evidence for assigning a Pergamene origin to this group comes from an examination of the type of Kybele riding a lion (**57**). The only close parallels for **57** come from Mamurtkale, and the general sculptural type of Kybele riding a lion is thought to be Pergamene in origin (see p. 26).

This connection between Celtic Gordion and Pergamon seems at first anomalous in light of our knowledge of the adverse relationship of the Pergamenes and the Celts in the Hellenistic period. However, there is substantial information that the Attalids maintained an interest in controlling the Celts through alliances (R. E. Allen 1983: 136-144). At least Eumenes II maintained a "cooperative" relationship with Celtic tribes in some periods of his reign. We are told by Livy (38, 18) that Manlius Vulso, the Roman consul in charge of the 189 B.C. expedition to bring the Celtic tribes under control, sent envoys to Eposognatus, the chief of the Tolistoagii who controlled the area around Gordion. Livy describes Eposognatus as the only one of the chiefs who had remained friendly to Eumenes, and thus one can assume that Eumenes II had managed alliances of some kind with Eposognatus and other Celtic chiefs earlier in his reign. The precise nature of the alliance between Eumenes and Eposognatus is not known, but both Gordion, as a headquarters of the Tolistoagii, and Pessinus, as the most important sanctuary in the region of this tribe (Lambrechts *et al.* 1972: 156-173), must have enjoyed an unusually open relationship with the Pergamenes in these times of peace. We know that the Attalids of Pergamon took a great interest in the cult of the Great Mother goddess at Pessinus, as is evidenced by the introduction of the Romans to that cult by Attalos I (Hansen 1971: 50-51) and by a series of letters, copied on stone in the 1st century B.C., written by Eumenes II and his brother Attalos II between 163 and 156 B.C. to the high priest of Pessinus (Virgilio 1981: Welles 1934: nos. 55-61; Hansen 1971: 126). Some of these letters indicate that by the 160s B.C., a Celt was a high priest of that cult at Pessinus (Virgilio 1981: 26, letter no. 2; 28, letter no. 4; 29, letter no. 5; 31, letter no. 7).

The relationships between Pergamenes and Celts were complicated, sometimes duplicitous, but there is no mistaking the literary sources as to the side the Attalids took in the 189 B.C. campaign of Manlius Vulso to rid Asia Minor of the dreaded Celts. It was Eumenes, among others from the Greek cities, who urged the Roman Senate to undertake the campaign and it was Attalos II, Eumenes' younger brother, who accompanied Manlius Vulso to Gordion and participated in the victory at Mt. Olympus nearby (Hansen 1971: 90). It was in this very period of Celtic domination of the Gordion region, during the end of the 3d and early 2d century B.C., that the large Kybele statuette (**52**) was manufactured at Gordion using a Pergamene model and that the probably Pergamene terracotta products of Group I were imported to Gordion. The figurines which form this group are restricted in type to representations of Kybele and standing females; all can be assigned functions as votives, probably in a cult of Kybele (see pp. 66-67 and 69-70 for Terracotta Deposits 3 and 6). It is interesting to note that the imported ceramics, on the other hand, show little if any connection with Pergamon (F. A. Winter, forthcoming), except in the SET "Level 2 House," where Pergamene units of measure are inscribed on five pithos fragments (see above, Terracotta Deposit 3). The Pergamene connections with Gordion seen in these figurines of Kybele and votives to Kybele can be explained by the presence of a community of Greeks at Gordion (see above, pp. 74-75) and by the shared interest of the Celts, Phrygians and Pergamenes in the cult of the Mother Goddess at Pessinus, just sixty kilometers southwest of Gordion (see also Burkert 1979: 104-105). It is likely that Pessinus was the link between the sometimes rivalrous and sometimes friendly Pergamenes and Celts, and that it was at least partially through Pessinus and the cult of Kybele that Gordion appears to be so Hellenized, despite its mixed population of Phrygians, Celts and Greeks, in a period of Celtic domination of the region.

GROUP II

60   Enthroned Kybele
61   Enthroned Kybele

70 Standing Female
73 Standing Female
74 Standing Female
76 Group Composition: Dancing Females
99 Eros in Flower
92 Female Head
96 Drapery Fragment

Although there are variations in the clays of the figurines in this large group, these variations may be accounted for by firing conditions and slightly different clay sources. There are enough stylistic cross-links to further corroborate that all these figurines probably come from the same manufacturing site or region.

The consistencies in the clay composition of these figurines lie in its micaceous character and red-orange firing color (Munsell: 5YR 6/4 [light reddish brown]-6/6-6/8 [reddish yellow] or 2.5YR 5/6 [red]-6/8 [light red]). These figurines are mostly very hard-fired, sometimes with tiny dark and light inclusions, creating a speckled surface effect (e.g., **60**). Rarely are the figurines fired gray at the core (e.g., **73**).

Stylistically, the features which link this group are the precise use of line, as seen in the sharply defined edges of the drapery and in the angular facial features of **92**, and an understanding of the variety of textures and how they can be achieved in a coroplastic medium. A sense of the dramatic is displayed in the unusual poses of the women in the group composition (**76**) and in the flowing locks of golden hair of one of these women. The use of thick painted decoration in well-preserved pastel colors, especially pink, is another characteristic of most of the figurines in this group.

The absolute identification of a single manufacturing site for the figurines in Group II is not yet possible, but in the general region around the Black Sea their possible origins may be found. Close stylistic and typological parallels for one of the figurines in this group can be found at sites in the Black Sea region: the enthroned Kybele (**60**) has parallels from Amisos, on the southwest shore of the Black Sea, and from Myrmekion in the Crimea. In addition, the rich polychromy of the figurines in this group is paralleled by many at Amisos (Mollard-Besques 1963: 81), although the descriptions of the clays used at Amisos for figurines in the Hellenistic period (D. B. Thompson 1963a: 15-16; Mollard-Besques 1963: 81) are not compatible with the description of the clay of the Gordion figurines. A figurine of an enthroned Kybele from Histria (Istros) in the Pontic region is identified as locally produced and the description of the clay as brick red with fine micaceous particles and granules of lime is very close to the Group II clay descriptions (Boardman 1962-63: 39, fig. 13; Coja 1961: 217, figs. 3-4). The clay of one group of the locally manufactured figurines and molds from Callatis (Mangalia) in the Pontic region is also described as brick red (Canarache 1969: 26). Further connections between Turkish Thrace and Galatian Gordion can be seen in the ceramics from Gordion and in the funerary architecture (see F. A. Winter 1984: 216-220). Thus, although the general region of the Black Sea can be pointed to for the possible origin of this group, it is not yet possible to further pinpoint the locale (see Russayayeva 1982; SAI 1970-1974 for summaries of terracottas from various sites north of the Black Sea).

THE GORDION FIGURINES IN THEIR CENTRAL ANATOLIAN SETTING

Due to a dearth of major systematic excavation at sites in the vicinity of Gordion and to a lack of publications on terracotta figurines and figural vessels from sites in Anatolia, it is not yet possible to critically compare the terracotta assemblage at Gordion to those of other major and minor centers in Central Anatolia in all periods. For the Early, Middle and Late Bronze Age, it is difficult because of the limits of the archaeological evidence from Gordion to assess the relative importance of this site, yet it is clear that there was a substantial Hittite-period settlement. Hittite centers, especially the capital of Hattuša-Boğazköy and Alaca Höyük, have been well excavated and the results and finds amply published. Specific comparisons in style and typology can be made between the small number of Hittite figurines from Gordion and those from Hattuša-Boğazköy (see esp. **120**, **121**) and general comparisons with the animal figurine types from both Boğazköy and Alaca Höyük (Kosay and Akok 1966: pls. 25-30).

For the Early and Middle Phrygian periods, we have few comparative data from the region. Major nearby centers in these periods were at Ankara to the northeast, Dorylaion (Eskişehir) to the west, Hattuša (Boğazköy) to the east (Schirmer 1969: 12-14) and sites in the Phrygian highlands to the southwest, where the most important of the religious centers was Midas City (Yazilikaya).

The limited excavations of a large tumulus at Dorylaion (Eskişehir) have produced no terracotta figurines or figural vessels (for Roman finds see Mellink 1973: 190) and the settlement mound has not yet been excavated. At Boğazköy, no figurines of the Middle Phrygian period have appeared in the significant publications of the small finds (Boehmer 1972, 1979). At Midas City, remains of a small Late Phrygian/Hellenistic sanctuary were excavated on the Midas Kale and terracotta figurines of the 2d century B.C. were found in pits (Haspels 1951: 21-22, 89-90, pl. 37b-c; 1971: 154-155, fig. 495, section U). None of the published examples bear any similarities to the Gordion figurines, despite the fact that the figurines are dedications to Agdistis (Kybele). (For the mythological relationship between Agdistis and Kybele see Vermaseren 1977b: 90-91.) Yalincak, a Phrygian site in the vicinity of Ankara with occupation into the Late Phrygian/

Hellenistic period, has produced at least one terracotta figurine (Tezcan 1964: 15: Kybele statuette) and no figurines have been published from the soundings and excavations on the Phrygian mounds in Ankara (Özgüç and Akok 1947; Buluç 1979).

In the Late Phrygian/Hellenistic period, Gordion's importance as the Phrygian capital had waned and the site had become probably a town of the Tolistoagii, while Pessinus, Ancyra (Ankara) and Tavium (beyond the Halys River) served as the major strongholds of the three Celtic tribes. No terracotta figurines have been published from Ankara, Tavium or any other Celtic fortress site in Anatolia (e.g., Blucium-Karalar or Peium-Tabanlıoğlu: Arik 1934; Arik and Coupry 1935; Mitchell 1974). The "Hellenistic" levels and remains at Boğazköy have been outlined (Kühne 1969) but no systematic study of the terracotta figurines has been carried out.

We know from historical sources that the sanctuary of Kybele at Pessinus assumed a role of great importance in the Late Phrygian/Hellenistic period in Central Anatolia, and its proximity to Gordion, its Celtic control, combined with the interest in Kybele at Gordion logically makes Pessinus a site whose terracotta figurines should be comparable to those at Gordion in the Late Phrygian/Hellenistic and Roman periods. The Belgian excavations conducted thus far at Pessinus, however, have uncovered almost exclusively Roman-period monuments and levels (Devreker and Waelkens 1984), while there is almost nothing Roman at Gordion with which to make comparisons. The temple, once identified as the Attalid temple of Kybele (Lambrechts *et al.* 1972: 156), is now recognized to be Imperial Roman in date and unrelated to Kybele (Devreker and Waelkens 1984: 52; Waelkens 1985; 1986: 48-60).

There is, in summary, no published corpus of terracotta figurines from any Central Anatolian site which can be adequately compared to that from Gordion. Gordion's size, long history, changing populations and rich cultural transformations from a Bronze Age center to a Phrygian capital to a market town and Graeco-Celtic center make it unique in the archaeological and historical record. It will thus be to Gordion that archaeologists and historians will look in the future for comprehensive comparative data on Phrygian terracotta figurines and many other categories of archaeological material.

Concordance

Inventory Number	Catalogue Number	Inventory Number	Catalogue Number	Inventory Number	Catalogue Number
MC 119	7	P 3698	98	T 26	74
MC 151	157	P 4157	162	T 27	164
MC 212	160	P 4247	150	T 28	63
MC 264	159	P 4388	117	T 29	148
MC 311	171	P 4437	22	T 30	123
P 486	18	P 5138	32	T 31	101
P 648	33	ST 169	105	T 32	35
P 666	15	T 1	27	T 33	38
P 810	80	T 2	8	T 34	60
P 1153	19	T 3	93	T 35	52
P 1154	26	T 4	89	T 36	83
P 1157	20	T 5	66	T 37	158
P 1160	28	T 6	59	T 38	163
P 1403	3	T 7	57	T 39	87
P 1411	1	T 8/9	68	T 40	29
P 1412	2	T 10	67	T 41	139
P 1424	4	T 11	134	T 42	12
P 1425	5	T 12	85	T 43	118
P 1664	34	T 13	53(a)	T 44	91
P 1694	81	T 14	106	T 45	102
P 2174	168	T 15	71	T 46	31
P 2234	21	T 16	82	T 47	55
P 2248	9	T 17	140	T 48	169
P 2237	30	T 18	124	T 49	109
P 2497	10	T 19	53(b)	T 50	119
P 2555	25	T 20	110	T 51	92
P 2576	6	T 21	137	T 52	70
P 2583	14	T 22	113	T 53	61(a)
P 2611	122	T 23	125	T 54	41
P 3229	24	T 25	42	T 55	69

CONCORDANCE

Inventory Number	Catalogue Number	Inventory Number	Catalogue Number	Inventory Number	Catalogue Number
T 56	**73**	T 85	**155**	T 114	**141**
T 57	**146**	T 86	**62**	T 115	**61(b)**
T 58	**99**	T 87	**76**	T 116	**46**
T 59	**36**	T 88	**167**	T 117	**47**
T 60	**37**	T 89	**88**	T 118	**114**
T 61	**58**	T 90	**112**	T 119	**40**
T 62	**97**	T 91	**94**	T 120	**96**
T 63	**100**	T 92	**135**	T 121	**43**
T 64	**84**	T 93	**149**	T 122	**75**
T 65	**13**	T 94	**142**	T 123	**48**
T 66	**86**	T 95	**51**	T 124	**145**
T 67	**103**	T 96	**77**	T 125	**115**
T 68	**65**	T 97	**147**	T 126	**154**
T 69	**170**	T 98	**116**	T 127	**128**
T 70	**50**	T 100	**78**	T 128	**126**
T 71	**44**	T 101	**165**	T 129	**136**
T 72	**108**	T 102	**111**	T 130	**49**
T 73	**95**	T 103	**11**	T 131	**127**
T 74	**45**	T 104	**17**	T 132	**152**
T 75	**132**	T 105	**16**	T 133	**151**
T 77	**166**	T 106	**104**	T 136	**72**
T 78	**64**	T 107	**144**	T 137	**54**
T 79	**138**	T 108	**161**	T 139	**107**
T 80	**156**	T 109	**23**	T 141	**121**
T 81	**131**	T 110	**153**	T 142	**130**
T 82	**133**	T 111	**120**	T 143	**56**
T 83	**39**	T 112	**143**	T 144	**90**
T 84	**79**	T 113	**129**		

Türkce Özet

Bu kitabın konusu olan 171 *terracotta* figürin ve resimli kaplar Pennsylvania Üniversitesi Müzesi tarafından 1950-1973 yıllarında Gordion'da yapılmış olan kazılarda bulunmuştur. Bu çalışmanın kapsamı, kalıp ve elle yapılmış insan, tanrı, diğer tabiat üstü yaratıklar ve hayvanlar, minyatürler, maskeler, madalyonlar, figürin kalıpları veya kaplar, ayrla, kap olmayan malzeme ile kalıp ve elle yapılmış resimli kaplardır. Kaplara ait parçalar olduğunu zannettiğimiz bir grup el yapısı hayvan figürinleri de hayvanlı kaplar kategorisi kapsamında etüd edilmiştir.

Terracotta figürinler Gordion'da Eski Tunç Çagı'ndan, Geç Frig/Helenistik Çağ'a kadar bulunmustur. Gordion'un 8ci yüzyıl öncesi çağlarına ait bilgimiz çok kısıtlıdır; ancak, Tunç ve Erken' Frig çağlarına tarihlenen az sayıda figürin bulunmuştur. M.Ö. 7. yüzyilda itibaren, Kimmerler tarafından tahrip edildikten sonra, M.Ö 4. yüzyılın sonlarına kadar (Orta Frig Çağı), Büyük Iskender'in fethini kapsıyan devirde, Gordion'da bulunan toprak malzeme sayısında büyük bir artış görülür. En tamam arkeolojik verilerin bu çağa ait olması da rastlantı değildir. Orta Frig Çağına ait buluntuların çoğu hayvan biçimli kaplardan (rhyton) veya hayvan figürinlerinden oluşur, bir de Orta Anadolu malzemesi olan çarık biçimli kaplar ve küçük arabalar bulunur. Ayrıca, bu devre ait çok sayıda kalıpdan çıkmış ithal Grek malı kaplar da vardır.

Geç Frig/Helenistik Çağ'da artış gösteren malı ithal Grek toprak malzeme arasında çoğunlukta olanlar Kybele tasvirleri, giysili kadın figürleri, Eros ve tiyatro maskeleridir. Bu devirde ithal figürinlerin sayısı Orta Anadolu`nun yerli malzemesine esittir. Ithal mallarının çoğu Gordion'un terk edilmesinden hemen önce, M.Ö. 189 'a tarihlenir. Bu devrin "koroplastik" repertuarının en canlı örnekleri arasında *bust-flower thymiaterion* (bk. levha 11-14), büyük Kybele heykelcikleri ve de Attis vardır.

Anadolunun surlarla çevrili en önemli şehirlerinden olan Gordion M. Ö. 189'da şehir terkedildikten sonra önemini yitirdi. Buradaki seyrek Roma yerleşmelerini ancak iki figürinle saptayabiliyoruz.

Fırınlarda bulunan kalıp parçaları veya yarıda bırakılmış figürinler ve gelişmiş çömlekçiliğin simgesi olan, kalıp ve figürin parçalarına bakıldığında, Gordion'da yapılmis olan terracotta figürinlerin Geç Frig/Helenistik Çağ'a ait olduğu görülür. Bütün verilere dayanarak diyebiliriz ki M.Ö. 3. ve 2. yüzyılda Yunanlılar ve Frigyalılar *terracotta* sanatını birlikte yaptılar. Yunan malzemesi Gordion'da Yunanlılar tarafından yapılmış veya onlar tarafından yaptırılmış olabilir. Kelt halkının Koroplastik atölyelerindeki çalışmaları hakkında birşey bilmiyoruz. Az sayıdaki Kelt stili bezekli ürünler Kelt olmayan halk tarafından yapılmış olabilir. Frigyali *terracotta* sanatçıları geleneksel figürinleri elle yapmaya devam etmiş veya onların yapımını etkilemişler veya çok özel eserler gri maldan yapılmıştır (*grey ware fabrics*). Aynı zamanda, Orta Anadolu'nun hayvan biçimli kaplarında, bu bölgede yaşamiş olan Anadolulu Iranlılar'ın etkisini görebiliyoruz.

Tüm figürin ve şekilli kapların yaklaşık yüzde ellisi ithal malı figürinlerden (Frig veya Orta Anadolu malı olmayan) oluşur. Gordion'da 6 yüzyıldan itibaren batının ve özellikle Yunan etkisinin ve ticaretinin nedenli geniş çapta olduğunu değişik tipteki ithal malı figürinlerden ölçebiliriz. Altıncı yüzyılda Doğu Yunan yerleşmelerinin tipik buluntuları olan hayvan şekilli kaplar, nar stili kaplar, ve *kore*ler'in Gordionda da 11 tane kaptan oluşan bir grup buluntu olarak ele geçirilmesine şaşırmamak gerekir.

Gordion'daki ilk ithal mali *terracotta* figürinler M.Ö. 5. yüzyıla tarihlenir. Geç Frig/Helenistik çağlarda ithal malı Yunan figürinlerin Gordionda rağbette oluşunu sayılarının çoğ almasından anlıyoruz. Kadın tasvirleri, özellikle ayakta duran ve giysili tipler, diğer kategorilere göre daha fazladır. Çoğu Yunan bölgelerinden ithal edilen bu figürinler, herhalde adak olarak özel tapınaklarda kullanılmıştır. Figürinler arasında, kadın ve *bust-flower thymiateria*'dan sonra, çoğunluğu Kybele figürin grupları oluşturur. Eros da popüler bir tanrı temsilcisi olarak Gordion'daki terracotta malzeme arasında bulunur. Diğer Grek tanrıları içinde Nike, Tyche, Artemis, Dionysos ve Ariadne, ayrıca Herakles ve diğer mitolojik konuları içeren Medusa ve iki *satyr* de bulunur.

Geç Frig/Helenistik Çag'a ait önemli iki ithal malı Yunan figürin grubunu, hamuru, boya tekniği ve uslubu ve yapıldıkları atölyelere göre ayırabiliriz. Bunlar arasında, sadece bir tanesinin kesin olarak Bergama atölyelerinde, diğerinin de Karadeniz yöresinde yapıldığı söylenebilir. Bu iki grup, geç Frig/Helenistik Çağ'da uslup ve teknik açıdan Gordiona ithal edilen figürinler arasında en kaliteli ve çarpıcı olanlardır.

Gordion figürinlerini Orta Anadolu toprak figürinleri ile karşılaştırmalı etüd edebilmek icin elimizde bir neşriyat yoktur.

Gordion'un hacmi, uzun tarihi, değişen nüfusu ve zengin kültür evreleri ile, —Eski Tunc Çağında merkez, Frig döneminde başşehir ve pazar yeri, Greco/Kelt devrinde yine merkez olarak–, arkeoloji ve tarih kayıtlarında eşsiz bir yeri vardır. Frig arkeolojik malzeme ve buna dahil olan toprak figürinler hakkında ileride yapılacak geniş çaptaki karşılaştırmali araştırmalar icin sanat tarihcileri, arkeolog ve tarih uzmanları Gordion neşriyatlarına muhakkak başvuracaklardır.

Tesekkür:

Bu kitabin hazırlanmasi sırasında bana yardımcı olan herkese, özellikle Gordion projesinde çalışan ve aşağıda isimleri yazılı kişilere teşekkürlerimi sunarım: Keith De Vries, Jean Carpenter Efe, Ann Gunter, Ellen Kohler, Lynn Roller, G. Kenneth Sams, Karen Vellucci, Robert ve Frances Vincent ve Frederick A. Winter. Ayrica, 1981 yaz aylarında *terracotta* figürinlerini Türkiyede çalışabilmem için bana destek olan konuksever, asağıda isimleri yazılı Türk ve diğer meslektaslarıma da teşekkürlerimi iletirim: Ekrem Akurgal, Ankara; Nusin Asgari, Istanbul Arkeoloji Müzesi, Kudret Ata, Ayfer Aker ve Meral Gözübüyük, Eski Eserler ve Müzeler Genel Müdürlüğü; Selahattin Erdemgil, Selcuk; merhum Kenan Erim, Aphrodisias; Crawford Greenewalt, Sardis; Pontus Heilström, Labraunda; Kubilay Nayir ve Rafet Dinç, Antalya Müzesi; Wolfgang Radt, Bergama; ve Raci Temizer, Anadolu Medeniyetleri Müzesi.

Index

Abdera (Thrace) 43
Aegina 27
Aizanoi 28
Alaca Höyük 80
Alexander the Great 2, 3, 24, 28, 36, 45, 59, 71, 74
Alexandria 35
Amisos (Samsun) 18, 23, 27, 44, 80
Amphipolis 42
animal(s) 1, 37, 49–59, 62, 65–67, 68, 71, 73, 75, 77, 80
　attachment 1, 5, 9, 49, 51, 52, 57–58, 59, 65, 71, 74
　birds 9, 13, 49, 50, 51, 58, 66
　　cock 49, 50, 59
　　dove 10, 12, 13, 28, 49, 50, 58, 59
　　duck 9
　　goose 5–6, 58, 65
　　hawk 9, 66
　quadruped 10, 49, 50, 51–58, 65–66, 68
　　dog 5, 6, 7
　　hare 10, 11, 13
　　hedgehog 10, 11, 65–66
　　lion 5, 6, 7–8, 10, 15, 22, 23, 24, 25, 26, 27, 28, 37, 42, 49, 50, 57–58, 66, 74, 78, 79
　　ungulate 49, 50, 51, 53, 54, 55
　　　bull 6, 9, 49, 50, 51, 53, 54, 56, 57, 58–59, 65
　　　deer/stag 6, 8, 10, 49, 50, 51, 56, 65, 75
　　　goat 6, 8, 31, 44, 57, 65, 67
　　　horse/stallion 49, 50, 51, 52, 53, 55, 57
　　　ram 6, 10, 11, 14, 49, 50, 52, 65
　　　sheep 10
　vessels (*See* plastic vessels, animal)
Ankara 2, 80, 81
　Museum of Anatolian Civilizations 1
Aphrodite (*See under* divinities, gods)
archetype 15, 21, 46, 58, 63–64, 69, 74
Ariadne 45, 47, 77
Artemis (*See under* divinities)
aryballoi (*See also* perfumed oils; unguent bottles) 10, 11, 13, 15, 61
Asia Minor 2, 22, 27, 38, 45, 46, 73, 78, 79
Assyria/Assyrians 2

Athens 13, 25, 33, 47
attachment (*See under* animal; plastic attachments)
Attica/Attic 10, 38
Attis (*See under* divinities)
attributes 16–17, 20, 22, 25, 26, 27, 36, 42, 73, 76, 77
Balıkesir 18
bird (*See under* animal)
Bithynia 2
　King Nikomedes 2
Black Sea 23, 27, 28, 29, 80
Blucium-Karalar 81
Boğazköy (Hattuşa-Boğazköy) 52, 61, 62, 71, 80, 81
boots and shoes 4, 23, 24, 26, 34, 49, 61–63, 68, 71, 72, 73, 77
Bronze Age 1, 2, 4, 5, 50, 51–53, 61–62, 72, 77, 80, 81
　Early 2, 49, 50, 51–52, 71, 75
　Middle 2, 50, 71, 75
　Late 2, 50, 71, 75
bull (*See under* animal, ungulate)
burials 1–2, 6, 7, 13, 14, 31, 44, 47, 51, 54, 56, 59, 61, 65, 71, 80
burnish (*See under* surface treatment)
bust-flower thymiateria 17–22, 24, 25, 67–68, 69, 71, 72, 73, 74, 75, 76, 77
busts 14, 15, 17–20, 21, 42, 47, 65, 68, 69, 73, 76
cake model 64
Callatis (Mangalia), Rumania 23, 27, 28, 37, 44, 80
Caria/Carian 78
cart model 49, 55, 59–61, 65, 71, 72
Carthage 18
Celts/Celtic 69, 74, 79
　presence in Asia Minor 2, 3
　tribes 2
　　Tectosages 2
　　Tolistoagii 2, 79, 81
　　Trocmi 2
cemeteries 1–2, 31, 47, 56, 61
Central Anatolia 1, 2, 61, 80, 81 (*See also* manufacture, place of)
Centuripe 48
chariot model 49, 55, 59–61, 65, 71, 72

chiton 17
chronology of objects 5, 25, 26, 27, 29, 31, 33, 34, 35, 36, 37–38, 39, 40, 42, 43, 44–45, 46, 47, 48, 49, 52, 53, 54, 55, 56, 57, 58, 59, 60, 61, 62, 65, 66, 67, 69, 70, 71–81
City Mound 1, 2
clay/fabric 5, 9–10, 11, 13, 14, 16, 23, 28, 29, 30, 32, 34, 35, 36, 40, 42, 44, 46, 48, 53, 58, 66, 67, 69, 70, 72, 73, 74, 75–76, 78–79, 80
Clazomenian 14
cock (*See under* animal, bird)
coiffure 14, 15, 16, 18, 19, 20, 21, 28, 30, 32, 35, 36, 37, 38, 39, 40, 45, 47, 48, 76–77, 80
Comedy
  New 46, 47, 48
  Middle 46
Corinth 11, 12, 18, 35, 45, 47
cornucopia 16-17
coroplasts 18, 23, 31, 71–73, 74–75, 79
  signatures 74, 78
costume (*See* boots and shoes; drapery; headdress)
Crete 43
Crimea 23, 27, 80
Cumae 14
Cyprus/Cypriote 32, 78
decorative techniques (*See* surface treatment)
deer/stag (*See under* animal)
Delos 37, 43
Demeter (*See under* divinities)
deposits 4, 8, 10, 13, 30, 32, 65–70, 78
Dionysos/Dionysiac (*See under* divinities, gods)
divinities 1
  goddesses
    Aphrodite 42, 78
    Artemis 16, 24, 69, 74, 77
    Demeter 18, 47, 78
    Kybele 3, 16, 17, 18, 22, 23, 24, 25, 26, 27, 28, 29, 30, 34, 35, 36, 42, 48, 59, 66, 67, 68, 69, 70, 71, 72, 73, 74, 75, 76, 77, 78, 79, 80, 81
    Agdistis 80
    Muses 24, 36
    Nike 10, 15, 16, 24, 30, 67, 72, 74, 75, 77
    Tyche 10, 16, 17, 24, 68, 69, 77
  gods
    Attis 24, 25, 30, 41, 42, 69, 70, 71, 72, 73, 75, 76, 77, 78
    Dionysos 15, 41, 45, 47, 64, 77
    Eros/Erotes 18, 21, 31, 41, 42, 43, 44, 69, 70, 71, 78, 80
    Herakles 15, 37, 41, 42, 74, 77
    satyr 15, 18–19, 45, 47, 67, 73, 76, 77
    Silenos/Silenoi 15, 18, 19, 36
dog (*See under* animal)
dolls 30–31
Dorylaion (Eskişehir) 80
dove (*See under* animal, bird)
drapery 13–14, 15–16, 17, 20, 21, 23, 24, 25, 26, 27, 29–30, 31, 32, 33, 34, 35, 36, 39, 40, 41, 42, 43, 44, 45, 63, 68, 72, 76–77, 80

duck (*See under* animal, bird)
earthquake 2, 3
East Greece (*See* manufacture, place of)
East Greek plastic vessels 7, 9–14, 18, 61, 65–66, 72, 77
Egypt 16, 18, 78
  Ptolemaic 16
Eleon (Thrace) 13
Eleusis 61
Emborio, Chios 61
Eros/Erotes (*See under* divinities)
Erythrai 12, 57
Etruria 11
Failaka Island (Ikaros), Kuwait 18
fertility figurines 51, 78
flower cups 17–22, 68, 69, 73, 76
function 10, 16, 18, 23–24, 25, 30–31, 45, 46–47, 51, 59, 61, 66, 67, 71, 72, 77
  funerary 7, 13, 14, 18, 31, 47, 51, 59, 61, 65
  votive 24, 30, 47, 51, 59, 64, 77, 78, 79
Galatia/Galatians 2, 16, 46
garland 19
Gela 13
glaze (*See under* surface treatment)
goddesses (*See under* divinities)
gods (*See under* divinities)
goose (*See under* animal, bird)
Greek
  -inspired objects 2–3, 4, 5, 9–17, 18, 22, 24, 25, 26–28, 29, 33, 35–36, 38, 41–43, 48, 66, 67, 72, 73–76, 77–78, 79
  inscriptions 2–3, 17, 24, 66–67, 68, 74, 79
groundcoat (*See under* surface treatment)
Hajji Firuz Tepe (Iran) 51
hairdo (*See* coiffure)
Halikarnassos 18
Halys River (Kizil Irmak) 81
hare (*See under* animal)
harness (*See also* yoke) 49, 50, 51, 52, 53, 55
Hasanlu (Iran) 61
hawk (*See under* animal, bird)
headdress 13, 15, 16, 18, 19, 21, 23, 26, 27, 28, 30, 31, 32, 38, 39, 40, 41, 42, 43, 48, 66, 76, 78
head vase 15, 74
hedgehog (*See under* animal, quadruped)
Herakles (*See under* divinities, gods)
Histria (Istros) 80
Hittite period 2
holes for suspension 24, 43, 46, 47, 48
horse/stallion (*See under* animal, ungulate)
human representations 1, 35, 36, 42, 47, 49, 61
  dancers 4, 29, 30, 35–36, 78, 80
  females 4, 15, 17–18, 19–20, 21–22, 23, 24, 28, 29–41, 48, 63, 66, 67, 68, 69, 71, 72, 73, 74, 77, 78, 79, 80
    head kantharos 15
    kore 10, 13–15, 31, 47, 77
    bust 10, 14–15, 66
    head 10

standing 10, 13–14, 15
  males 4, 35, 36, 37, 41, 45–46, 47–48, 68, 73, 74
  Negroes 15
incense burners (*See also* bust-flower thymiateria) 17–22
incision (*See under* surface treatment)
Isthmia 61
jewelry 12, 13, 14–15, 16, 19, 23, 24, 25, 26, 31, 37, 38, 39, 40, 41, 42, 46, 68, 69, 72, 75
Kallipoli (Aetolia) 32
Kamir-Blur, Urartia 61
Kamiros (Rhodes) 11, 14
kantharoi 15
kiln 17, 21, 34, 46, 64, 67–69, 71–73, 75
Kimmerians 2, 3, 6
Körte brothers 2,
Kourion, Cyprus 59
Küçük Hüyük 1, 2, 53
Kululu 61
Kybele (*See under* divinities, goddesses)
Kyzikos 24
Larisa on the Hermos 23, 79
Lefkandi 61
"Level 2 House" 24, 66, 67, 79
Lindos (Rhodes) 14, 36
lion (*See under* animal)
Lipari 47
Livy 3, 79
Lydia/Lydians 2, 9
Lydian period 2
lydion 7, 12, 62, 63, 66
Lysippos 45
Macedonia 32
maenad 15, 36
Mamurtkale 22, 23, 24, 26, 28, 35, 46, 48, 66, 77, 78, 79
Manlius Vulso 3, 79
manufacture, place of
  Anatolia 9, 10
  Central Anatolia 5–9, 16, 22, 25, 29, 42, 46, 49, 65, 67, 71, 72, 74, 75, 76, 77
  Greece 29
  East Greek workshops 9–10, 13, 14, 61, 66, 77
    Miletos 10, 13, 14
    Rhodes 9, 11, 13, 14, 61, 67
  Gordion 17, 19
  Lydia 7, 9, 14
  Phrygia 72, 74
mask 1, 4, 21, 41, 46–48, 71, 73
medallion 1, 37, 41, 42, 45, 47, 74
Medieval period 3
Medusa 37, 74, 77
Midas 2, 18
Midas City (Yazilikaya) 80
Miletos/Milesian 10, 12, 14
miniatures (*See also under* vehicle, wheel) 1, 4, 25, 35, 44, 47, 49, 51, 59–61, 65
Mirmeki 18
Mithradates II 2

models (*See also specific types*) 1, 49, 59–61, 64, 71, 72
molds 1, 15, 20–22, 26, 27, 28, 29, 31, 32, 33, 39, 40, 41, 43, 44, 45, 47, 58, 63, 66, 68, 69, 71–74, 76, 80
Morgantina 18
Munsell Soil Color Charts 5
Muses (*See under* divinities, goddesses)
Myrina 16, 29, 31, 32, 33, 34, 36, 42, 43, 44, 78
Myrmekion 23, 27, 80
Mysia 18
Naukratis 13
Neo-Attic reliefs 22
Nike (*See under* divinities, goddesses)
Nola 11
nymphs 36
Olbia 18, 38
Olynthos 15, 18, 31, 36
paint (*See under* surface treatment)
Peium-Tabanlioğlu 81
perfumed oils (*See also* unguent bottles) 10, 77
Pergamon/Pergamenes 2, 22, 23, 24, 25, 26, 28, 29, 32, 33, 35, 38, 45, 46, 48, 66, 67, 74, 77, 78, 79
  Attalids 3, 77, 79
  Attalos I 79
  Attalos II 79
  Eumenes II 79
Persian period 2
Persians 2, 3
  Achaemenid 8, 9
  Cyrus 2
Pessinus 2, 3, 25, 38, 77, 78, 79, 81
phiale 22, 24, 26, 27, 28, 42, 73, 76
Phrygia/Phrygians (*See also* manufacture, place of) 2, 16, 22, 24, 51, 77, 78
  rock-cut monuments 24
Phrygian cap 23, 28, 42, 78
Phrygian helmet 28
Phrygian inscriptions 2, 51
Phrygian period
  Early 1, 2, 3, 5
  Middle 1, 2, 3, 5, 8, 9
  Late/Hellenistic period 1, 3, 5, 8, 9, 12, 15, 17
Pitane (Çandarlı) 12, 61
plaster used in ancient repairs 19, 20, 24–25, 41–42, 70, 72–73, 76
plastic attachments 9, 29, 30, 36, 37, 41, 49, 51, 52, 56, 61–63, 71, 72, 74–75
  handle, Nike protome 10, 15–16, 24, 30, 67, 72, 74–75, 77
plastic vessels 1, 4, 9–17, 36, 44, 49, 61, 67–69, 71, 77
  animal (*See also* animal) 4, 5–9, 10, 14, 49, 51, 62, 65–67, 71, 73, 74, 75
    Central Anatolian 4, 5–9, 10, 65–66, 67, 71–77
    Greek or Greek-inspired 1, 4, 7, 9–12, 65–66, 71, 72, 73, 74, 77–80
  chronology 5, 10, 11–14, 16, 17, 18, 65–66, 67, 69–70, 71–77
  pomegranate 10, 11, 12–13, 65–66, 77

polish (*See under* surface treatment)
polos (crown) 18, 22, 23, 24, 26, 27, 28
pomegranate (*See under* plastic vessels)
Pontus 2
pose (position/stance) 4, 10, 11, 13, 15, 16, 21, 22, 24, 25, 26, 27, 28, 29–30, 31–36, 41, 42–43, 44, 68, 79–80
Pottery Establishment 17, 21, 28, 67–69, 71–73, 75
    kiln 17, 21, 46, 67–69, 71–73
Priene 22, 23, 27, 28, 33, 42, 43
protome 10, 15–16, 21, 28, 29, 36, 67, 72, 74–75, 77
Punic 18
quadruped (*See under* animal)
quiver 20, 26, 43, 73, 76
ram (*See under* animal)
repairs, ancient (*See* plaster used in ancient repairs)
rock-cut monuments (*See under* Phrygia)
Rhenia (Delos) 32, 33
Rhodes 9, 11, 13, 33, 38, 45, 61
rhyta 5, 6, 7, 8–9, 10, 31, 44, 51, 62, 67, 72, 77
Roman period 1, 2, 18
Samos/Samians 11, 13, 14
sandals (*See* boots and shoes)
Sangarius River 1
Sardis, Lydia 11, 13, 61
Sargon II, annals 2
Sarkiné, Georgia 47
satyr (*See under* divinities, gods)
sculpture in stone 13–14, 16, 17, 22, 24, 25, 26, 33, 38, 45, 68, 74, 79
Seleucia on the Tigris 18
Seleucids 2
    Seleukos 44
shoes (*See* boots and shoes)
Sicily 18, 61
Silenos/Silenoi (*See under* divinities, gods)
slip (*See under* surface treatment)
Smyrna (Izmir) 28
Sotades Shop 10
Southern Italy 18,
sphinx 22, 24, 25, 27, 76
spouts 1, 6, 7, 8, 11, 12, 13, 14, 16–17, 49, 71, 72
stamping (*See under* surface treatment)
stone (*See* sculpture in stone)
Strabo 3
surface treatment
    burnish 5, 6, 9, 48, 53, 54, 56, 58, 62, 63, 66, 67, 75
    glaze 5, 7, 8, 10, 11, 12, 14, 15, 16, 36, 37, 57, 61, 62, 63, 66, 67, 71
    groundcoat 5, 8, 9, 16, 19, 20, 21, 24, 26, 27, 28, 31, 32, 33, 34, 35, 36, 37, 38, 39, 40, 41, 43, 44, 45, 46, 47, 48, 55, 57, 58, 59, 60, 62, 63, 72, 76, 77, 79
    incision 6, 7, 9, 12, 15–16, 21, 24, 25, 30, 31, 34, 35, 37, 38, 39, 40, 43, 46, 53, 54, 57, 58, 59, 64, 76–77
    paint 5, 6, 7, 8, 9, 11, 12, 13, 14, 15, 16, 18, 19, 20, 21, 23, 24, 25, 26, 27, 28, 29, 30, 31, 32, 33, 34, 35, 36, 38, 39, 40, 41, 42, 43, 45, 46, 47–48, 49, 53, 55, 57, 58, 59, 60, 61, 62, 63, 65, 69, 70, 72, 76, 77, 78, 79, 80
    polish 5, 6, 7, 8, 9, 10, 16, 17, 21, 49, 52, 53, 54, 55, 56, 57, 58, 60, 61, 62, 63, 65, 66, 67, 69, 72, 75, 77
    slip 5, 7, 11, 12, 14, 16, 19, 24, 31, 32, 36, 39, 40, 41, 42, 47, 48, 49, 51, 52, 53, 54, 55, 56, 57, 58, 59, 60, 61, 62, 63, 72, 75, 76, 77
    stamping 6
suspension of vessels/figurines/masks (*See also* holes for suspension) 10, 11, 24, 30, 43, 46, 47, 48
Tanagra 42
Taranto 13
Tarsus 32
Tavium 81
technique
    figural vessels 1, 4–5, 8, 13–17, 65, 68–69, 71–77
    figurines 1, 4–5, 23, 25, 27, 49, 68–69, 71–77
    handmade 1, 7, 8, 9, 12, 23, 25, 26, 31, 33, 39, 41, 46, 49, 51, 52, 53, 54, 55, 56, 57, 58, 59, 60, 61, 62, 63, 64, 72, 75, 76, 77
    hand-modeled 1, 6, 7, 8, 9, 14, 18, 19, 20, 21, 24, 26, 27, 37, 38, 39, 40, 41, 45, 47, 48, 49, 53, 54, 60, 65, 72, 74, 76
    moldmade 1, 9–16, 18, 19, 20–22, 24, 25, 26, 27, 28, 31, 32, 33, 34, 35, 36, 37, 38, 39, 40, 41, 42, 43, 44, 45, 46, 48, 58, 63, 66, 68–69, 72–74, 76
    plastic 1, 4, 45, 76–77
    wheel-turned 6, 7, 8, 9, 10, 11, 12, 13, 14, 24, 49, 53, 60, 65, 72, 76
Thera 13
Thrace 80
thymiateria (*See also* bust-flower thymiateria) 17–22, 24, 25, 42, 44–45, 47, 67–68, 69, 70, 71, 72–73, 74, 75, 76, 77, 78
Tocra 10
torque 16, 46, 68, 72, 75
toys 30–31, 50, 51, 55–56, 65
Troy 16, 18, 25, 29, 31, 34, 43, 78
Tumulus A 13, 15, 31, 59
Tumulus P 5, 6, 51, 59, 65, 75
Tyche (*See under* divinities)
tympanum (tambourine) 22, 23, 24, 25–26, 27, 28, 35, 63, 68, 76, 77
unguent bottles (*See also* aryballoi; perfumed oils) 10–17, 31, 61, 66, 67, 69, 70, 77
ungulate (*See under* animal)
vehicle, miniature 4, 49, 51, 55, 59–61, 65, 72, 73
vent holes 18, 19, 20, 26, 31, 33, 35, 39, 44, 76
vessels, (*See* plastic vessels)
wheel, miniature 49, 55, 59–61, 71, 72, 73, 75
West Anatolia/West Anatolian 61, 62, 72
Xanthos 12
Yalincak 80
Yassıhöyük 51
yoke (*See also* harness) 49, 50, 51, 55

Figures

FIGURE 1

General site plan of Gordion

FIGURE 2

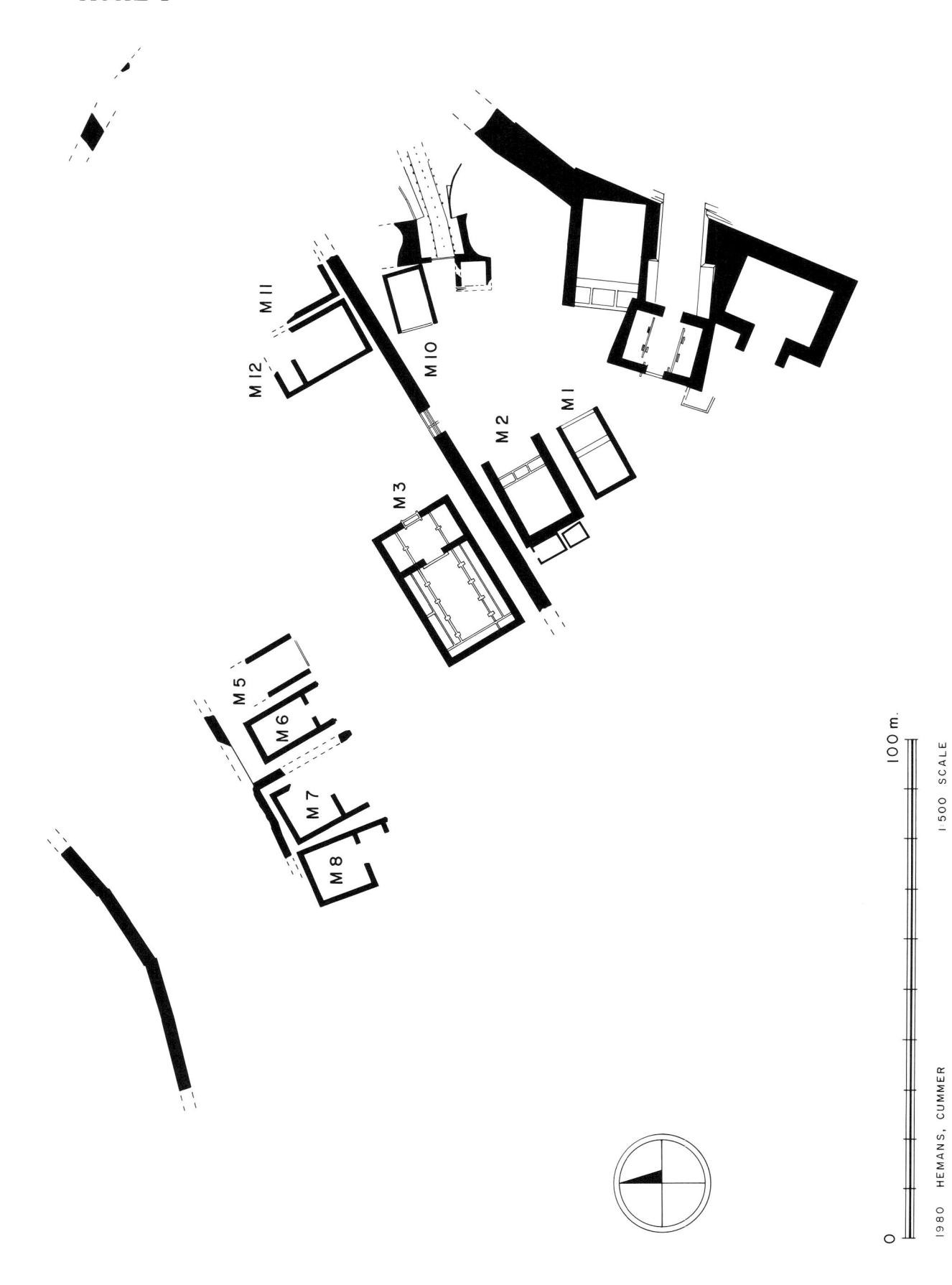

Early Phrygian City Mound

FIGURE 3

Middle Phrygian City Mound

FIGURE 4

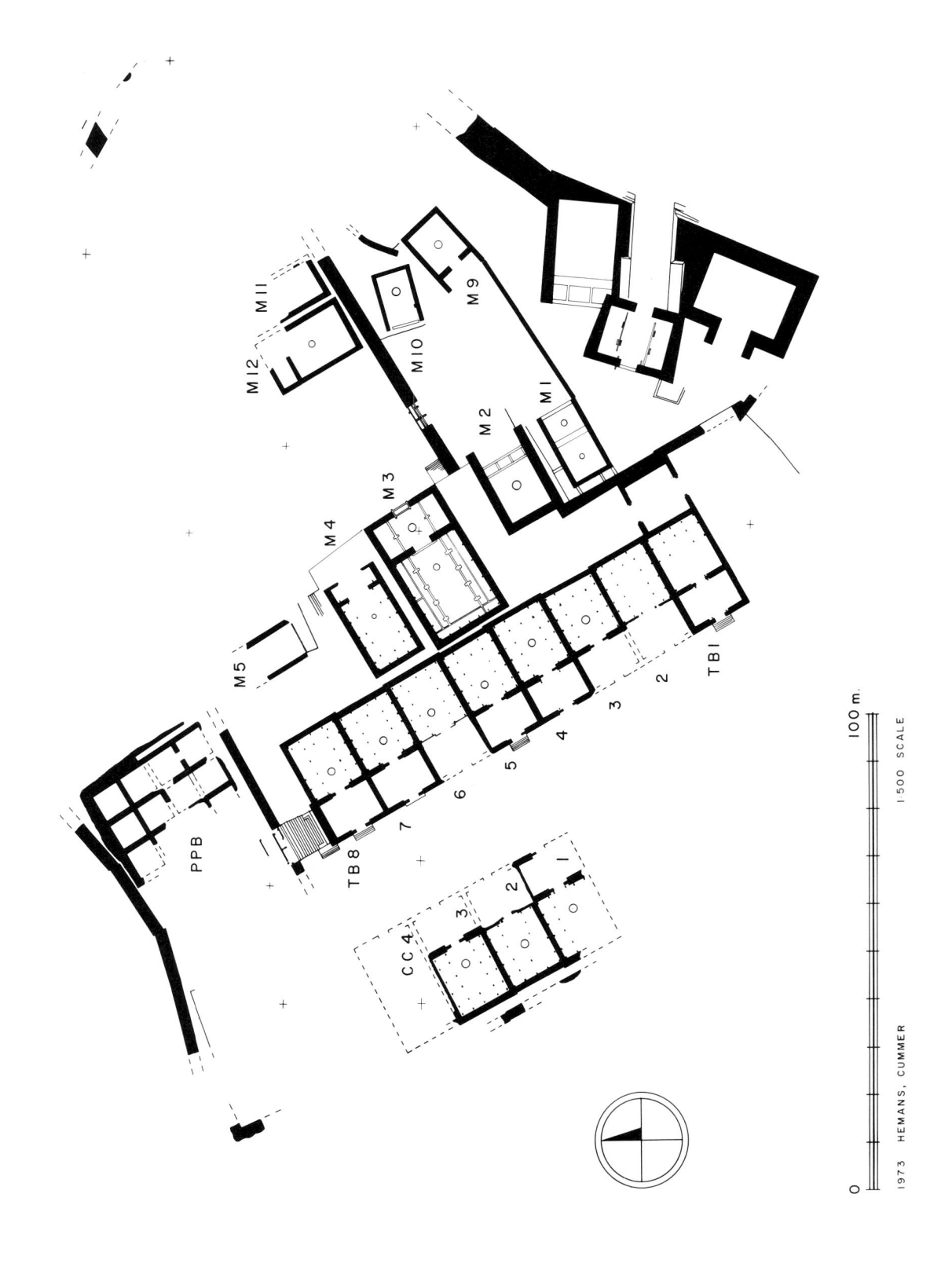

Late Phrygian/Hellenistic City Mound

FIGURE 5

Deposit 1: Reconstructed Floor Plan of Chamber of Tumulus P (*Gordion* I, fig. 5)

FIGURE 6

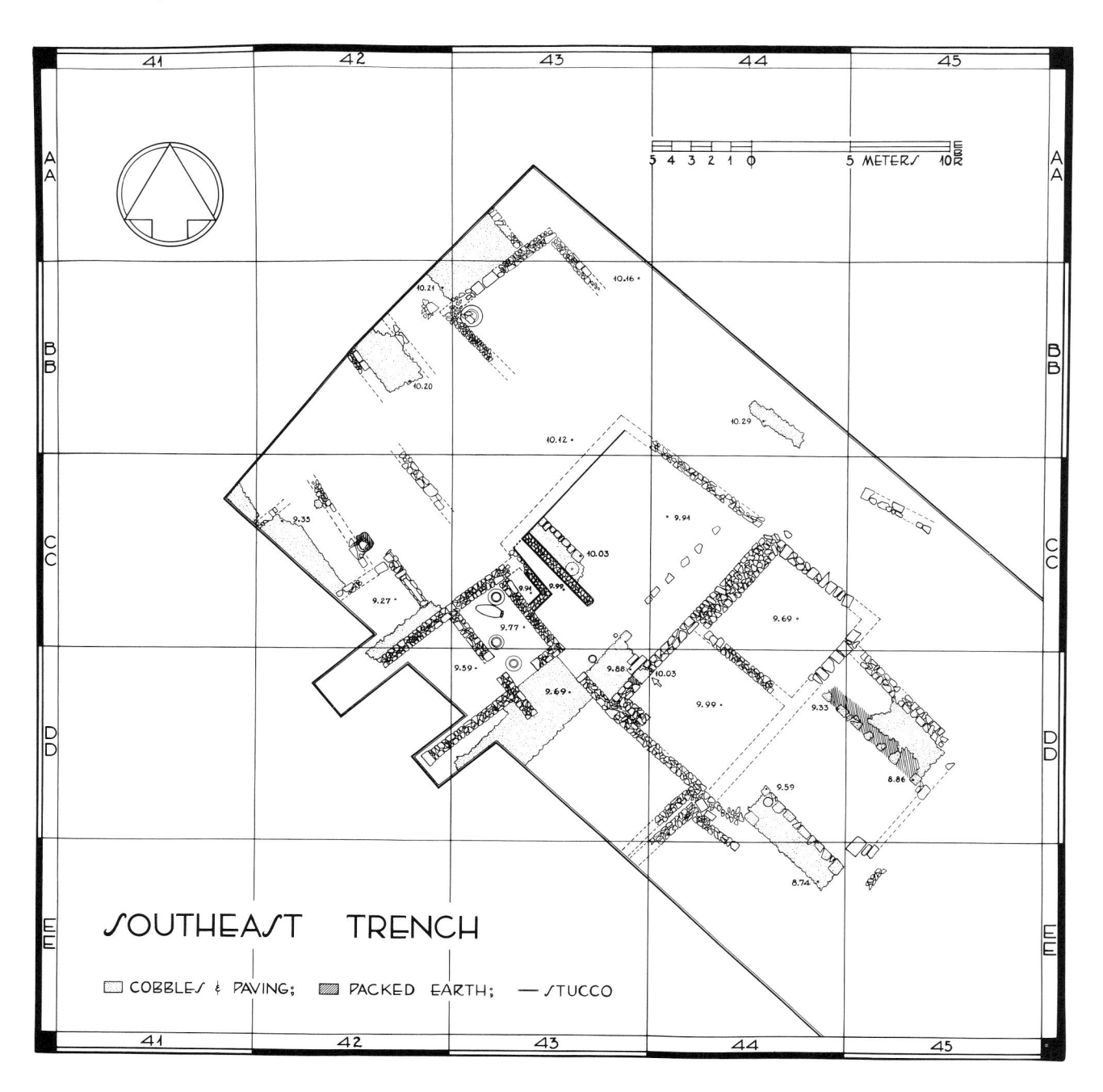

Deposit 3: Plan of Level 2 House

FIGURE 7

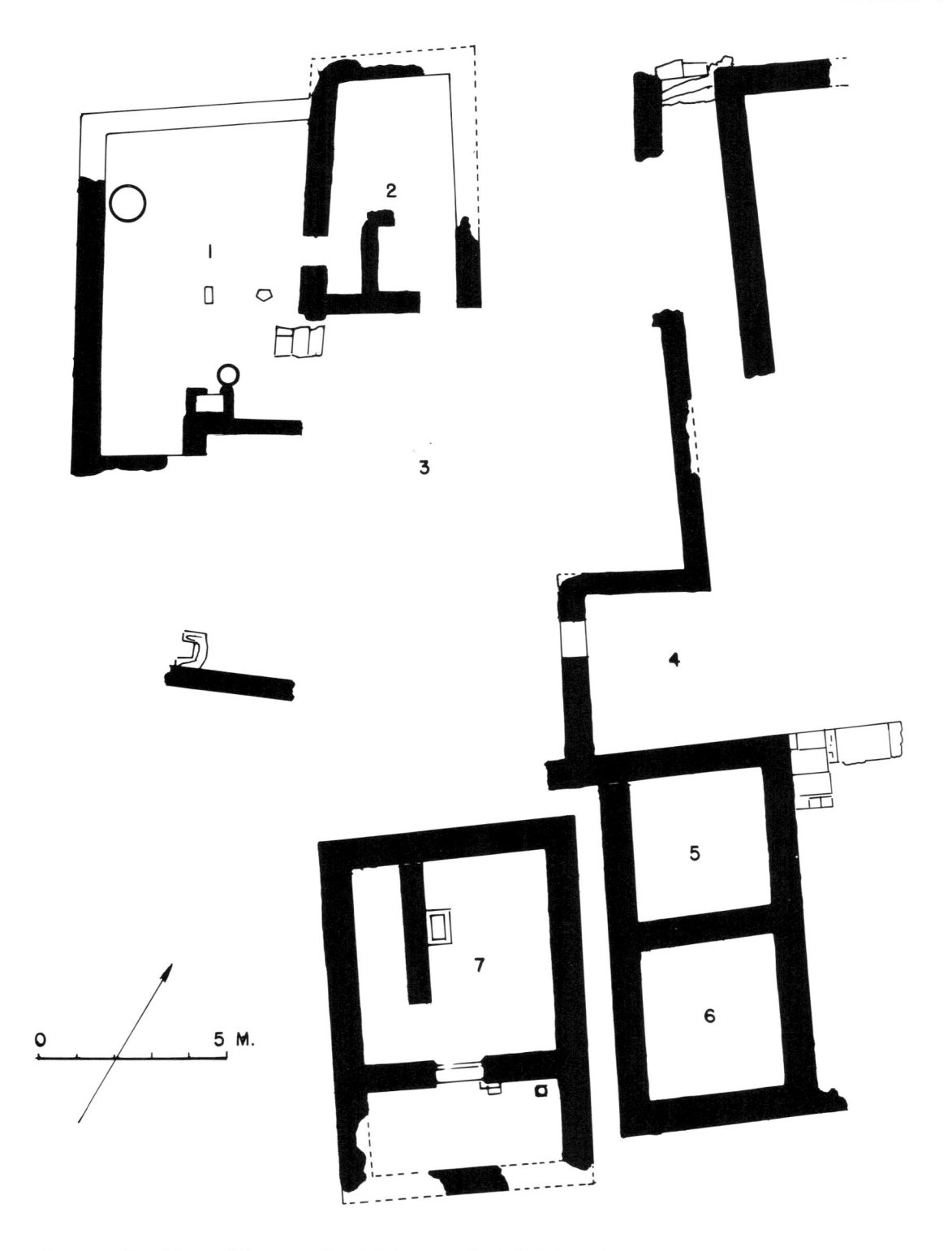

Deposit 5: Plan of Pottery Establishment & Adjoining Structures

Plates

COLOR PLATE I

33

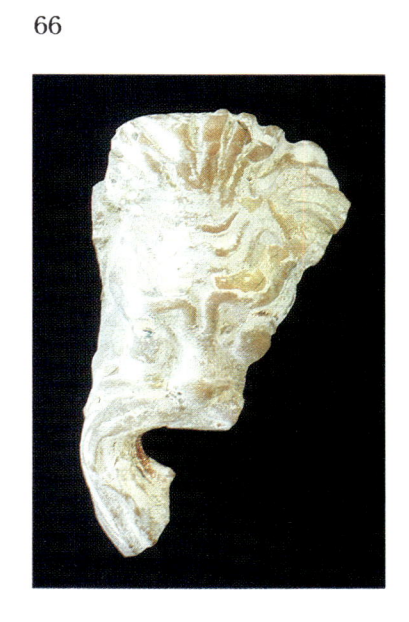

52

66

68

76

111

N.S.

COLOR PLATE II

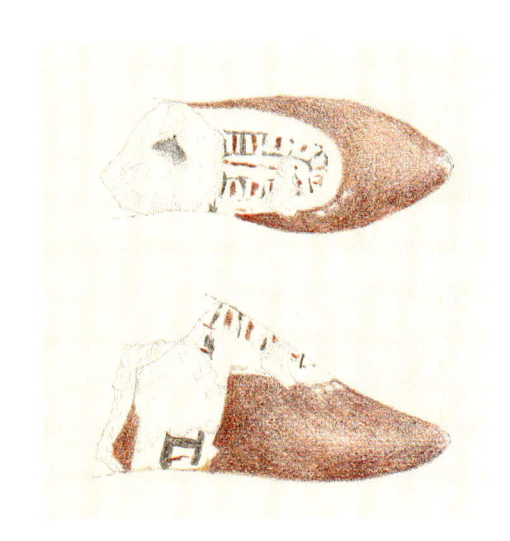

163

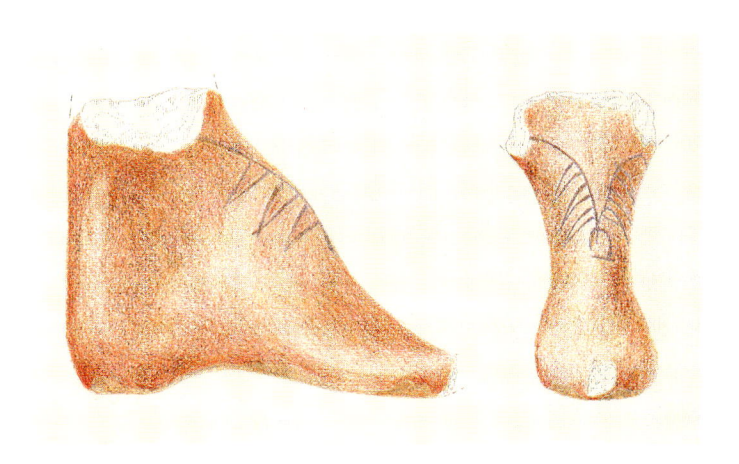

164

165

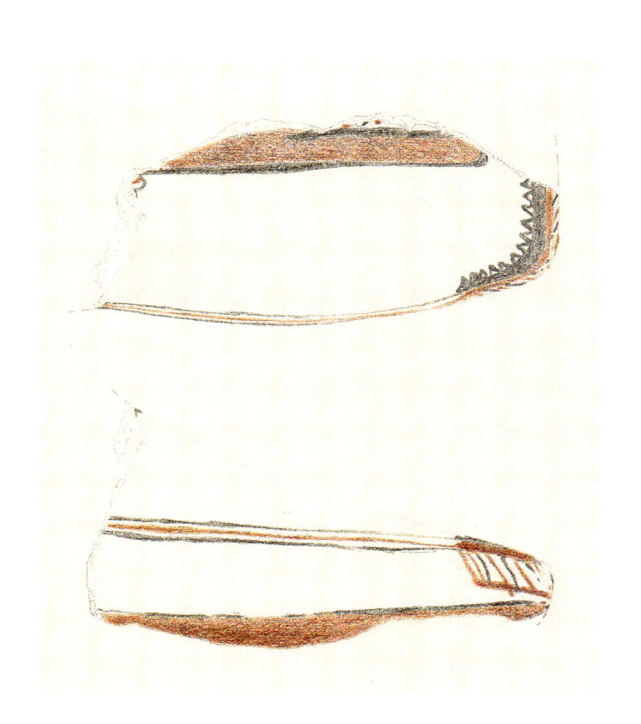

167

168

1:2

ANIMAL VESSELS   PLATE 1

1

2

1:4

PLATE 2 ANIMAL VESSELS

3

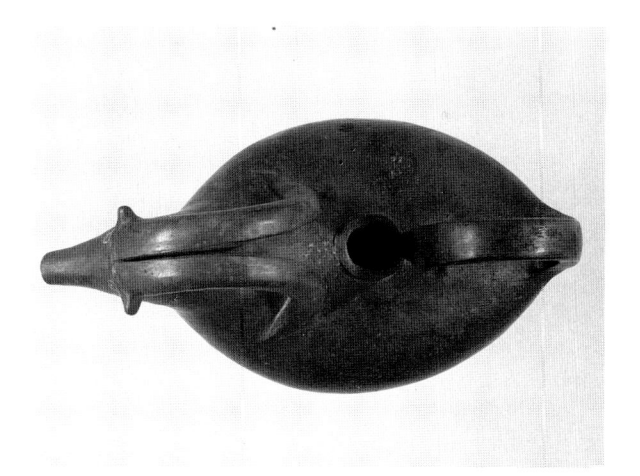

4

5

1:3

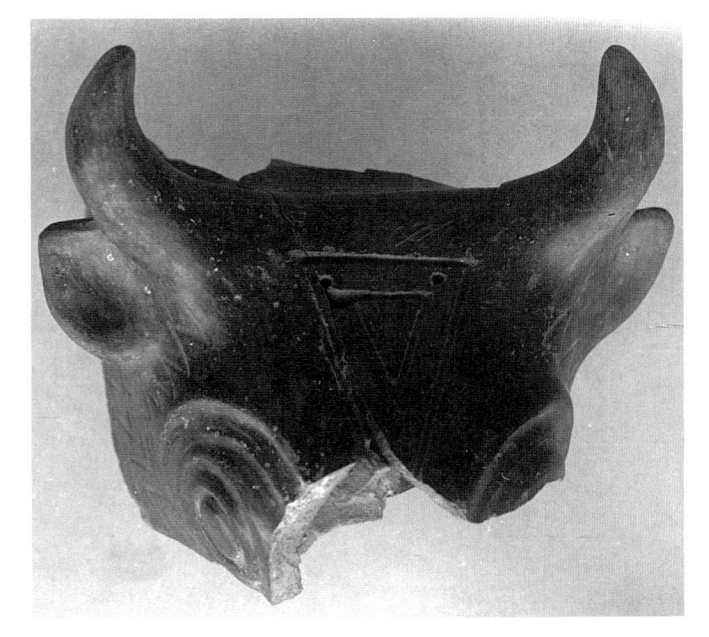

ANIMAL VESSELS PLATE 3

6

7

8  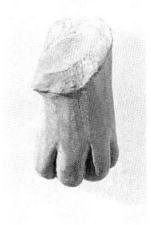 9

3:5

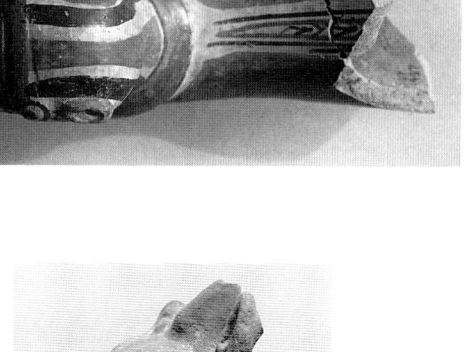

PLATE 4　　　　　　　　　　　　　　　　　　　　　　　　　　　ANIMAL VESSELS

10

11

12

13

1:2

ANIMAL VESSELS PLATE 5

14

15

16

17

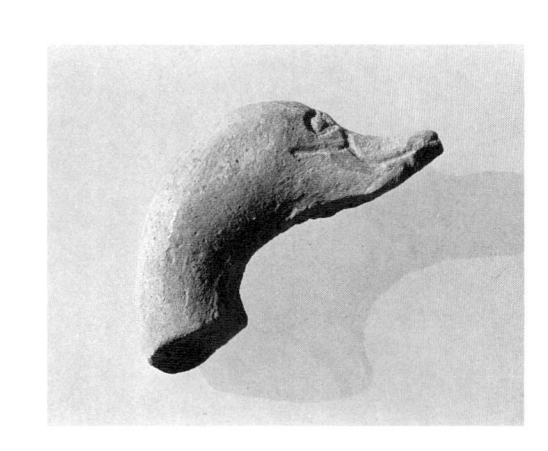

18

1:1
14,15 - 1:2

PLATE 6 PLASTIC VESSELS

19

20

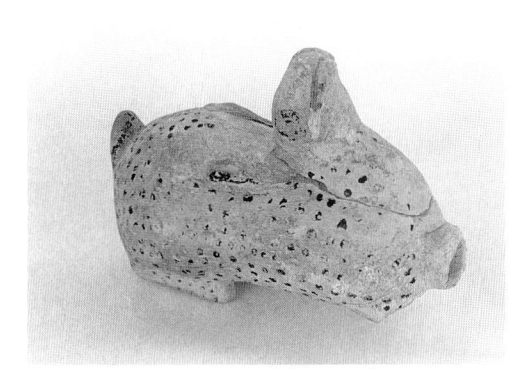

21

22

23

2:3

PLASTIC VESSELS PLATE 7

24

25

26

PLATE 8 PLASTIC VESSELS

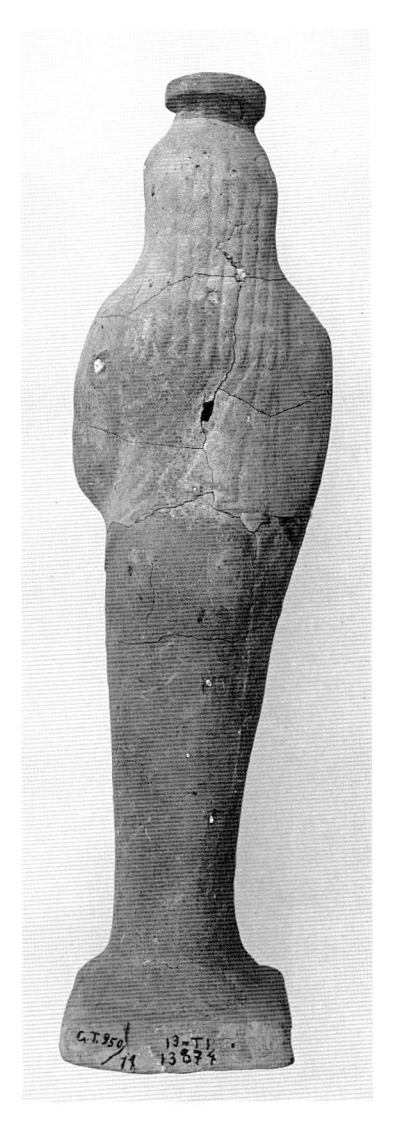

27

Detail: Arms with bird

1:2
27 detail - N.S.

PLASTIC VESSELS
PLATE 9

29

30

28

1:1

PLATE 10 PLASTIC VESSELS

31 A. mold   B. cast   32

33   34

BUST-FLOWER THYMIATERIA

PLATE 11

35

36

37

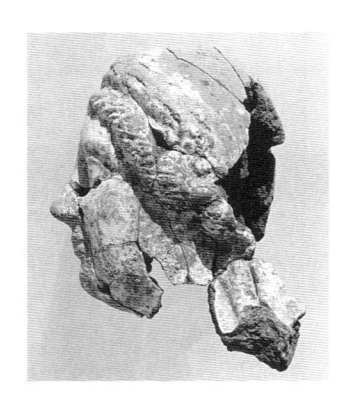

1:2

PLATE 12 BUST-FLOWER THYMIATERIA

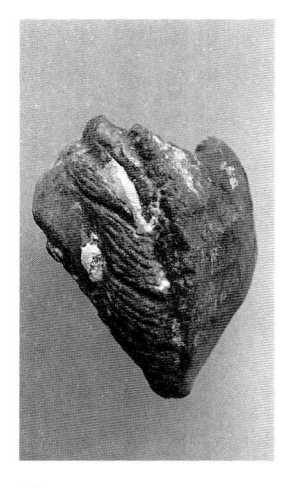

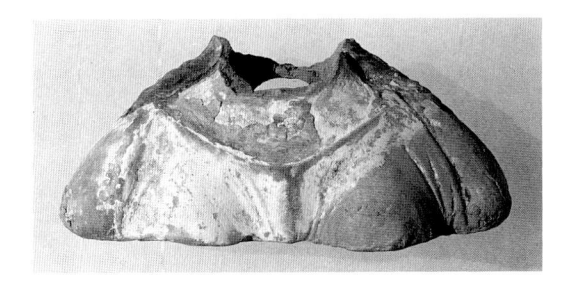

38

39 40 41

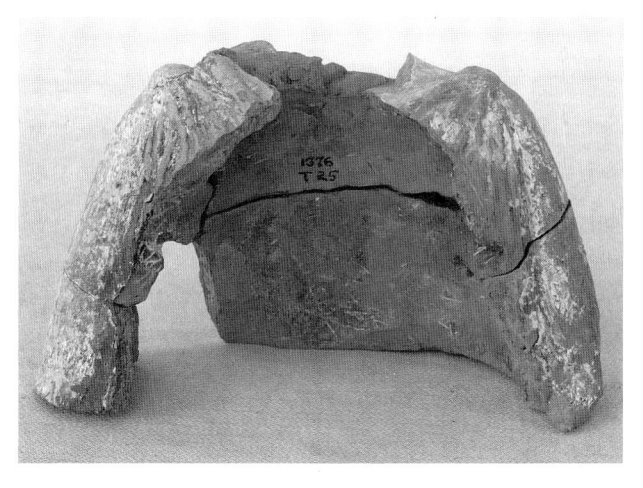

42

1:2

BUST-FLOWER THYMIATERIA　　　　　　　　　　　　　　　　　　　　PLATE 13

43

44

45

46

47

48

49

1:2

PLATE 14

BUST-FLOWER THYMIATERIA

50

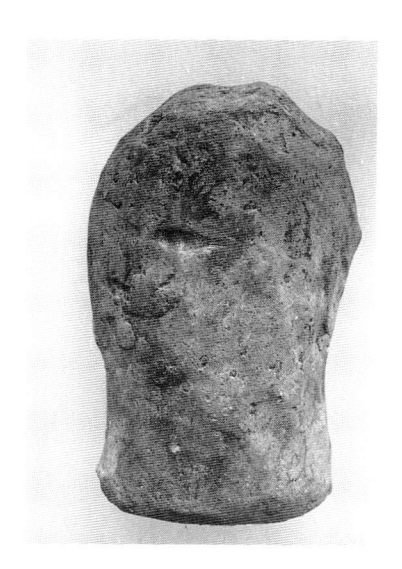

51 Mold: Front   Mold: Back   Cast

50 - 1:3
51 - 1:2

KYBELE AND RELATED TYPES   PLATE 15

52   Detail: left side, tympanum and sphinx

1:4
details - N.S.

PLATE 16   KYBELE AND RELATED TYPES

52   Detail: right side, phiale, sphinx   Detail: hand and phiale

1:4
details - N.S.

KYBELE AND RELATED TYPES PLATE 17

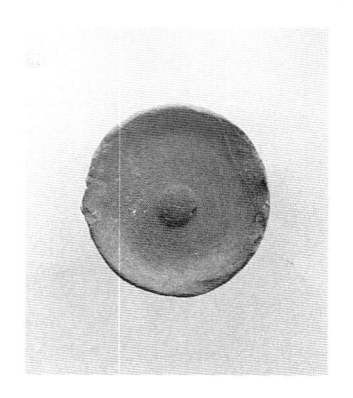

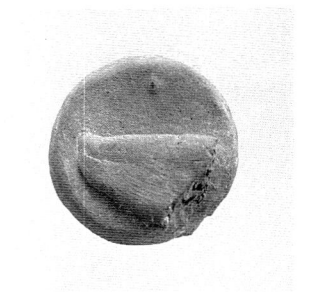

54

53 55

56

3:4

PLATE 18   KYBELE AND RELATED TYPES

57

58   59

KYBELE AND RELATED TYPES PLATE 19

60

61

62

63

64

1:2

PLATE 20 FEMALES

65

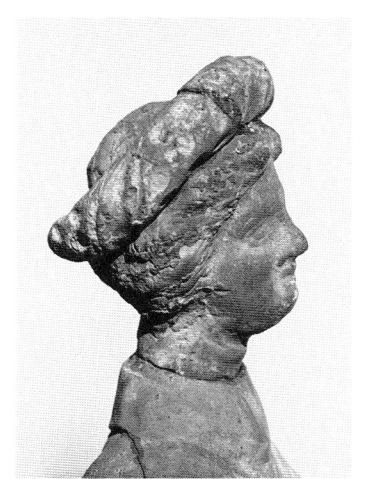

66

66 details - N.S.

FEMALES
PLATE 21

67

68

1:2
68 details - N.S.

PLATE 22 FEMALES

69

70  71  72  73

1:2

FEMALES PLATE 23

74

75

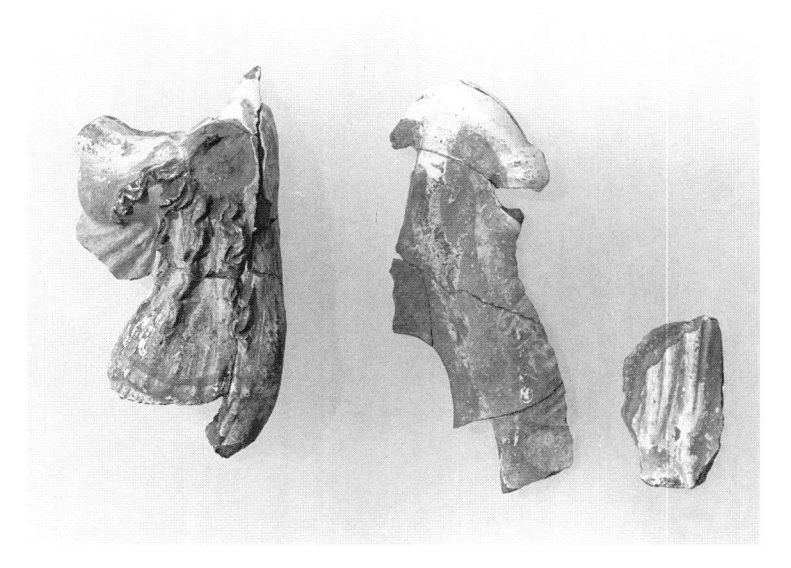

76

1:2

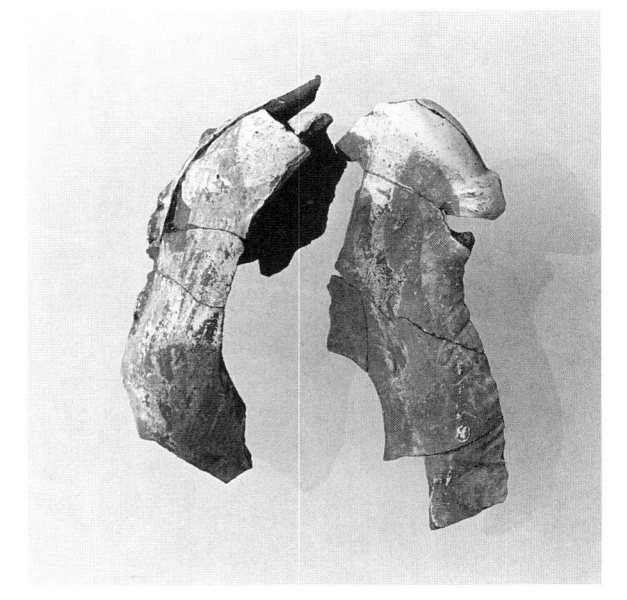

PLATE 24
FEMALES

77

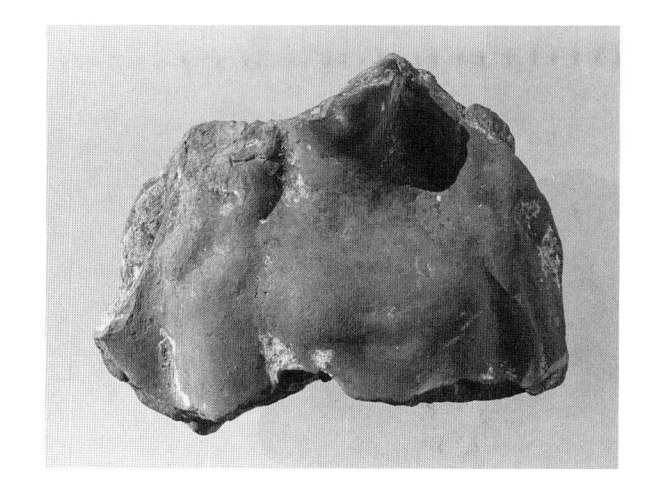

78

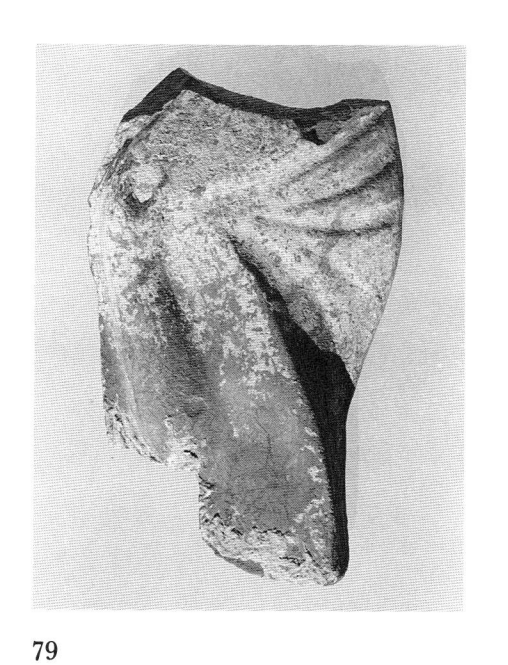

79

80

81

1:1
77, 79 - 1:2

FEMALES

PLATE 25

82

83

1:1

PLATE 26
FEMALES

84

85

86

87

88

89

1:1

FEMALES
PLATE 27

90

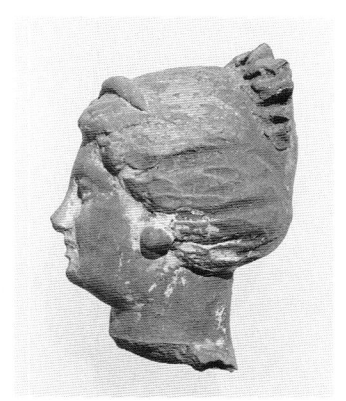

91

92

93

94

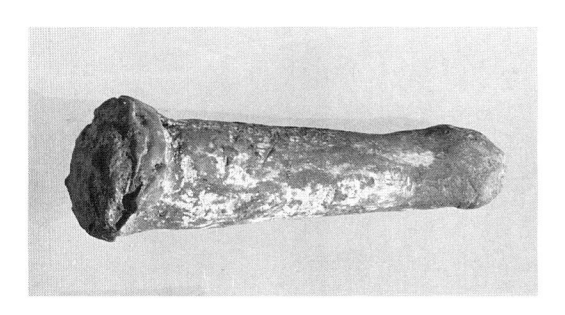

95

96

1:1
96 - 1:2

PLATE 28
MALES

97

98

99

97 - 1:3
98 - 1:1
99 - 1:2

MALES

PLATE 29

100

101

102

103

1:1

PLATE 30

MALES

104

105   A. mold

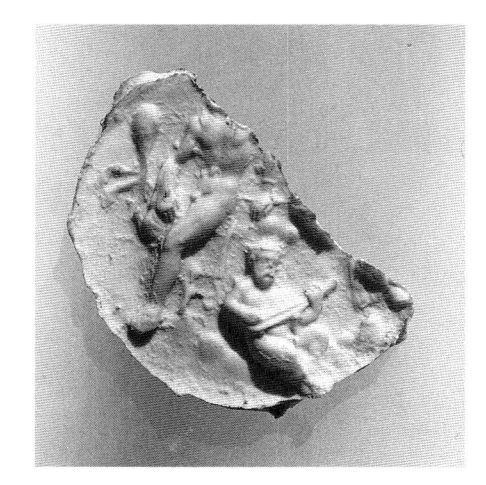

B. cast

106

1:2
106 - 1:1

MALES/UNIDENTIFIABLE HUMANS PLATE 31

107

108

109

1:1

PLATE 32
MASKS

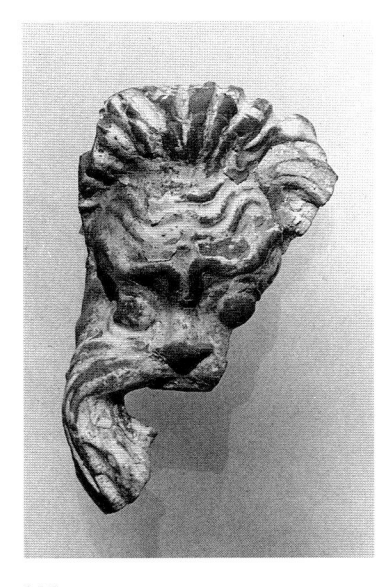

110

111

112

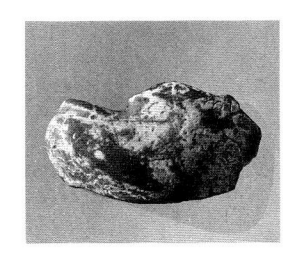

113

114

2:3

ANIMALS PLATE 33

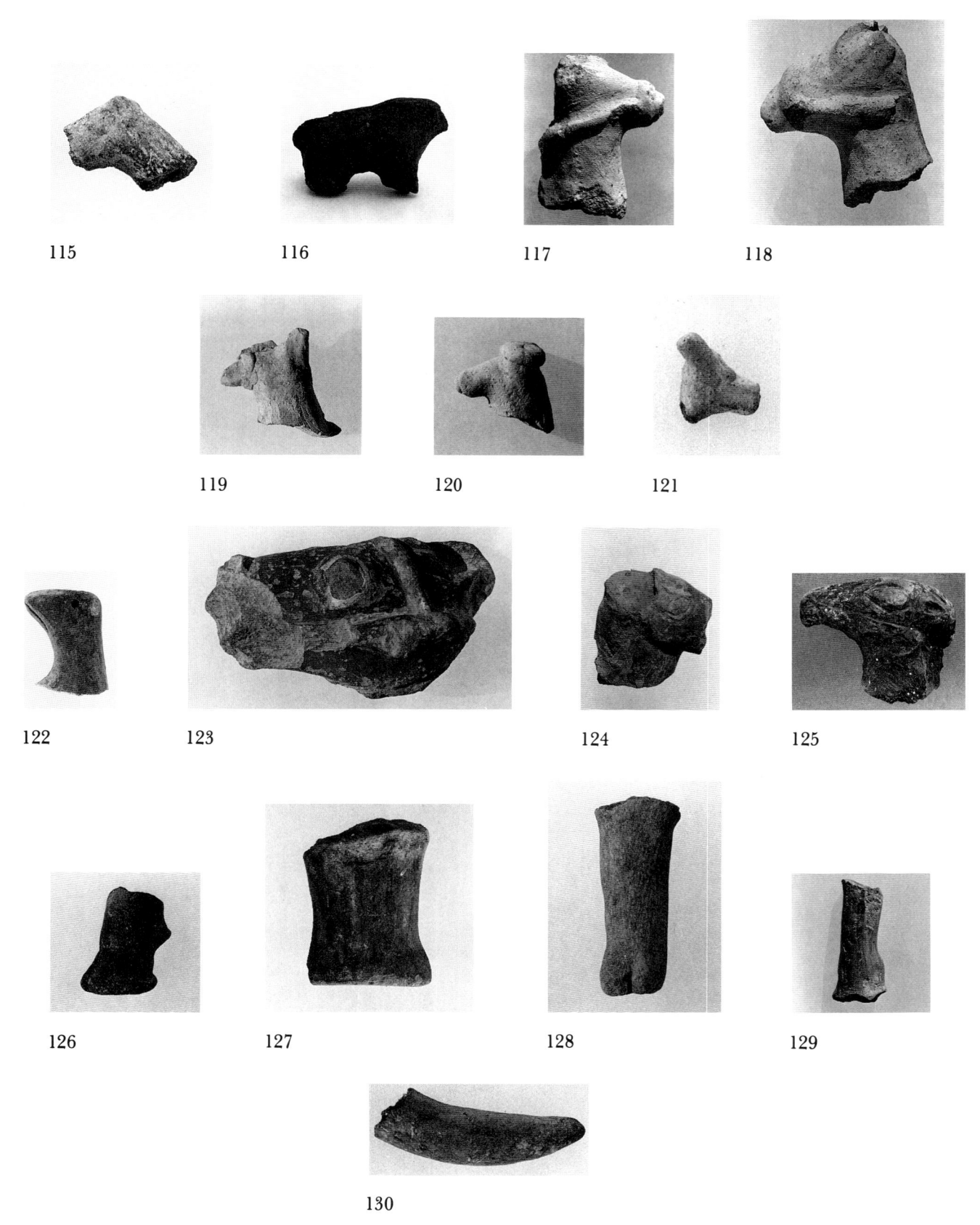

115 116 117 118

119 120 121

122 123 124 125

126 127 128 129

130

1:2

PLATE 34   ANIMALS

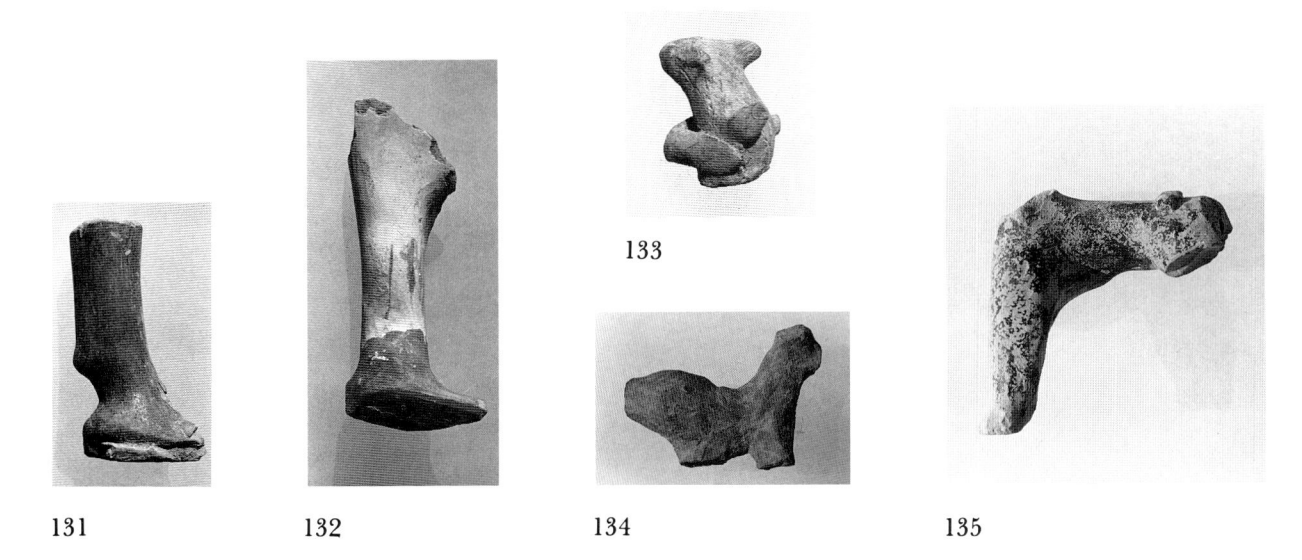

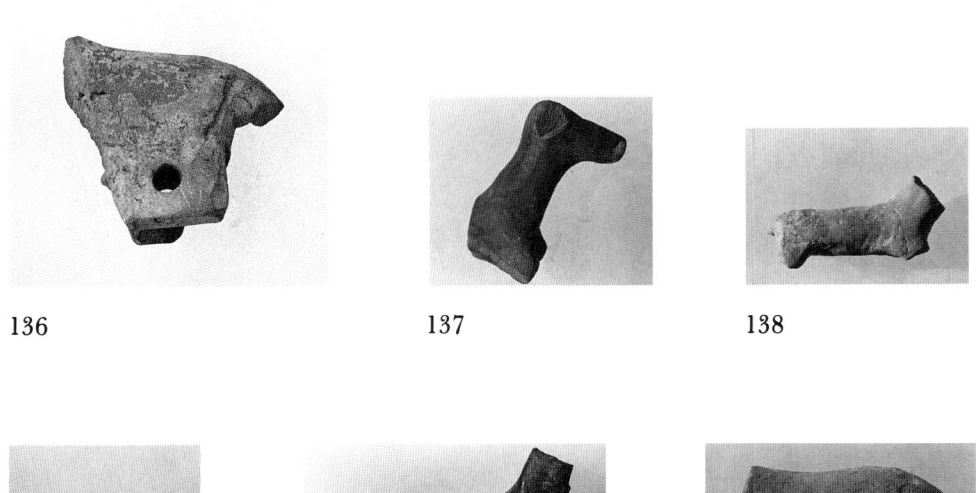

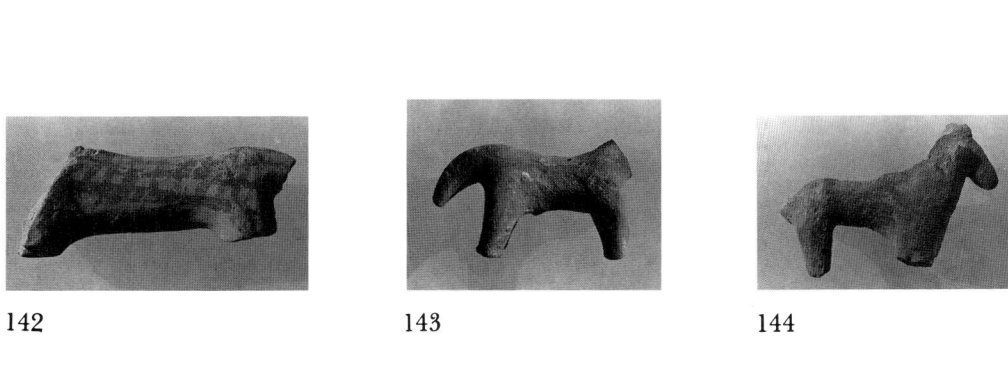

131 132 133 134 135

136 137 138

139 140 141

142 143 144

1:2
133 - 1:1

ANIMALS   PLATE 35

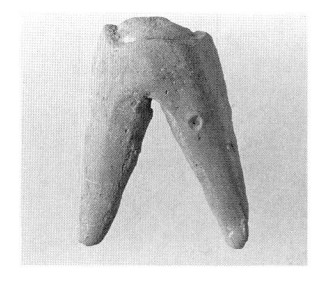

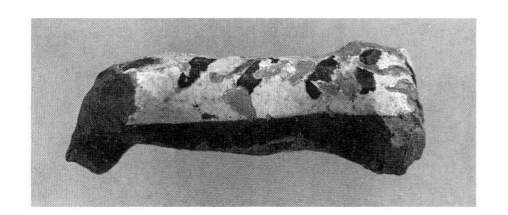

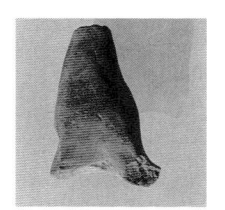

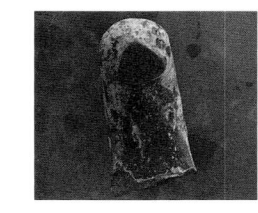

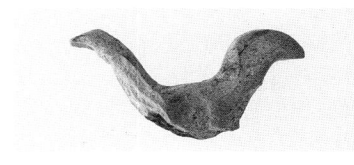

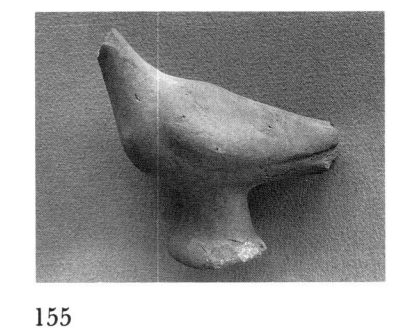

145

146

147

148

149

150

151

152

153

154

155

1:2

PLATE 36   MISCELLANEOUS: VEHICLES AND WHEELS

156

157

158

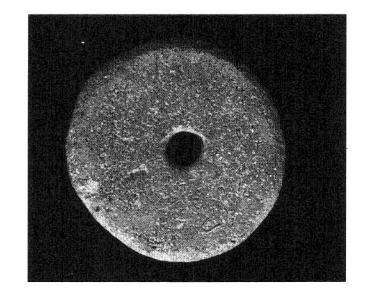

159

160

161

1:2

MISCELLANEOUS: BOOTS AND SHOES   *PLATE 37*

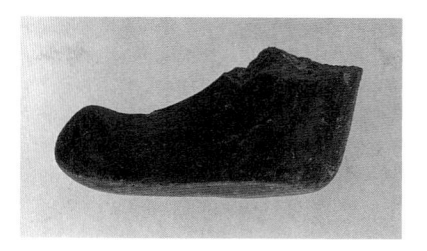

162

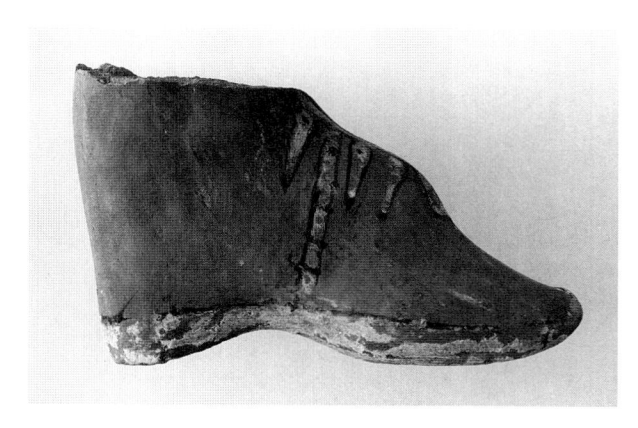

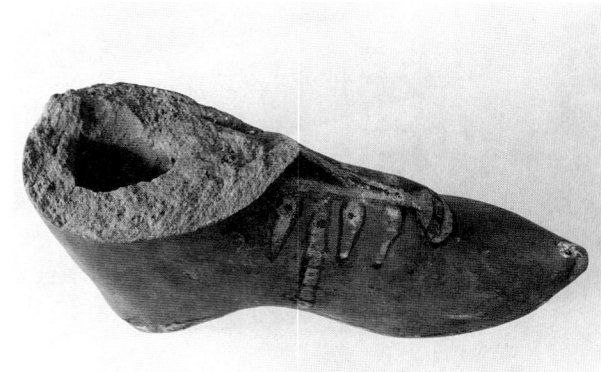

163

164

165

1:2
162 - 1:1

PLATE 38
MISCELLANEOUS

166

167

168

169   170   171

1:2

COMPARANDA

PLATE 39

Hedgehog Unguentarium
from Çandarlı
Istanbul Archaeological Museum Inv. 9967

Goose Unguentarium
from Çandarlı
Istanbul Archaeological Museum Inv. No. 10269

Terracotta Figurine of Kybele
from Priene
Istanbul Archaeological Museum Inv. No. 1617
(Mendel 1908, no. 204)

PLATE 40

Marble Statuette of Seated Kybele
from Gordion (Inv. No. S 81)

COMPARANDA
PLATE 41

Alabaster Statuette of Seated Kybele
from Gordion (Inv. No. S 103)

Terracotta Female with Wreath
from Macedonia
Istanbul Archaeological Museum
Inv. No. 1449 (Mendel 1908, no.
3069)

Terracotta Female with Wreath
from Macedonia
Istanbul Archaeological
Museum Inv. No. 1450
(Mendel 1908, no. 3068)

Terracotta Standing Female
from Myrina
Istanbul Archaeological
Museum Inv. No. 354
(Mendel 1908, no. 2579)

1:2

Other Books on Gordion from University Museum Publications

GORDION EXCAVATIONS: FINAL REPORTS, I
Three Great Early Tumuli
Rodney S. Young

1982. University Museum Monograph 43. Hard. xxvii + 326 pp., 3 color pls., 148 figs., 101 photographic pls., appendices, biblio., index. ISBN 0-934718-39-3

GORDION EXCAVATIONS: FINAL REPORTS, II
The Lesser Phrygian Tumuli Part 1: The Inhumations
Ellen L. Kohler

1995. University Museum Monograph 88. xxxvi + 422 pp., 72 figs., 85 pls., 9 tables, appendices, index. ISBN 0-924171-33-2

GORDION EXCAVATIONS: FINAL REPORTS, III
The Bronze Age
Ann Gunter

1991. University Museum Monograph 71. Hard. xx + 116 pp., 32 photographic pls., 31 figs., foldout section, biblio., concordance, Turkish summary. ISBN 0-934718-95-4

GORDION EXCAVATIONS: FINAL REPORTS, IV
The Early Phrygian Pottery
G. Kenneth Sams

1994. UNIVERSITY MUSEUM MONOGRAPH 79, two volumes. Text volume: xxxii + 347 pp., index. Illustrations volume: xv + 3 pp. of color pls., 4 pp. of plans, 65 pp. of figs., 8 pp. of site photo pls., 170 pp. of object photo pls., endpaper map. Hard. ISBN 0-924171-18-9

GORDION SPECIAL STUDIES I
The Nonverbal Graffiti, Dipinti, and Stamps
Lynn E. Roller

1987. University Museum Monograph 63. Hard. xxii + 103 pp., 52 figs., 7 photographic pls., 3 plans, indices, biblio., Turkish summary. ISBN 0-934718-70-9

FROM ATHENS TO GORDION:
The Papers of a Memorial Symposium for Rodney S. Young
Keith DeVries, editor

1980. UNIVERSITY MUSEUM PAPERS 1. Paper. xix + 168 pp., frontispiece, 144 figs. ISBN 0-934718-35-0

A Third Century Hoard of Tetradrachms From Gordion
Dorothy Hannah Cox

1953. University Museum Monograph 9. Paper. vi + 20 pp., 8 pls. ISBN 0-934718-46-6

UNIVERSITY OF PENNSYLVANIA MUSEUM
of Archaeology and Anthropology

215-898-4124
Call for information on other Gordion titles

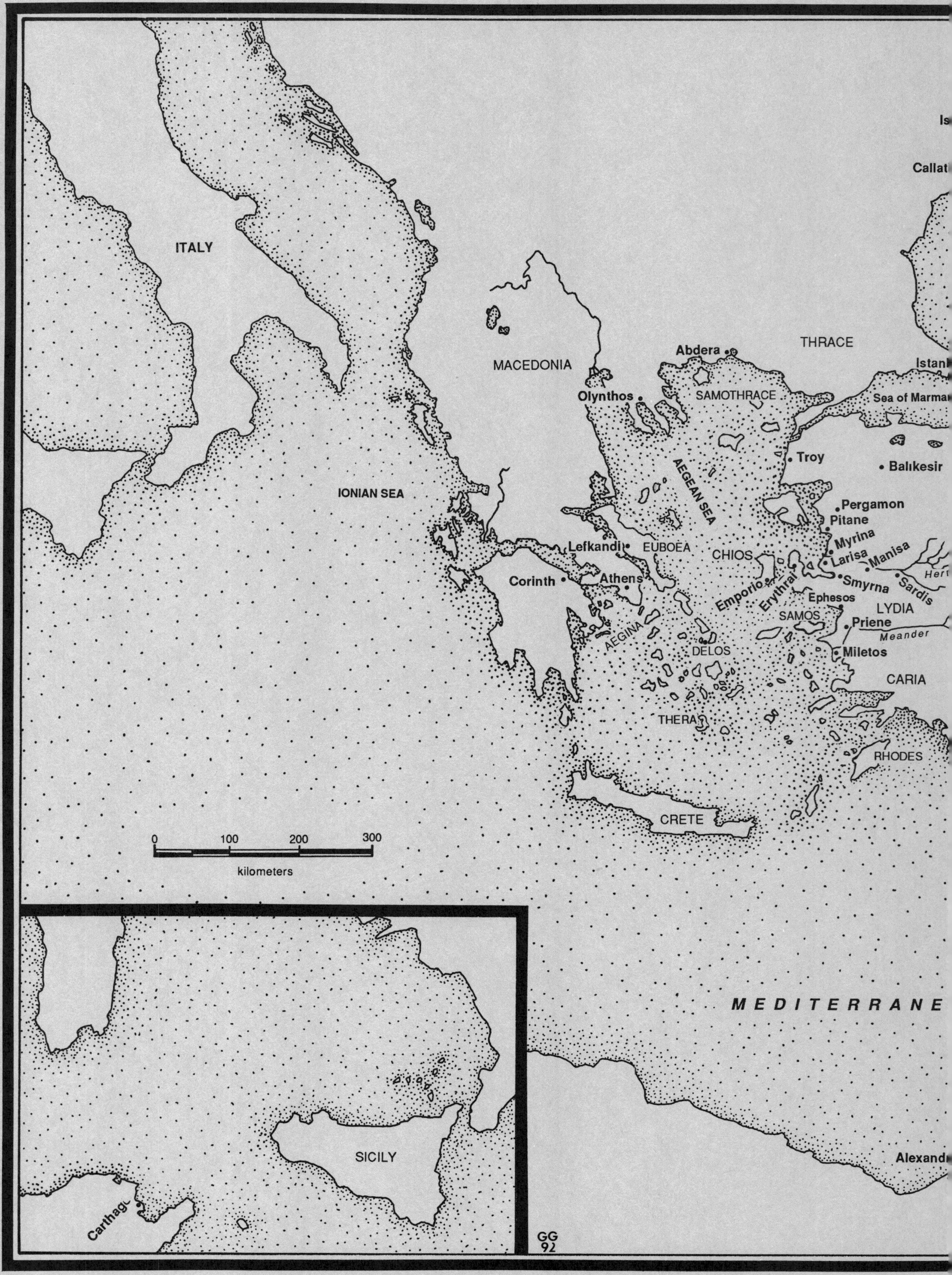

ITALY
MACEDONIA
THRACE
Abdera
Olynthos
SAMOTHRACE
Sea of Marmar
Istan
Is
Callat
Troy
Balıkesir
AEGEAN SEA
IONIAN SEA
Pergamon
Pitane
Myrina
Larisa
Manisa
Lefkandi
EUBOEA
CHIOS
Corinth
Athens
Smyrna
Sardis
Emporio
Erythrai
Ephesos
LYDIA
SAMOS
Priene
Meander
AEGINA
DELOS
Miletos
CARIA
THERA
RHODES
CRETE
0
100
200
300
kilometers
MEDITERRANE
SICILY
Carthag
Alexand
GG
92